The Economy of Anonymity

The Economy of Anonymity

Power in the Age of Identification

Hector Amaya

STANFORD UNIVERSITY PRESS
Stanford, California

Stanford University Press
Stanford, California

Library of Congress Cataloging-in-Publication Data
Names: Amaya, Hector author
Title: The economy of anonymity : power in the age of identification / Hector Amaya.
Description: Stanford, California : Stanford University Press, [2026] | Includes bibliographical references and index.
Identifiers: LCCN 2025028533 (print) | LCCN 2025028534 (ebook) | ISBN 9781503645554 cloth | ISBN 9781503645813 paperback | ISBN 9781503645806 ebook
Subjects: LCSH: Anonymous persons | Identity (Psychology) | Online identities
Classification: LCC HM753 .A455 2026 (print) | LCC HM753 (ebook)
LC record available at https://lccn.loc.gov/2025028533
LC ebook record available at https://lccn.loc.gov/2025028534

Cover design: Jan Šabach
Cover art: Unsplash

The authorized representative in the EU for product safety and compliance is: Mare Nostrum Group B.V. | Mauritskade 21D | 1091 GC Amsterdam | The Netherlands | Email address: gpsr@mare-nostrum.co.uk | KVK chamber of commerce number: 96249943

Contents

	Foreword	vii
Introduction	**A Subaltern Theory of Anonymity**	1
One	**The Dialectic of Anonymity and Identification**	38
Two	**Anonymity and Ontology**	63
Three	**The Myth of Anonymous Publicity**	89
Four	**Trust Among Anonymous Strangers**	125
Five	**Bordering, Anonymizing, and Inscription Technologies**	165
Six	**Unnaming, Renaming, and the Economy of Anonymity**	197
Conclusion	**Thirteen Properties of the Economy of Anonymity**	235
	Notes	255
	Bibliography	261
	Index	279

Foreword

I began this book unaware that the learning, thinking, and researching would take me away from current scholarship on anonymity. If each project is an exercise in growth, this one has helped me grow in most unexpected ways. I cannot think about the social or about identity the same way after writing these chapters and after arguing for the importance of anonymity to the subject, to ontology, and to our understandings of the social sciences. Like others interested in anonymity, I was also interested in power, but I found the power of anonymity not only in the open locales of the political but also in the intricate spaces of the subjective. Anonymity, as I now think about it, is an element of human life as common and important as is identity, one of the essential mechanisms of the social, and one of the few trickster elements designed specifically for entropy.

While a fair amount of thinking has been spent figuring out social order, entropy is as real as order is difficult. Entropy is neither good nor bad, but it is essential for change. Theories of social order, some of which are explored in this book, are the enemies of entropy and are so for good reasons. To many people, entropy appears on the horizon as scary, chaotic, violent, and unpredictable. Entropy, we are told, is the universe before God, lawless. It is Hobbes's state of nature, the decay after civilization.

But there is more to entropy than its bad publicity as there is more to the elemental forces like anonymity that may produce it. As scholarship on anonymity has shown, entropy is often needed to exist because, to many individuals and communities, order is scary, violent, lawless, and uncivil. To the subaltern, the revolutionary, the iconoclast, the rebel, the relatively controlled entropy of agentic anonymity offers the gift of hope. And hope to the hopeless is precious, which is why so much fiction and scholarship have been invested in this almost mythical view of anonymity, one that brings some entropy to the social.

But even this mythic perspective does not do justice to everything that anonymity may engender. There is more to the entropic power of anonymity, more that it brings and makes possible. To important minorities, this entropic power is, also, change, the tilling of soil needed for germination, the undoing required to flourish, the unbeing required for being. The trickster element, anonymity, tricks onlookers, but it also tricks the past and the future and helps individuals by opening pathways for action and being.

If tricksters destabilize and entropy unsettles, what remains is a crumbling totality, the type of imaginary universe that houses my views on anonymity. This made sense as this is the work of a scholar who has read too many times Octavia Butler's *Parable of the Sower* and *Parable of the Talents*. "Change is God," proposes Lauren Olamina, the process philosopher at the heart of the two books. God is change, and the only totality she and I would have is a crumbling totality.

Anonymity has been my "positive obsession," to again reference Olamina. It began the year I was a member of the Institute of Advanced Study (Princeton, NJ), a year that allowed me to write the first insights that define this book. If anonymity is indexical dissociation, then anonymity must also be a social technique crucial to subjugation and being. Once I began to see anonymity in this way, I began seeing it everywhere, including in coverture, slavery, and immigration. The obsession began.

This book is indebted to many people and institutions. I am thankful to IAS School of Social Science, in particular director Didier Fassin, and guest leading faculty Axel Honneth. Joan Scott was extremely helpful in the early versions of my first analytic steps, and other IAS members were wonderful guides. These included Michael Walzer, Munira Khayyat,

Robin Celikates, Greta Wagner, and Rodrigo Cordero. The University of Virginia supported my year at IAS. The Department of Communication at Stanford University and the Center for Latinx Digital Media at Northwestern University allowed me to share early versions of these ideas, and their feedback undoubtedly strengthened the project.

I am particularly thankful to the University of Southern California, the Annenberg School of Communication, and Dean Willow Bay, who have supported my research and writing for the last few years. This has been the intellectual home that encouraged my work and growth. Annenberg colleagues who read my work and gave me wonderful feedback include Troy Mikanovich and Julianna Kirshner. Robert Mejia's mastery of theory, including Latine theorizations, strengthened the work. Several research assistants were also crucial to the project, and I am particularly thankful to Javier Rivera, Zahraa Badr, and Eduardo Gonzalez. These wonderful RAs helped my research in many ways but also gave me crucial writing and theoretical feedback. These communities of scholars have provided the intellectual landscape that nurtured every page.

Last, I need to thank Jennifer, my wife and my intellectual partner. Although I am certain that whatever I write will fail to capture the depth and breadth of her influence on my work, I must at least try. Jennifer has taught me about science and technology studies (STS), history, and theory; she has debated with me my sometimes-dubious ideas and pushed back against my bad intellectual habits, helping me see my limitations. She has been patient with my ideas and intellectual obsessions and has shown me the potential in my work. She has kept my faith in intellectual inquiry and my ambition. But Jen is more than my intellectual partner. Jen is my life partner, and, at times, when the writing was obsessive (and a positive obsession is still an obsession), Jen was the person who reminded me that there was more to life than work and that family and friends mattered. Thank you.

The Economy of Anonymity

Introduction

A Subaltern Theory of Anonymity

Increasingly, we are anonymous to those around us, but not to "the eye of power," to use the phrase Michel Foucault made famous (1980, 146). In our digital lives, we use nicknames and avatars to play video games and hide our true identity; we create multiple email addresses to partially hide what we do and who we are in different contexts; we use VPNs and BitTorrent to mask our identities and activities and to fool other machines and surveyors; and we troll or enthusiastically comment on social media posts under the guise of pseudonyms, letting go of social constraints like politeness or fear. In the digital realm, anonymity is everywhere, a persistent option for those who wish to hide, experiment, and deceive.

But we are anonymous in more contexts than the digital. In a world in which urbanization is increasingly the norm, many of us experience the anonymity of the crowd on a daily basis. We experience the pleasure of feeling free because people do not know who we are, and we can behave without fear of harming our reputations. And, the crowd indeed can be freeing, but the anonymity in the crowd can also be experienced as an angst, the dread of being unseen, anonymous, without the ability to convey to passing others our worth and our history. Both feelings are real and common.

While our digital and material lives provide many opportunities to routinely experience anonymity, the eye of power is always upon us. In the digital realm, this is due to the technological capabilities of computers and sensors that keep records of every activity we carry out. It is easy to use anonymity horizontally, when interacting with other web users, but it is actually quite hard to be truly anonymous to corporations and governments. And, in urban spaces, the eye of power is omnipresent in the myriad surveillance technologies that routinely surround our every move and pervade more and more places. It is hard to walk in downtown Los Angeles, my city, without being seen. Cameras are everywhere, and new technologies like facial recognition and gait recognition are added to the forensic utility of fingerprints and DNA to remind us that our bodies are identifiable and traceable. We may hide our identities from those who are right beside us but cannot hide from the state or the digital corporations that want, use, and profit from our data and biological traces. We are identifiable even while experiencing anonymity.

Many scholars and studies have explored Foucault's "eye of power," a term he used to refer to the way the panoptic had become central to modern governmentality (Foucault 1980, 146). Inspired by Jeremy Bentham's circular prison design, with a watchtower in the center that allowed for the constant observation of prisoners, the panopticon became a metaphor that Foucault used to illustrate modern forms of control through surveillance (Foucault 1977). The digital revolution brought about by computation made Foucault's concerns about surveillance ever more present. Our lives, we know, are subject to systematic data collection and surveillance, and the literature on datafication, critical platform studies, critical algorithm studies, and surveillance studies helps us understand the social and political ramifications of this state of affairs.

Clearly, surveillance and datafication matter because anonymity and privacy matter, but while a great deal of intellectual investment is spent in exploring the connections between surveillance, datafication, and privacy, relatively few have studied the fact that anonymity is common, routine, and important to our lives. As the United States and other democracies flirt with authoritarianism and absolutism, the possibility or impossibility of anonymity will become increasingly important in the West, just as it is already in many other places. From the perspective of subalterns and those wishing to participate in civic actions, it is anonymity, not privacy, that holds the promise and possibility of political and social change, and it is anonymity, not privacy, that defines the value and worth of studies of surveillance and datafication.

This book is an attempt to rebalance our intellectual investments and expand our understandings of anonymity by focusing on anonymity's relations to life, politics, and the social. The book shows that placing anonymity under the microscope reveals much more than a reaction to the overreach of power of corporate and state actors. There is more to anonymity than the important dialectic relationship of anonymity to surveillance and datafication. Let me illustrate this "more" by quickly referencing the central fictional character in Margaret Atwood's *The Handmaid's Tale* (1986), a story about a woman who is navigating existence in her own authoritarian state. We know this character as Offred, and it is only well into the story that we learn that Offred was a name imposed on her:

> My name isn't Offred, I have another name, which nobody uses now because it is forbidden. I tell myself it doesn't matter, your name is like your telephone number, useful only to others; but what I tell myself is wrong, it does matter. I keep knowledge of this name like something hidden, some treasure I'll come back to dig up, one day. I think of this name as buried. This name has an aura around it, like an amulet, some charm that's survived from an unimaginably distant past. I lie in my single bed at night, with my eyes closed, and the name floats there behind my eyes, not quite within reach, shining in the dark. (84)

This "more" I am referring to can be glimpsed in Offred's words. Named, unnamed, renamed, Offred is anonymized yet an object of constant surveillance. Her birth name, her identifier, her most concrete index, is both part of the structure of social power and also part of her deepest sense of self. What she has lost when she was dissociated from her birth name is just alluded to, but it is clear that this loss is connected to her unmentioned name, her treasured identifier.

Identifiers, indexes, do more than identify or point, and it is this "more" that I elaborate on in these pages. I first place anonymity in history and show the role it typically plays in our social and political imaginaries, which likely fuel our suspicion, fear of, and anger toward systematic surveillance and ever-expanding datafication. But instead of claiming that anonymity matters only because of the role it plays in our social and political imaginaries, in the following section I define anonymity as a social technique that produces indexical dissociation, the separation of an individual from their personal identifiers, from the signs (names, Social Security numbers [SSNs], fingerprints, and others) that point toward them. I argue that there is much more that anonymity can teach us if we see it as such. This definition of anonymity expands our understanding of what anonymity is and what it does and adds welcome complexity to a social technique that many treat simply as hiding an identity. The next section justifies this expansion of anonymity and explains why it is necessary. I follow with an explanation of how the book relates to and differs from scholarship on privacy. And this introductory chapter finishes with a substantive section that explains why the connection of anonymity to the indexical matters.

Anonymity, History, and the Imaginary

In its most quotidian sense, anonymity is imagined as making some types of freedom possible. This is why I began the book by creating a dramatic difference between anonymity and the eye of power. Helen Nissenbaum (1999) would agree. She writes:

> For situations in which we judge anonymity acceptable, or even necessary, we do so because anonymity offers a safe way for people to act, transact, and participate without accountability, without others "getting at them," tracking them down, or even punishing them. This includes a range of possibilities. Anonymity may encourage freedom of

> thought and expression by promising people a possibility to express opinions and develop arguments about positions that, for fear of reprisal or ridicule, they would not or dare not take otherwise. Anonymity may enable people to reach out for help, especially for socially stigmatized problems like domestic violence, HIV or other sexually transmitted infection, emotional problems, or suicidal thoughts. (142)

We, Nissenbaum and I, write aware that most readers would see an opposition between anonymity and power because to most readers anonymity would connote the possibility of rebellion and freedom, the opposite to power from above. And this connotation is not new. It is predictable because it is ensconced in our historical understanding of the good society, particularly after the Enlightenment. What would the history of the United States be without anonymity, which allowed political dissenters to act on and publish dangerous and rebellious ideas? Can we imagine this history without Thomas Paine's *Common Sense*, the forty-seven-page pamphlet he first published anonymously in 1775? Without the legal guarantee of the privacy of postal correspondence that afforded anonymity to abolitionists who organized against slavery? What would the history of literature be without anonymity? Would we have the work of Jane Austen, Mary Shelley, or the Brontë sisters, to name a few famous authors who published anonymously in order to bypass patriarchal restrictions on cultural production and property? Can we imagine systems of power in the era of big data without WikiLeaks, a publisher of anonymously "leaked" documents, or the systematic work of the hacker organization Anonymous?

The connection between anonymity and freedom is evident if we think of modernity in relationship to the European Enlightenment, the passing of feudalism, the rise of secularism, the erosion of monarchic rule, colonialism, the Atlantic slave trade, and the rise of new nations thanks to independence movements in places like the Americas. All these dramatic changes could not have happened without the rise and support of new types of subjectivities and social technologies. Among them, Hannah Arendt (1958), Jürgen Habermas (1989), and Reinhart Koselleck (1988) argue for publicity and the rise of public spheres as essential to social change. Indeed, without publicity and public acts of dissent, social change would not be possible.

However, inspired by Koselleck and the recognition that publicity theory marginalized the subaltern (Fraser 1990), I have argued that anonymity must also be considered among the social technologies essential to a modernity shaped by patriarchy, colonialism, slavery, and capitalism (Amaya 2020). I learned this from scholars like James C. Scott (1990), who reminded us that when and if the subaltern speaks up, they do often by avoiding direct confrontations with the powerful and instead "adopted the safer course of anonymous attacks on property, poaching, character assassination, and shunning" as political tactics (17). Throughout history, many groups and individuals could speak to power only because of anonymity, and it is unwise to place publicity as essential to modernity without acknowledging the role and importance of anonymity, a social technology particularly suited to undermine power structures (Amaya 2020; Asenbaum 2018).

The connotation of anonymity to freedom has become mythical, in the sense Roland Barthes (1972) used the term, and, as myth, it has become central to dystopian narratives about socio-technical overreach like the film *Minority Report*, the Apple+ television series *Silo*, the classic novel by George Orwell *1984*. These stories connect corporate and/or political totalitarianism with the erasure of anonymity, with constant surveillance, and with the inability to escape the eye of power. And, as we move closer to producing or creating the socio-technical capabilities of full surveillance, as digitation envelops us all, the future seems ever more scary, inhospitable to freedom, political subversion, and social change, particularly if these depend on anonymity. Surveillance technologies are everywhere, and true agentic anonymity seems rarer every day. Importantly, surveillance technologies are improving, and the likelihood that our future will be even less hospitable to anonymity is quite high. This is particularly true for subaltern populations who, like Simone Browne (2015), Nick Couldry and Ulises Mejias (2019), and Torin Monahan (2015, 2022) have taught us, are subject to even more radical forms of surveillance and data extraction.

Yet, holding too close to the myth of anonymity is dangerous because all myths, Barthes would remind us, are powerful, convincing, *and* limiting. We can glimpse the limitations of the myth of anonymity by quickly analyzing the word *anonymous* itself, which is a rather old word. Anonymous is found in ancient Greek (ἀνώνυμος), and already in that context, the word referred to a writing or an action not bearing the name of the author or actor.[1] Over time, particularly as the term's use spiked in the sixteenth century in the English context, anonymity acquired other meanings and connotations. As an adjective, anonymous became a synonym of untraceable, unrecognized, uncelebrated, unremarkable, bland, generic, nondescript, impersonal, undistinguishable from others of its kind. From referring to the removal or hiding of a personal name, an identifier, and thus of an author, actor, the markers of an individual, the term has become also an argument about lack of individuality within a set, within a group or category. This is the meaning of anonymity when we use it in the phrase "the anonymous crowd." In the context of anonymity, the individual and the concrete or direct identifier are entwined. One meaning, the one bound to authorial and agentic practices, attends to the human as an author, creator, and an individual. The other attends to humans as generic, unremarkable, members of groups. Anonymity has thus crucial connections to these two important meanings, which are interrelated. The meanings speak to the dialectic of the individual and the collective, perhaps the most human of all dialectics. In both meanings of anonymity, the term points us toward the defining characteristics of individuals, represented in the act of creation, in the freedom to speak to power without repercussions, and in the capacity to be unique even when belonging to a community or human category. In both meanings of anonymity, individuality and group identity are entwined.

The myth linking anonymity to freedom seems convincing because it describes only one type of anonymous activity, the one attending to agency, counterhegemonic acts, and creativity. In this type, anonymity refers to actions by individuals, often subalterns, who try to hide their identities to act in public, as when Mary Wollstonecraft Godwin Shelley, a woman, used anonymity to publish *Frankenstein; or, The Modern Prometheus* in 1818 (Vareschi 2019) in a publishing world unfriendly to women. I call this type of anonymity "agentic anonymity." But, as Thomas DeGloma (2023) and Anon Collective (2021) argue, anonymity has two other important uses by individuals and societies. We also use anonymity to describe institutional norms that hide the identity of individuals in order to do something public, as when we talk about anonymous voting (the secret ballot) or anonymous organ donation. I call this "institutional anonymity." And, as shown by the connotations that the term acquired over time, we also use anonymity to describe contexts in which an individual becomes invisible, unremarkable, nondescript, as in the expression "the anonymous crowd." I call this "contextual anonymity."

Anonymity is simply more than the myth and more than the dialectic pairing to the panopticon. I argue first that to fully explore anonymity, we must step away from the quick association of anonymity and freedom and examine what anonymity actually is and what it does in each of the different types of anonymity. Luckily, even the quickest examination gives us an important clue that can help us advance a study of anonymity, one rooted in the primary denotation of anonymity. In all these types, agentic, institutional, and contextual, *anonymity is indexical dissociation due to identifier substitution, erasure, or suppression*. I use here the term "identifier" in its indexical capacity, in the capacity an identifier like a name has to point toward an individual, or the capacity an identifier like "woman" has to point toward a group of individuals. In this capacity, an identifier is an index, which means that a shortened version of this book's first insight reads as follows: *Anonymity is indexical dissociation*. An individual becomes disconnected from their identity when they are disconnected from their indexes, and whatever public act or product is produced while anonymous (a novel, as in Shelley's case, or a vote, as in the secret ballot), this act or product cannot be traced back to any particular individual. This basic definition of anonymity applies to every instance of anonymity that I can think of, from anonymous trolling to anonymous data in a statistical set and all the in-between. So, it is a good beginning, one that avoids the myth by focusing, as Barthes may suggest, on the primary denotation of anonymity.

Yet, all beginnings should be cautious. Anonymity may always be indexical dissociation, but, is the opposite true? Should all cases of indexical dissociation (which refers to the substitution, erasure, or suppression of indexes) be understood as anonymity? This needs careful consideration, and the easiest way of answering is as follows. I think it is hard to think about all cases of indexical dissociation, but I believe that most cases of indexical dissociation produce the conditions of anonymity. That is, they have the effect of hiding an individual's identity, biography, and specific history. *As a general rule, indexical dissociation anonymizes.*

There is a second complexity that has to do with neighboring terms or terms that sometimes are used to describe some experiences of indexical dissociation. I am thinking in particular of "social invisibility" and "social erasure," two terms that are common and powerful descriptors of forms of indexical dissociation. Social invisibility refers to the experiences of individuals, often subalterns, who are meant to sit in the visual background, not foreground, and are often unseen (Dilhara 2019; Howard-Wagner 2021; Monahan 2022). We use the term "social erasure" to refer to more systematic ways of making some subjects unseen, unacknowledged, not subject to analytic or political consideration. Insofar as these subjects and groups are unseen, invisible, or erased, they are also anonymized, and, for this reason, I use the term "anonymity" as a common condition in all of these cases. That said, that anonymity is a common condition in instances of invisibility and erasure does not mean that these experiences and phenomena can be reduced to anonymity. They are distinct phenomena that include aspects of anonymity, and when I use erasure or invisibility in this book as synonymous with anonymity, I use them only in that capacity.

Prioritizing anonymity's primary denotation (indexical dissociation) proves generative immediately because, if so understood, anonymizing starts showing up in unexpected places, in places that traditionally have not been analyzed as anonymity but fit the criteria. Consider the way in which slave systems have often forced individuals to change their names (indexical dissociation) in order to reduce these individuals to chattel. I believe these are cases of anonymizing in which the institutions central to slavery (slave traders, the church) used anonymizing to dehumanize; slavery erases part of an individual, and the erasure was carried out partly by the imposition of names (I elaborate on this in Chapter 6). Or consider the way women under coverture have been forced or seduced by tradition to change their names after marriage as a way of marking that they belong to their husbands. Coverture anonymizes. Coverture erases part of an individual, and the erasing often includes the imposition of names. Even Gayatri Chakravorty Spivak, in her famous essay "Can the Subaltern Speak?" (1988), uses naming and unnaming to partly explain the erasure and silencing of the subaltern subject. Contextual anonymity also has powerful effects. Sometimes, the anonymity of the crowd makes us feel free, unburdened. Other times, like in Ralph Ellison's (1989) novel *Invisible Man*, invisibility is dehumanizing. Just as Torin Monahan (2022) argues about the ambivalence of visibility, invisibility is full of trappings (5).

I expand on all of these examples and issues in the book. Here, let me simply use them to note that anonymity, understood as a common outcome of indexical dissociation, is neither good nor bad. It may be hard to imagine a good society without anonymity, but I can easily imagine a terrible society that uses anonymity to dehumanize some of its members. I live in one. *Strictly speaking, anonymity is a means by which individuals and institutions can change or bypass power arrangements. Anonymity is also an identity possibility that enables or forces individuals to live in what Mariana Ortega (2016) calls the "in-between," the space between multiple identities, their constraints, and their power* (see also DeGloma 2023). Paine could be a loyal British subject one moment to some people, and in some contexts, and a seditious person in another moment to other people in other contexts. Shelley could be a "proper" woman at one time and an author at another, which, in this context, was a masculinized identity. But Paine and Shelley exemplify also different manifestations and possibilities of the in-between and of anonymity. Paine was not born a dissident. Shelley was born a woman, and this identity marker, this index, placed boundaries over which she had no control. Paine could have remained a royalist. Shelley could not stop being a woman, at least within the gender norms of the time. An ascriptive (by birth) identity marker can thus produce anonymizing effects that the individual experiences as inauthenticity, the inability of the identity marker to represent the true self. Trans, nonbinary, and intersex individuals often struggle with identity markers and seek to change them when possible. In these cases, anonymity is indexical dissociation, but identity is not represented by identity markers, and individuals often seek to change identity markers in order to feel in harmony with their identifiers (Spade 2015).

Over the course of history, the bad uses of indexical dissociation (in slavery or coverture) have shaped history and modernity, and they are as important as the good outcomes of anonymity (political freedom and subversion of oppressive norms). Our lives have been partly the product of an economy of anonymity, which has allowed for its positive and negative effects to be part integral of our lives. With the phrase "economy of anonymity" I mean to highlight a distribution system that dictates who can have anonymity, who cannot, what institutions can use it and for what ends, and in what contexts individuals are likely to become anonymous. The phrase also tries to make sense of anonymity as a social technique that becomes a currency that people and institutions use in order to exist or in order to carry out their goals and objectives. The currency of anonymity may not be tradable, but it is subject to heavy investment. When it is worthwhile, we invest heavily in being known and in moving away from anonymity; when it is worthwhile, we invest heavily in becoming invisible, as when we use any of the products like VPNs that allow us to use the web anonymously.

It is difficult to determine whether the economy of anonymity has produced more good than bad. Are the negative outcomes of coverture more important than the revolutionary potential of anonymous writing? It depends on who answers the question. Those who have needed or used the in-between less for their primary identity because their primary identity offers the privilege of power may answer differently than those who by history, choice, or nature had needed to live in-between. I suspect that those in the former would value a great deal of institutional anonymity and the tactical deployment of anonymizing techniques toward the marginalized. I also suspect that the latter would value agentic anonymity. But if we think of anonymity as a social technique, then we can answer this question more confidently, as it is not whether anonymity has produced more good than bad but rather what kind of political outcomes anonymity enables, for whom, and under what circumstances, and how anonymity structures particular forms of power and for whom.

Even if it is difficult to determine whether anonymity has produced more good than bad, in a modernity increasingly shaped by technology and datafication, *I can state with certitude that the economy of anonymity is transforming*. True agentic anonymity is at risk of disappearing, while the power of institutions, corporations, and governments to use anonymizing tactics remains the same or is expanding. As I note earlier, increasingly, we have the option of being anonymous to those around us, but not to the eye of power.

I am compelled by the insight that the economy of anonymity is changing and, as mentioned before, by the fear that we have not yet grasped the significance of what this means. Scholars who say otherwise, I believe, tend to be scholars who attend to anonymity only from a narrow, ends-focused, often mythic, perspective, and, to these scholars, anonymity is relatively easy to understand and evaluate. If someone thinks about anonymity only in the context of anonymous publishing or political dissidence, they think of anonymity as a social good that we should protect. Period. If someone thinks of anonymity in relationship to the way anonymity helps the proliferation of hate speech on the web, they think of anonymity as a social evil that we should police. Period. We ought to instead hold on to all the facets and complexities of anonymity in order to understand what anonymity means to society today and what it may mean tomorrow. So, if the question driving this book is, What will happen to individuals and societies as we lose agentic anonymity at the same time that institutional and contextual anonymity continue or gain strength?, then I first have to ask the questions, What is anonymity? And, what does it mean to theorize anonymity in a way that attends to all its social and individual outcomes? But, first, what does it mean to theorize anonymity from a subaltern position?

Subaltern Theorizing and Anonymity

The term "subaltern" is associated with several interconnected traditions, including Marxism, postcolonialism, South Asian studies, and Latin American studies, to name the few more relevant to this book. While recent uses of the term connect it to the lived realities of colonial subjects, in particular those in India (e.g., the work of Ranajit Guha) and Latin America (e.g., the work of Ileana Rodríguez), the way the term "subaltern" first entered our theoretical imaginaries was through the work of Antonio Gramsci. In this book, I return to Gramsci but do so thankful that the South Asian and Latin American subaltern groups have added depth and complexity to the term.

In Gramsci's work, the subaltern relates, broadly speaking, to marginal groups and communities dominated by hegemonic forces. In Gramsci's writings, the original use of the term was sometimes metaphoric, as when Gramsci (Gramsci and Buttigieg 1992) writes on Engels as occupying "a subaltern position in relation to Marx" (Notebook 4, §1), and other times descriptive of specific social classes: "Subaltern classes are subject to the initiatives of the dominant class, even when they rebel; they are in a state of anxious defense" (Notebook 3, §14). While both of these uses are important, I am interested in a third use of the term by Gramsci implicit in his goal of developing a subaltern historiography. This goal, which was shared also by South Asian subaltern studies and Latin American subaltern groups, matters because it implies that theorizing and historicizing have perspectives and that only some theorizing is subaltern. I believe that subaltern theorizing is not necessarily about the experiences or histories of subaltern communities or individuals. Subaltern theorizing is about the perspective of theory and the type of questions one asks.

Eduardo Mendieta (2008) writes a powerful explanation of what subaltern theorizing means, one particularly useful to my project. In illustrating the difference between postcolonial theory and subaltern studies, he writes:

> What is at stake on one [postcolonial] side is to think from the larger canvas of history, not assuming the givenness of this canvas, but pre-

> cisely to question the existence and nature of the canvas as the very condition of the possibility of painting something like the scene of history, that is, not just how history happens, but why history is required in order to think the very possibility of agency at a macrolevel, as the agency of social ensembles. On the other [subaltern] side, what is at stake is to think the space of subjectivity as one that is already occupied by the sociohistorical, to think how the subjectivities of the master and the slave are co-determined and co-determining. In this way we may think of subaltern studies as an ensemble of investigations into modes of subjection, an analytics not of *dasein* but of subjected and revolted agency, an analytics in which one is not only and always the subaltern of another, but in which this one is also an insurrected and resisting other. Subaltern studies thus always imply a theory of insurrected agencies, agencies that inaugurate and disclose new modalities and horizons of praxis, or social action. (300)

At issue in subaltern theorizing, Mendieta argues, are modes of subjection, particularly those given shape by forms of domination. In this book, the question "what is anonymity?" is answered precisely in reference to the subject and domination, attuned to anonymity's capacity to shape subjectivity and interiorized forms of power.

This book presents a subaltern theory of anonymity first because it analyzes the way anonymity shapes subjectivity and anonymity's role in the interiorization of power. Second, because the book is rooted in questions, issues, perspectives, and theoretical insights developed first by subaltern theorists like Gloria Anzaldúa, Mariana Ortega, Ulises Mejias, and Nick Couldry. And, third, because the project is centrally concerned with understanding anonymity as it relates to subaltern subjectivities and experiences. This means that most of the examples and cases I explore come from subaltern communities and individuals (e.g., Latine, Indigenous groups, women, sexual minorities, and immigrants), but not every case listed here refers to subalterns. The reason is simple. Anonymity shapes everybody's lives and subjectivities, and I am interested in the human condition and how this condition is partly constituted by indexical dissociation. One more note. Not every theorist or scholar referenced here fits the criteria of subaltern scholar, partly because I personally believe that the measure of good work is not provenance but insight. This means that my bibliography is not a litmus test of who has written on anonymity from a subaltern perspective but my honest assessment of who has shown us the way to clarity and understanding regarding issues and questions pertaining to anonymity.

So, I set my quest on the difficult task of thinking anonymity conceptually, from a subaltern perspective, in such a way that this conceptualization can explain anonymity in relation to the subject; in different social domains; in relationship to individuals, institutions, and contexts; in relationship to epistemology and ontology; and in relationship to history and society. This can be achieved only by first demystifying anonymity, and an effective way of achieving this is seeing anonymity before the mystification happens, before the effects of anonymity, good or bad, settle down, at the moment of mediation, at the moment in which indexical dissociation happens.

Anonymity and Other Approaches to Indexes

Engaging anonymity at the moment of mediation, as indexical dissociation, makes anonymity an object of research analytically connected to other intellectual pursuits that focus on the study of identification and indexes (personal identifiers). These traditions include surveillance studies, privacy studies, and socio-technical approaches to classifications. In these strong analytic approaches, anonymity is often addressed, is implied, or exists like a black hole, a concept that we cannot quite see except for the effects on the concepts around it. Yet, these traditions' importance to this project is significant, even if anonymity is sometimes not mentioned, for it is through some of these studies that we can learn the potential epistemological, social, political, and ontological consequences related to changes in the economy of anonymity.

Surveillance studies are invested in explaining how institutions, governments, and communities use socio-technical systems like CCTV (video surveillance) technologies to identify populations and individuals. Privacy studies care about the human and legal need to carry out activities in spaces away from surveillance, without the burden of identification. Socio-technical approaches to classification explore the epistemological, social, and ontological effects of being identified or classified in a particular way. Anonymity is indexical dissociation, a technique that "presents" individuals in public without their identifiers being attached to their action or publications. Identification and indexes are thus the common thread in these analytic approaches.

These approaches are so connected that sometimes they are hard to distinguish. In the nineteenth century, the Brontë sisters, like other female authors, published anonymously to bypass patriarchal restrictions on cultural production and property. They did so to avoid social surveillance, and thus personal consequences, but these consequences were rooted in the fact that their names, their indexes, were women's names. Charlotte Brontë writes a historic preface to the 1850 *Wuthering Heights* edition, a year after her sister Emily, the author, had died of tuberculosis:

> Averse to personal publicity, we veiled our own names under those of Currer, Ellis and Acton Bell; the ambiguous choice being dictated by a sort of conscientious scruple at assuming Christian names positively masculine, while we did not like to declare ourselves women, because—without at that time suspecting that our mode of writing and thinking was not what is called "feminine"—we had a vague impression that authoresses are liable to be looked on with prejudice; we had noticed how critics sometimes use for their chastisement the weapon of personality, and for their reward, a flattery, which is not true praise. (Gaskel 1985, 286)

Their names, Brontë reminds us, pointed specifically to her and her sisters, and categorically to women, which meant that their indexes activated classifications and power constraints specific to women that they personally wanted to avoid. These classificatory constraints mattered to the Brontë sisters because these names pointed specifically, not generally, to them. That is, the name Emily Brontë at the time pointed to a concrete person, a specific body, who would suffer the consequences of acting "inappropriately." And even though the basis of this judgment or "chastisement" (as written by Brontë) was gender categories, it is the direct identifier Charlotte or Emily Brontë that would specify the target of the punishment. Accountability of the type that Nissenbaum discusses in the quotation at the beginning of the chapter thus exists in at least two registers: in the register of categories and classifications like "woman" or "seditious" (as in Thomas Paine, mentioned earlier) and in the register of direct identifiers or concrete indexes like personal names, which make possible for social norms, juridical structures, and knowledge systems to have specific targets (Hacking 1986).

Like the case of Charlotte and Emily Brontë illustrates, events pertaining to anonymity are often implicitly or explicitly also about surveillance, classifications, and others are also about privacy. The reason is simple and important. The analytic cluster of anonymity, surveillance, privacy, and classifications is connected by a focus on the capacities and possibilities of indexes as identifiers. Yet, even the quickest review of the literature on the cluster reveals asymmetries. Today, studies of classifications are driven by the importance of indexes to datafication and computation. Studies of privacy, which obviously connect to identification, are common because datafication has made it a pressing issue to academics, activists, and pundits. To my surprise, rarely do studies of surveillance or privacy engage anonymity as the opposite of identification. Seminal work in surveillance studies like David Lyon's *The Electronic Eye* (1994) does not attend to anonymity and instead places privacy as the opposite of identification, and this tendency has persisted. Shoshana Zuboff's massive and influential book *The Age of Surveillance Capitalism* (2019) echoes Lyon's approach. She does not consider anonymity as central to her concerns and instead considers privacy the key issue opposite to datafication. The same is true in Sarah Igo's *The Known Citizen: A History of Privacy in Modern America* (2018) and Colin Koopman's *How We Became Our Data: A Genealogy of the Information Person* (2019). In these exceptionally great books, indexes are in a dialectic relationship to privacy, not anonymity.

To the credit of the authors, the reasons are quite important. Privacy issues are at stake, for instance, at the moment that our personal data when shopping on the internet is kept, bundled, and sold to third parties. For this reason alone, privacy has become a huge concern today. Yet, privacy is different from anonymity, and issues related to anonymity also have significant social, personal, and political importance. Troublingly, at times, the terms "privacy" and "anonymity" are conflated, and it is tempting, in the current socio-technical context, to see them as confusingly overlapping. Yet, they are always different.

Privacy is about being able to carve a space away from political, social, and capitalistic surveillance (Lyon 1994, 14; 2004). Privacy is a spatial category that denotes three locations: an outside, the position of the onlookers; an opaque boundary that limits the possibility of, from the outside, looking in; and the private space in which actions can be carried out without outside witnesses. So, privacy is a concept describing activities that you keep entirely to yourself or to a limited group of people. In privacy, your identity is known within the private space but hidden to those outside that space. From the perspective of those outside, your identity is hidden and so are the activities in which you engage in privacy.

In contrast, anonymity is about public actions. Mary Shelley wanted her novels in public, with the public. She wanted people to read what she created. She did not want her ideas to remain private. But for her ideas to be public, her identity needed to remain hidden. Such is often the burden of the subaltern. She needed anonymity, not privacy. To blow the whistle on abuse of power or other forms of crime in your organization without risking career and social standing in that group is similarly about anonymity, not privacy, which is why we typically have strong laws that protect sources of the free press. In anonymity, your identity is hidden but not your actions. Although both privacy and anonymity produce secrets and use indexical dissociation techniques, privacy and anonymous behaviors are actually the opposite (Amaya 2020; J. Dean 2018; Lyon 1994, 187).

This is not to say that privacy is always clearly the opposite of anonymity. I believe that concerns about privacy often overlap with concerns over anonymity because of the changing nature of our social lives and the very materiality in which we exist. At one point, the universe of our social interactions was given shape by physical matter, by walls, by streets, by rooms, by alleys. And we constructed ideas, and even policies and laws, about privacy and publicity that were pertinent to this material logic. Privacy was associated with the home; publicity, with the plaza or the town hall. The home was important for its walls; the agora, for its openness. As Zizi Papacharissi (2010) reminds us, the digital complicates the distinction between public and private, opened and closed, commercial and public (Monahan 2022). In digital contexts, privacy and anonymity seem rather similar. But they are not. Anonymity should always be about an individual's public life, even if this public life is carried out in privately owned social spaces such as TikTok or 4chan. Importantly, life is not equal to digital contexts, and anonymity plays a role in all material contexts.

Because anonymity is always about public life, anonymity is the result of public and shareable means of signification and experience that give meaning and value to a person's identity. In all its forms, agentic, institutional, and contextual, anonymity is anchored on identificatory language and practices. Simply, if anonymity is indexical dissociation, to understand anonymity requires that we also understand indexical association and the way indexical association relates to public life. Last, if our goal is to understand the power effects of surveillance or datafication from a subaltern perspective, we need to ask questions about anonymity, which happens in public, the realm for "insurrected agencies," "praxis, or social action," to borrow Mendieta's words. Privacy matters, but, for subalterns, the possibilities or impossibilities of social action matter more.

Anonymity, Identifiers, and Index Types

Personal identifiers, indexes, are at the center of the analytic cluster of anonymity, surveillance, privacy, and classifications, and this is the first clue as to what it means to define anonymity as indexical dissociation. The capacities and possibilities of anonymity are singularly connected to the capacities and possibilities of indexes. And what is the defining capacity of indexes? Indexes point: They point toward an individual or a group of individuals. Indexes connect a sign (a name, a race) to a specific body or set of bodies. The name Charlotte Brontë would have associated her novels to her person, her body, and her gender. The pseudonym Currer Bell did not. In fact, the pseudonym also pointed, but it pointed away from her as a person and from her gender. Charlotte Brontë was able to remain anonymous, in the in-between, not because her novels lacked attribution but rather because the someone they pointed toward was a fictive person represented by a name, Currer Bell, that pointed to an empty space, to no-body.

Anonymity is not lack of identification. Even the term "Anonymous," sometimes used to fill the space of the author, identifies. Anonymity thus depends on the capacities and possibilities of indexes. The most important one of these capacities is the capacity to point toward an individual. In the next chapter, I elaborate on how this indexical capacity connects to the work of Charles Peirce and other philosophers of language. Here, it is sufficient to state that the cluster of anonymity, surveillance, privacy, and classifications is connected to the indexical capacity of personal identifiers, and I understand this to be a technical connection. The cluster shares, and depends on, a technique. Just as human indexes are important for their capacity to point toward an individual, anonymity always refers to the technique of pointing away from an individual or group. Indexes create an association, a link between a sign (a name, an SSN, a racial classification) and a person or a group. Anonymity breaks that link and thus dissociates an individual or a group from their identity. But dissociation is complex.

First, dissociation does not mean lack of association. Every action has an actor; every publishing has an author; every human has a history and a body. Charlotte Brontë used the pseudonym Currer Bell to publish her work. She broke the associational link between her name and her person but constructed another link toward a fictive human named Currer Bell. Even a manuscript without an author is presumed to be authored; thus the term "someone" stands for the author, and that someone has a history, a place, and a social location. That we don't know the specifics means only that the author built a link away from their person. Anonymity depends on substitution, and thus anonymity uses the principle of identification. Anonymity is indexical, but it points toward another human with another body and history.

Second, we can dissociate from our names and use a fake name or nickname in some settings; some may be able to dissociate themselves from ethnicities or genders, and the histories of ethnic and racial passing as well as the histories of gender fluidity attest to this; but we cannot dissociate ourselves from every personal identifier. Our DNA, for instance, is with us always, and we leave DNA traces often without us knowing it. Some indexes like names are thus movable or subject to interpretation, while others like DNA are, arguably, not. I expand on this issue in the next section.

Third, anonymity is also contextual, not only agentic. In some contexts, we are and we feel anonymous. A person can be dissociated from their identity when a person is ignored, as in cases of social invisibility (e.g., as in the experiences of Brown and Black women in some social and professional settings) or in cases in which an individual is simply part of a crowd. These dissociations may not be initiated by the individual (the anonymity of the crowd), and some may be experienced against an individual's wishes (to be socially invisible), but they produce forms of anonymity. We feel and are anonymous when caught in the dialectic of visible invisibility (Taylor 2016).

I have walked into supermarkets as a Brown male person to find myself under surveillance from security people who, I am certain, would implicitly trust me if they knew I was a respected professor at an esteemed academic institution. One identity marker, my brownness, identifies me, and, in that context, it also makes me anonymous, without a specific history or social standing. Hypervisibility and invisibility are often dialectical, and the reason, Monahan (2022, 70–73) helped me understand, is that we are subject to multiple and sometimes contrasting interpellations. We feel and are anonymous in a crowd, and this opens up some opportunities for behavior and closes others depending on the spectrum of interpellations our bodies activate. Strictly speaking, we are different social beings when we are in a crowd, with different forms of power. We have some degree of impunity, and we may be rude to others under the cover of anonymity, as when we bump our shoulder against someone else's and do not apologize. Perhaps this is why rules of politeness seem more prevalent in small communities, human organizations where bumping against another is rarely anonymous. But we also have less power in a crowd. The person who suffers rudeness in a crowd suffers it partly because they are not seen as worthy of the utmost respect and the interaction is seen as inconsequential, a type of social calculation that is less common in a small town or a tight community, where people encounter each other all the time and one cannot presume that social interactions do not have consequences. In a crowd, for instance, hard-earned social standing may be gone. Indexical dissociation is simply complex, as these examples begin to illustrate.

The complexities do not end there. If we understand anonymity as indexical dissociation, then we can find instances or forms of anonymity in other practices seldomly defined as anonymous but often considered as instances of indexical dissociation. I mention two at the beginning of the chapter, slavery and coverture. What about the branding of numbers on prisoners' skin in Nazi concentration camps, which reidentified them as numbers? What can we make of the forced or disciplinary removal of names during colonization in the Americas? I was compelled to change my name when I took US citizenship. Didn't a part of me become anonymous, hidden from public view, forced into invisibility? While anybody can become anonymous or be anonymized, the experiences of the subaltern often include forms of anonymity.

As Gary Marx (2001) has noted, different types of indexes perform different social, legal, administrative, and cultural tasks, and it is important to note these differences. Indexes have specific affordances, including different anonymity possibilities. These possibilities are the most consequential to subaltern individuals and communities whose lives are more constricted by power structures and forces. I believe there are at least four types of indexes derived from semiosis or the nature of the signs we use as indexes: *natural language indexes* like names or racial designations; *alphanumeric indexes* that are needed to interact with specific institutions (SSNs) or technologies (email address); *digital indexes*, which are central to computation; and *biological indexes* such as DNA, fingerprints, and biometrics. They can all be used for anonymity, but they tend to present particular possibilities depending on the type.

Natural Language Indexes

Natural language indexes exist within traditional signifying systems and exist in culture and history. For that reason, these indexes have the capacity to connote and denote and even have rich discourses centered around them, as would the index "woman" or "foreign." The semiotic capacity expands their social uses and connects them to a wide array of power arrangements. This expansion is socially productive and reductive, for it allows a synthetic sharing of information through the use of a single word. With a concrete index like José Pérez, others can identify an individual as a specific individual, but also as a Latine and an ethnic minority. The word *Pérez* calls attention to an array of discourses, from specific histories (e.g., the history of US expansionism into the West) to theories of ethnicity and race that become precedent and context to actions. Once the person has been identified as Latine, the actions of that individual, their words, movements, and the objects that surround them, become the testing ground for theories of ethnicity. Those interacting with that individual would perhaps routinely ask themselves, "Does he talk like a Latine?"; "Does he think like a Latine?"; or "Does he eat spicy food like many other Latines do?" This set of questions and answers would confirm the ethnic discourses, histories, and theories activated by the name, expand them, or place them in the category of exceptions to the rule.

Famous examples of people choosing anonymity by changing their names to escape ethno-racial connotations of natural language indexes abound. In places like Hollywood, where names mean casting possibilities, the practice has been common. Martin Sheen was born Ramón Estevez. Chloe Bennet was Chloe Wang. Kal Penn was Kalpen Suresh Modi. Mindy Kaling was Vera Mindy Chokalingam. Larry King was born Lawrence Harvey Ziegler. Almost invariably, cases like these involve the removal of an ethnic name and the adoption of an Anglo-sounding name. In cases like Martin Sheen and Larry King, as in many others, changing names was also about manufacturing whiteness and displacing or hiding subaltern status. In this simple move, a minority becomes a majority, at least partly. All of these cases are instances of anonymity quite similar to that of Mary Shelley or the Brontë sisters. New names are meant to change the meaning of a person's work in public. All these are efforts by the actors to control how others will perceive them and even to control their chances of employment.

There are many reasons that people choose to live under a name different from the one they were given at birth, but most reasons relate to the fact that names connote categorical indexes. Categorical indexes like racial and gender designations live in natural languages and are so rich that there are full academic disciplines partly and even centrally concerned with the study of what some categorical indexes mean, including gender studies, African American studies, queer studies, Chicano studies, and so on. From psychological-driven studies about stereotypes, to critical cultural studies about discursive and semantic connotations of terms like "women," "Black," "Mexican," and so on, the study of categorical indexes is multidisciplinary and quite ambitious. The concern is not, however, too different. Almost every study about categorical indexes, regardless of method or discipline, proposes that these indexes shape the life possibilities of groups and of individuals. To be designated a woman is to be offered the life, economic, political, and historical possibilities the term references and, sometimes, no others. Unsurprisingly, these markers of identity have been at the center of emancipatory projects, which sometimes we term "identity politics," which are a significant proportion of emancipation projects in pluralistic societies.

The anonymizing effects of natural language indexes often relate to the signifying and cultural power of natural language. It is because these indexes are embedded in culture that they matter, and individuals and institutions use them to change the meaning of a life or mark life changes, as in the cultural imposition of making a woman change her birth name after marriage. Natural language indexes have been crucial to administration, and, for that reason, they have become central to our administrative identities. Until relatively recently, natural language indexes were the primary way by which governments kept track of populations. So, for most of history, state administration has centered on indexes like names, genders, caste, and race to administer and control populations, and the histories of taxation, conscription, slavery, and coverture illustrate my point.

It is only until very recently, in most cases in the nineteenth century or later, that states began using alternative modes of identification to supplement or complement natural language indexical systems. Many of these new index systems, though not all, are based on numbers (SSNs) or alphanumeric combinations, such as indexes in passports, driver's licenses, prisoner roles, and employee records.

Alphanumeric Indexes

Alphanumeric indexes use numbers and/or letters as digits, not as quantities or as a part of words. All alphanumeric indexes represent a unique individual, one person. My SSN is meant to single me out, to point toward me among the set of roughly three hundred plus million US citizens and residents. Alphanumeric indexes may be unique in that they connect one index to one person, but they are also contextual, as in prisoner numbers that are specific to a prison, school identification numbers that are specific to that school, or license plate numbers that are specific to the state. In these cases, an alphanumeric index is unique only in that prison, in that school, or in that state.

Alphanumeric indexes rarely index alone as identifiers and typically connect to a name and sometimes to an address or other individual indexes such as a race, an ethnicity, a gender, an age, and a date of birth. In some important cases such as with the SSN, they are unique and connect one index to only one person. Or at least that is the theory. The reality may be different, and what alphanumeric symbols actually provide is a unique combination of symbols that *represents* one person. Numbers and alphanumeric combinations are representational and can be understood as key symbolic mechanisms that attest to what Mary Poovey (1998) may call the facticity of an individual, and this facticity is not based on the onticity of humans as a species but on the onticity of *humans as a set of creatures* with individual characteristics, the ontology of life, if you wish. No two living things are the same, and this truism (it is, after all, a theory) could be represented only with alphanumeric indexes. At least theoretically, humans, a mere eight billion, could be shown unique with alphanumeric indexes.

In the United States, the SSN is perhaps the most consequential alphanumeric index, and it allows for particular types of anonymity. There are markets for buying SSNs that target undocumented immigrants and other individuals wishing to change identities. The reasons are multiple. SSNs are meant to be private and only be used between the citizen and/or legal resident and the institution in particular but consequential transactions. In most states, SSNs are needed to get a job, a credit card, a driver's license, and even a bank account. For undocumented immigrants, SSNs mean access to most labor markets, which makes SSNs crucial to their life goals. SSNs are mostly sold as part of data packets that include other kinds of personal information and indexes. According to experts in cybersecurity, an SSN alone may be bought for as little as $2 each, but packets of personal data that include health or medical records, passport information, and other contact information can cost over $1,000 and be used to create fake IDs and identities. This is why hackers target institutions that keep a multiplicity of these personal data.

Alphanumeric indexes have the advantage of easy storage and the capacity of full concreteness: that is, they can be, theoretically, unique. This makes them ideal for the administration of large quantities of people and for connecting different data points to specific individuals (credit records). This capacity for representational concreteness allows for alphanumeric indexes to open up new avenues for thinking about the management of individuals and the social and governmental capacities of surveillance.

A history of alphanumeric indexes does not have the same sequential form as the history of natural language indexes. Alphanumeric indexes follow the rise and popularization of statistical thinking in the nineteenth century and, later, the rise of computation at the end of the nineteenth and beginning of the twentieth century. They are great for ordering systems. Simply, alphanumeric indexes could make sense only if states and other institutions had the epistemic and technological capacity to handle the vast amount of data management that these indexes require. Names are social first and institutional second. Alphanumeric indexes are mostly institutional.

Digital Indexes

The complexities of personal data security in today's world have to do with the fact that most indexes can become *digital indexes*, which are binary and use only two digits: zeroes and ones. Digital indexes are unique because many binary indexes are created, invented, or crafted out of human/computer willful and consensual interactions (e.g., emails that rely on email addresses) and human/computer interactions independent of human consent, as when a digital surveillance camera captures your image. Most indexes, including natural language indexes, alphanumeric indexes such as SSNs, and biological indexes such as DNA, can be made digital, which means that today the digital index category is the most expansive of them all. Importantly, current computational practices have made digital indexes unique also in that they are typically created alongside metadata, which allows the index to be concrete (e.g., name) or categorical (e.g., woman) but always associated with a context for the metadata that often includes a time stamp and geolocation. The uniqueness of digital indexes has compelled many to believe that the essence of power is changing, and, because of this, humans are also transforming.

Because digital indexes are ubiquitous, and because they are sometimes self-assigned (digital nicknames, avatars, email addresses), individuals use them to craft anonymous identities that can be used for play (as in the use of a nickname to play a video game), for identity experimentation (when individuals create an avatar in MOOC to experience what it means to be of a different sex or species), for avoiding accountability (when individuals create a fake identity to troll), or for criminal activity. Self-assigned digital indexes have made anonymity a prevalent way of social interaction in today's society even if in many cases an individual is anonymous only to other individuals, not to the platform (e.g., TikTok or Facebook). True anonymity in digital environments is actually hard to attain.

There is a second and consequential way in which anonymity connects to digital indexes. Starting with the statistical turn in the nineteenth century and continuing today, most categorical statistical sets (e.g., the universe of "rural" or "republican") included large quantities of individuals. This meant that in most statistical imaginaries, such as the social sciences that created and theorized the data, individuals could be represented anonymously. Categorical indexes connected individuals to power but did so as members of sets, of classes, of ethnicities, of genders. In so connecting, individuals become partly anonymous, subject to theorizing as abstract, not real, members of the social.

The statistical turn lives in the data world, and so does group-based anonymization. But, in addition, privacy concerns have normalized or mandated practices of data collection that anonymize data, and this includes occlusion or erasure of concrete indexes like names and SSNs and the generalization of categorical indexes like age (the literature on data sometimes refers to this strategy as k-anonymity). Other strategies include reducing the granularity of data representation, which reduces the ability of sets to be useful for data management but attends to the need for privacy (sometimes these are referred to as L-Diverse and T-closeness strategies) (Jain et al. 2016; Smith and Waldo 2023).

Privacy advocates would be quick to note that data anonymization is far from being the norm or sufficient. There are algorithmic means by which to deanonymize data, and a lot of data is collected without these protections or expectations. The result, again, is that full digital anonymity is difficult to achieve, even though data anonymization exists and is expanding, at least in some nations and regions like the European Union.

Biological Indexes

Biological indexes are based on bodies as these exist or have existed in their environment and tend to be particularly consequential to subalterns. They are also more complex than the previous three categories because they are not based on signs alone, but the capacity of biological features to be used to constitute unique systems of identification and unique traces as in the case of concrete indexes such as fingerprints, footprints, DNA, facial features, voice, and even gait, as well as categorical indexes such as phenotypes, skin coloration, body types, and aurality. The complexity is twofold: Some biological indexes are mediated by natural language indexes like "woman" or "tall," and they thus inherit the linguistic, discursive, cultural, and semiotic possibilities of natural language. At this level, biological indexes become words that represent absences and relate to referents, as Ferdinand de Saussure (1959) helped us see, in arbitrary ways. Words like *woman* or *tall* represent biological indexes and should be treated like other natural language indexes.

But biological indexes have a second level of complexity. Biological indexes may also signify because they have become mediated through systems that make them "readable" even if they are not represented by words, as in the case of fingerprints that police forces have used since the nineteenth century to identify individuals. With fingerprints, the trace is an attestation of the presence of a specific body, and thus the relationship between sign (fingerprint) and referent (body) is a relationship of correspondence and dependency. Only one finger can yield a particular fingerprint. This relation, contra Saussure, is not arbitrary, which makes these types of biological indexes signs that truly stand in for the body and for the person. If natural language indexes account for absent bodies, biological indexes like fingerprints, faces, and voices account for present bodies, which makes them ideal for situations of legal accountability.

Many biological indexes like facial features and skin coloration have very active social lives, and, because of this, they shape social interactions. These indexes work alongside natural language indexes like names and racial categories to present an individual to others, and they help others produce inferences about the individual and thus about the way the individual should be understood and treated. We presume that these indexes are connected to race, gender, age, fitness level, and sexual orientation and routinely use them to identify and classify people. Someone is a woman; that other is beautiful; he must be Chinese; she is at least fifty years old; that person sounds like a smoker; that woman sounds like a little girl; that guy sounds queer and walks queer, and so on.

A history of biological indexes may be a mixture of histories of gender and race but also of beauty, fitness, and well-being, one that attends to the social work of reproductive organs, skin, phenotypes, body types, and coloring, particularly as these visual indexes connect with hierarchy, power, privilege, marginalization, and epistemology. On gender and sex, Elizabeth Grosz (1994) writes about the scope of questions pertinent to a history of biological indexes as follows:

> There are always only specific types of body, concrete in their determinations, with a particular sex, race, and physiognomy. When one body (in the West, the white, youthful, able, male body) takes on the function of model or ideal, the human body, for all other types of body, its domination may be undermined through a defiant affirmation of a multiplicity, a field of differences, of other kinds of bodies and subjectivities. A number of ideal types of body must be posited to ensure the production, projection, and striving for ideal images and body types to which each individual, in his or her distinct way, may aspire. Only when the relation between mind and body is adequately retheorized can we understand the contributions of the body to the production of knowledge systems, regimes of representation, cultural production, and socioeconomic exchange. (19)

Body types, of course, do not exist without biological indexes, and the public, political, epistemic, and cultural life of bodies, the way they are represented in our body politics, in our sciences, and in the stories we value, is always through reference to specific biological traces, often visual, but not always. When Mary Shelley (1993) anonymously writes *Frankenstein; or, The Modern Prometheus*, she describes the monster as a giant, eight feet tall, whose yellowish skin and appearance elicited nightmares: "No mortal could support the horror of that countenance. A mummy again endued with animation could not be so hideous as that wretch. I had gazed on him while unfinished; he was ugly then, but when those muscles and joints were rendered capable of motion, it became a thing such as even Dante could not have conceived" (46). From skin color to the visibility of muscles and joints, the height, and the countenance, the monster is so because of specific biological indexes that translate into ethical and social assumptions for which the monster will pay a debt never incurred. Such is the burden of the subaltern.

As Grosz and Shelley remind us, body types, biological indexes, rarely sit isolated in the field of description. They are almost always part of active discourses and theorizations about humanity, difference, and subjectivity. They represent morality (as in the discourse of obesity today), purity (as in discourses of beauty), education (as in discourses of race and ethno-racial difference), class, and so on, and, for this reason, biological indexes shape humanity; they are the essential markers that allow prejudice (positive or negative) to exist. They simplify the social by allowing for quick inferences about others (wrong as they may be) and make the social livable, even if in so doing they also make it unjust and even ghostly. That is, if the social is partly the result of the inferences we attach to biological indexes, the social is the product of those ghostly figures that, like the monster in Shelley's *Frankenstein*, populate our minds and move us toward miscalculated actions. We say to ourselves routinely, "that person is pretty," and we wish to interact with them; "that person looks dangerous," and we move away from them; "that person looks like family," and we use our warmest smile when facing them; "that person looks wealthy," and we use deference. Far from the rationality associated by some economists to human behavior, a genealogy of biological indexes would show social and economic structures shaped by things seen but unproven, the rational choice of humans as they relate to ghosts and monsters.

With the Enlightenment, biological indexes entered into the realm of science and have shaped profoundly disturbing epistemologies, including all the sciences that attend to gender, sex, race, and ethnicity, crucial categories for subalterns. From the disturbing works like Joseph-Arthur, comte de Gobineau, who writes in 1853 *An Essay on the Inequality of Human Races* (Gobineau 1915), to the systematicity of racial science found in Johann Friedrich Blumenbach's racial anthropology, which would influence deeply Samuel Morton's own *Crania American; or, A Comparative View of the Skulls of Various Aboriginal Nations of North and South America* (1839), science has fueled racism. Blumenbach, for instance, correlates craniums with intellectual and moral character, which allows him to assert that "the CAUCASIAN RACE . . . is distinguished for the facility with which it attains the highest intellectual endowments," and, of "the AMERICAN RACE," Blumenbach argued we were/are "averse to cultivation, and slow in acquiring knowledge; restless, revengeful, and fond of war, and wholly destitute of maritime adventure" (qtd. in Morton 1839, 3). Morton takes it from there and further specifies the characteristics of other Indigenous peoples, which become, like the monster in Shelley's work, the not-quite-human product of science who will suffer the consequences of having encountered men like Blumenbach and Morton.[2]

Just as the meaning of biological indexes shaped the racial and ethnic life of everyone in the last few centuries, other sciences participated in the constitution of meaning and understanding regarding the biological markers of gender and sex. The work on hysteria of influential French neurologist Jean Martin Charcot, for instance, shaped neurology and psychology and influenced popular ideas about gender and womanhood (see Evans 2019). Medicine, biology, and psychology colluded with cultural and political structures to reconstitute a science-backed patriarchal system that used biological indexes as markers of radical difference, radical because it was rooted in nature: wombs, hormones, breasts, penises, testicles, and so on. How convenient to have science-backed arguments about illnesses, weaknesses, and differences that would grant man the upper hand on leadership, success, and humanity, as Grosz would state it. Until very recently, the age of Enlightenment was not the age of human equality. It was the age of biological indexes justifying inequalities. Colonialism, racial patriarchy, the deep sexism of coverture, to past and some current anti-LGBTQ rhetoric and policies, are unequal structures supported, more or less consistently, by science.

The relationship between biological indexes and culture, politics, and science has meant that these indexes are both inevitable and sometimes feel oppressive. They are often public and thus have a social life that individuals do not necessarily control. But when they can, biological indexes provide the opportunity to change the social meaning of our bodies. Plastic surgery, for instance, allows individuals to fit standards of beauty, age, and even race. Nadia Kim (2008) shows how eyelid surgery became popular in postwar Japan and in Korea in the wake of the Korean War, and she argues that we must understand today's massive plastic surgery industry in nations like South Korea as the result of US occupation. She even presents evidence of army surgeons like Dr. Ralph Millard, who undertook these procedures on Korean army staff to correct "deformities" (his term): "A slant eyed Korean interpreter, speaking excellent English, came in requesting to be made into a 'round-eye.' His future lies in his relation with the west" (Millard qtd. in Kim 2008, 53). He then declared proudly that after the procedure, others may mistake him for Mexican or Italian. Markets of beauty follow imperial patterns and geopolitical asymmetries as in the previous case, and we see this also in the massive market for whitening products in places like India, Mexico, and Brazil (Rondilla and Spickard 2007). In many of these cases, the modification of biological indexes is initiated by the subject under cultural, political, and social pressures to conform to standards of beauty and race and thus to fit parameters of publicness that would give them social advantages. We don't typically group these cases or any other case of passing under the banner of anonymity, but I believe they fit the criteria if we understand anonymity as indexical dissociation that allows the individual to bypass power structures and restrictions.

Understanding anonymity depends on concretizing the properties of specific indexes and the way these properties constitute different social, ontological, epistemic, political, and technological possibilities for indexical dissociation. Indexes have affordances, and understanding these affordances allows us to understand their use and anonymizing possibilities. A public index binds people together; a natural language index constitutes complex connotations to individuals and groups; a digital index can easily be used by computers, but it is useless without computers; administrative indexes can be the grounds for politics and science; a biological index follows the individual everywhere, and it is highly concrete. Each category of index is a category of affordances, of the things that individuals and groups can do with indexes, and the way these indexes become part of our socio-technological lives.

But, quite importantly to this book, indexes are not important simply because they allow governments, economies, and technological systems to function more effectively. *Indexes matter to subjects. And so does indexical dissociation.* After the passing of the Thirteenth Amendment in 1865, which abolished slavery, many emancipated slaves changed their names to

US heroes such as Washington and Jefferson as ways of securing standing in white society and signaling patriotic values. Importantly, emancipated individuals performed their emancipation by choosing a name. To have or take an index, to give or to impose an index, and to lend or to steal an index are foundational actions, ontic operations that help define what is freedom and what is oppression.

Organization of the Book

This book is a wager that we can learn much about society, humanity, and power by analyzing the structural tensions and possibilities of anonymity and by analyzing how the economy of anonymity is changing in a modernity defined by computation. I believe that thinking deeply and historically on this issue opens up questions and realities that can help us understand broadly the type of modernity we had and the one we are entering. This book does that. It expands, deepens, and historicizes anonymity. I use lessons from those who study anonymity, but also those who study identity, classifications, privacy, and surveillance. Inspired by those who study indexes, I see anonymity as a means, but instead of moving away from this insight as many often do, I delve into it and ask how anonymity connects to social order, to identity, and to change. In common parlance, means refers to a method or an instrument necessary to achieve an end. For this reason, a means has a mediating, technical role; it occupies the space in between two social realities; and it connects and likely shapes them. If anonymity is a means, a method, an instrument, a type of mediation, what gives anonymity specificity? What type of method or instrument is it? How should we understand and account for its role in the social and in the subject?

Inspired by anonymity and identity scholars, Chapter 1 explores indexical dissociation by looking at indexes from a perspective afforded by their capacity to point toward an individual or a community. The chapter references the work of Charles Peirce and connects fundamental semiotic properties of indexes to anonymity and identification. Indexes, Peirce theorizes, point, and I add, indexes are the a priori of sorting (classifications), ordering (social groups), accountability (ethics and juridicality), and human onticity. The chapter introduces the notion of indexicalization, which highlights what is common to anonymity and identification and argues that the commonalities are technical manifestations of the possibilities of indexes. The section on indexical dissociation uses the complementary work of subaltern Latine theorist Gloria Anzaldúa and Bernhard Siegert to theorize indexicalization and its ontic capacities. Siegert helps me understand anonymity as a cultural technique, and Anzaldúa helps me see that this cultural technique is particularly useful to subjects who exist between realities, in-between, or what Anzaldúa calls "nepantla." Nepantla, Anzaldúa argues, is particularly important to subalterns and the type of identity negotiations many subalterns have to routinely perform.

Chapter 1 introduces the notion that anonymity has ontic effects on the subject. Does it have ontological effects? Chapter 2 answers this question by arguing that anonymity shapes human ontology because anonymity is a crucial cultural technique in and for human change. I arrive at this position in three stages. The first is based on the literature about the ontological capacities of classifications, which is a first step in showing the onticity of categorical indexes. The second stage argues that ontological arguments about classifications account for human change and, thus, for the need to expand these theories to account for anonymity and concrete indexes like personal identifiers. The last section explores human change by reference to the work of Anzaldúa and philosopher Mariana Ortega and her notions of identity in the borderlands to argue for an ontology that includes anonymity and change. Woven through these three stages are cases pertaining to individuals at the margins of classifications, including nonbinary and intersex individuals and migrants.

Anonymity at the level of the subject has ontological effects, but anonymity also has a social life. As I argued previously, anonymity is a cultural technique that has specific meanings in contemporary life. Agentic anonymity in particular has mythological meanings associated with anonymity's capacity to bypass power structures. Because of the promise of freedom, anonymity also has a role in ideas about citizenship and civic agency, but insofar as freedom, citizenship, and civic agency depend on the social, they also depend on the capacities of technology to allow, or not, agentic anonymity. In current socio-technological environments, in the era of digitation, the myth of anonymity is dangerous, and Chapter 3 shows a case that illustrates both the attractiveness of the myth of anonymity and the constricting capacities of the digital world. The case, which I began developing in my previous book (Amaya 2020), involves the anonymous blogger Lucy and her disappearance.

Lucy's case lays bare a powerful and deadly asymmetry in the economy of anonymity in datafication. Lucy could be anonymous to those around her, but she was never truly anonymous. Chapter 4 explores further this asymmetry, but the chapter also argues that this asymmetry is new and different from previous socio-technical realities. To argue this, the chapter shows how anonymity was theorized in sociopolitical theories of order in modernity. By understanding anonymity in sociopolitical theory, we can start to understand what is particular and different about anonymity in datafication. The chapter is particularly focused on strands of contractarianism, a way of sociopolitical thinking rooted in trust and the challenges to trust brought about by modernity. Contractarianism tried to answer the question, How could individuals build trust in others when these others are anonymous strangers who are no longer ruled by religion, tradition, and kinship? By contrast, this question is meaningless to a digital world ruled by profit, one in which agentic anonymity is available horizontally as a nihilistic force but mostly unavailable from the perspective of corporations and the state.

While I argue that the economy of anonymity in the digital world greatly diminishes the possibility of agentic anonymity, some forms of institutional anonymity are common and perform disciplinary roles in a type of social order that continues fighting with difference and diversity. Chapter 5 explores in detail how technologies of inscription have powerful anonymizing effects over immigrants who are routinely expected or forced to undergo name changes that have the effect of Anglicizing them. At the same time, immigrant populations are some of the most surveilled groups in the United States. These two realities, the routine institutional anonymizing of name changes and hypersurveillance, give form to another type of asymmetry in the economy of anonymity, one that echoes the invisibility/hypervisibility dialectic that Monahan has helped us identify and theorize.

Chapter 5 is an exploration of how technologies of inscription shape anonymity, but it is also a model of how to carry out anonymity research with technologies of inscription. The chapter shows, among other things, that different inscription technologies, from forms to keyboards, have specific anonymizing possibilities. Chapter 6 is also a different model of how to carry out anonymity research by referencing a single, and quite consequential, index: names. While different types of indexes have different and specific anonymity possibilities, no other index is more socially important than names, as Offred helps us see. Simply, most people think of anonymity first in relationship to names. I began this book with examples of anonymous publishing by Thomas Paine and Mary Shelley because I knew that these were archetypical examples of anonymity. But there is more to the archetype, particularly as you filter the archetype through a theory of anonymity as indexical dissociation, one that identifies agentic, institutional, and contextual anonymity, and one that defines anonymity as a cultural technique particularly powerful to those who are in-between. Just as Chapter 3 demystifies the idea that anonymity is entwined with freedom, Chapter 6 problematizes the archetypical notion that anonymity refers to the hiding or substitution of names. The chapter shows that unnaming and renaming are common social practices that give meaning to traditions, autonomy, change, and to power structures that use unnaming to discipline and coerce.

While the goal of the book is to understand anonymity as it relates to the social and to the subject, each chapter reveals different aspects of a system that I call the economy of anonymity. The Conclusion brings together insights from each chapter that help us identify some basic properties of the economy of anonymity. From exploring the distribution systems that dictate who can have anonymity, to the effects on subjects and identity, the Conclusion identifies thirteen properties that define the economy of anonymity. This book argues and shows that the economy of anonymity connects the intersubjective to the social, thus helping us understand current and future power structures. In short, the economy of anonymity helps us better theorize power, subjects, and the in-between.

One

The Dialectic of Anonymity and Identification

The organization Anonymous is a hacker activist organization that began on the imageboard 4chan in 2003. The collective uses anonymity in different ways, including in its name and in the way the organization functions publicly. The trolling, hacking, and other digital activities that characterize the organization have no authorship but the group's. Anonymity here is necessary to keep the members safe from the state, the law, and the institutions and organizations they hack, criticize, and sometimes coerce into action. Anonymous activities may be public, but members do not suffer the consequences of surveillance by the state and other actors and organizations.

Anonymous also uses anonymity as a type of performance that gives meaning to their activities. Members appear in public with their faces covered with a Guy Fawkes mask to hide their identities, but also to present another collective identity that they hope will be understood as antiestablishment. Guy Fawkes, after all, is best known for his involvement in the "Gun Powder Plot" that, in 1605, attempted to kill Protestant King James and substitute him with his Catholic daughter, Princess Elizabeth. So, while the mask allows for the hiding of identities, or what I have called "identity dissociation," the mask reminds us that dissociation means also association, and, while individual personas are discouraged, the organization has created a collective persona, Anonymous, that speaks from the standpoint crafted by a mythos that they work hard at preserving. Part trickster, part whistleblower, the Anonymous persona gives meaning and rhetorical direction to what the organization members say about their work. Individual members join for different personal reasons rooted in their experience and political visions and realities, but once a member, their personal goals become secondary and they embrace collective goals. Gabriella Coleman (2014)—an anthropologist who has written a powerful book on the organization—cites a member of the collective who explains why 4chan was important: "The posts on 4chan have no names or any identifiable markers attached to them. The only thing you are able to judge a post by is its content and nothing else. This elimination of the persona, and by extension everything associated with it, such as leadership, representation, and status, is the primary ideal of Anonymous" (47).[1] The explanation is as wise as it is timely: Anonymity allows for statements in 4chan to be only about the quality of the statements, not about the status of the individual—a reminder that statements are valued in conjunction with the speaker.

Even in the context of a collective organized around anonymity, names and titles matter—such indexes matter. They become the context that shapes the validity and power of ideas. Perhaps that is why Benjamin Franklin (2016) hid his name to publish opinionated newspaper pieces and instead used names tactically, rhetorically. He published on hypocrisy with the name Silence Dogood; he published on women's rights under the name Polly Baker; and he famously authored the *Poor Richard's Almanack* under Richard Saunders. Fearing prejudicial evaluations of their work, Emily, Anne, and Charlotte Brontë wrote under the pseudonyms Ellis, Currer, and Acton. We may advise children "not to judge a book by its cover," but we often judge an action, a statement, and an idea by the author's name.

Eliminating the persona, as stated in the quotation from Coleman, "and by extension everything associated with it," is possible because personal identifiers have an indexical property, the capacity to point toward an individual or human group and the ability to point away from them. This pointing, as implied by Anonymous, would be inconsequential if the index was not also the first in a sequence of other social mechanisms such as sorting, ordering, and the constitution of accountability. That is, anonymity matters not simply because it points away from a person or their history and persona. When Emily Brontë used the name Ellis Bell to publish *Wuthering Heights* in 1847, she used anonymity first to point readers away from her person and did so by inviting readers to believe that the author was the fictional—male—persona named Ellis Bell. Clearly, pointing away was not the only goal. Emily, for instance, did not use the name Mary Bell, which would have attracted biased readings. She chose Ellis because it was not a female given name, and thus she believed that the name would not diminish the book's ability to be read and judged by its merits. The name, in other words, pointed away from Emily and her gender, but also pointed specifically to Ellis and gender categories that were used hierarchically and would make the book accountable to particular judgments and interpretations. Anonymity bridged the gap between two social realities and allowed Brontë the possibility of an in-between, a liminal space that in her case granted power otherwise unavailable (Ortega 2016). Anonymity mattered because the index Ellis allowed Brontë to point to a gender popularly associated with authority and authorship, then sorted the work as male-authored and thus subject to traditional criticism, making it accountable to specific cultural, economic, and even juridical constraints.

And so, the first step in delving deeper into the nature of anonymity is to grapple with at least these technical dimensions of indexes and answer the question, "What do indexes do?" Indexes (1) point, and they are the a priori of (2) sorting (classifications), (3) ordering (how do classifications relate to each other?), and (4) accountability (obligations that shape judgment, economics, and legal frameworks). Scholars like Michel Foucault and Ian Hacking, among others, have also argued that human categories have ontic properties, which I discuss in the next chapters. Here, let me simply mark that indexes are also the a priori of (5) "human onticity," a term that refers to the properties and characteristics that humans have.[2]

Grappling with anonymity's technical dimensions forces us to reckon with questions untested and unanswered by most literature on anonymity. Most literature on anonymity, as I argued in the Introduction, is interested in ends or in the "after" of anonymity. Anonymity matters because it allows for something else to appear. In the case of Anonymous, anonymity matters because it allows for this antiestablishment organization to exist. In the case of anonymous publishing, anonymity matters because it allows authors otherwise marginalized to have a central stage in publishing. If we think of human activities in a timeline, most research on anonymity cares a great deal about the "after" of anonymity (freedom, women's publishing), and some care about the "before" (marginalized authors) of anonymity. Yet, the technical dimensions of anonymity and indexes are a way of attending to the "during." That is, the technical side of anonymity is about the process of anonymizing, about what happens between the before and after, what happens in-between.

Staying in this in-between means asking questions about how the technical aspects of anonymity become the a priori of their social effects and how these technical aspects are encountered, faced, and wrestled with by subjects. Imagine the Brontë sisters confronting a world in which their individuality, artistry, and craft would be judged with biases that may marginalize their value and their work. Imagine their pain, anger, and frustration. Imagine them confronting this as a problem that may be solved from the perspective of publishing, but not from the perspective of the prejudices they faced. Imagine them adopting anonymity as a means to be published, but on the condition that they hide their gender and, in so doing, reproduce the very patriarchal conventions they wished to escape. Imagine seeing your work recognized, judged favorably, and not being able to take credit or benefit socially from such distinctions. Every day their work was published with pseudonyms and had personal and social effects. The in-between, the anonymizing, extended for years.[3] Only the tragedy of the impending death of Emily compelled Charlotte to reveal their identities and the reasons for the ruse (Mullan 2007, 76–113). And only after confronting the risks of social ostracism and/or criticism could their work produce the social changes that would eventually allow other women authors to openly publish their literary works. Can one separate the social effects of anonymity from the subjective ones?

The social manifestations and effects of anonymity, I argue, are as important as their personal and subjective manifestations. For this reason, we need to ask: How does anonymity operate in the social? And also, how does anonymity operate in the subject? To my knowledge, no single conceptual framework allows me to do these two analytic operations, and, for this reason, in this chapter I introduce "indexicalization," which can be simply defined as the social and epistemological practice of needing and creating indexes to identify humans. We can know humans only by first assigning indexes to identify them. That is a "man" and that is a "woman." That is Charlotte and that is Emily.

Indexicalization is an analytic framework that has several peculiarities designed to attend to the complexities of anonymizing. First, because anonymizing (e.g., Currer Bell) is connected to and dependent on identification, indexicalization must be able to attend to both. My first proposal about indexicalization is that it is a process or a mechanism that produces or manifests possible variations rooted in the indexical, two of which are anonymity and identification, but also include privacy and classifications. Indexicalization presents in the real as anonymity, privacy, identification, and classifications that are different realities inherent in the play of indexes. Second, because anonymizing has social and subjective manifestations, indexicalization must be able to explain what happens at the level of the social and what happens at the level of the subject. To this end, I benefit from scholarship on identity and identification that also attends to liminality or what I have been calling the in-between. Two particular theorists have been crucial to my own understanding of liminality in identity and identification. Gloria Anzaldúa, a Latine and queer scholar who theorizes identity in moments of transition, uses the notion of "nepantla," a term that is connected to borderlands and the in-between and one that helps me understand anonymizing at the level of the subject. I also benefit from the work of Bernhard Siegert, a theorist associated with mediality, which is an intellectual tradition concerned with how processes of mediation constitute reality. Both Siegert and Anzaldúa propose, in very different ways, that the in-between has ontological effects. In their work, and in mine, the in-between of indexing, what I call indexicalization, has the capacity to shape reality and humanness.

The chapter emphasizes the mediality of anonymity, the fact that anonymity is a means, and focuses on that issue alone. It is thus a counterargument to those who look at anonymity simply as a means to an end. Focusing on the mediality of anonymity is a necessary step if we are to understand changes to the economy of anonymity. This focus is the only one that allows us to understand the diversity of ends that anonymity produces and/or serves. Contrariwise, if one starts with a focus on ends (Is anonymity good because it allows dissidence? Is anonymity bad because it allows hateful trolling?), one cannot explain or justify why anonymity matters given the multiplicity of ends for which it is used.

This chapter engages the first four technical dimensions of anonymity qua identification—pointing, sorting, ordering, and accountability—and is organized in two sections. The first explores further the implications of defining anonymity as indexical dissociation, which means that in order to make sense of anonymity, one must understand indexical association or, if you prefer, identification. Since indexing is the work of personal identifiers, the section starts by exploring what it means that identifiers point, and I use the work of Charles Peirce on indexes to set the analytic tone. The semiotic work of indexes is what constitutes the possibilities of identification and anonymity, which are two presentations of the same or similar mechanism that I call "indexicalization."[4] The second section develops the idea of indexicalization and its connections to the work of Anzaldúa and Siegert.

Anonymity and the Work of Indexes

The collective Anonymous hides the names of those who participate, and when a member of the collective must be in public, they use a mask resembling Guy Fawkes to hide their face. They do this not simply as performance but as a way of attending to the single, obvious, and more important power of names and faces. Names and faces point toward the person who is speaking or acting. Everything in anonymity starts with the property that some signs have to point toward a specific individual or toward a category of people. Not every sign can do this. Only some signs can. Names can identify a person, but the word *cloud* cannot. Faces can identify a person, but in our current state of technology and social norms, the back of someone's knee cannot. Everything in anonymity starts with some signs' capacity to identify, to index, to point to people. So, a first and necessary step for understanding anonymity is understanding the signs, which one may call personal identifiers or indexes, that have such capacity.

Personal identifiers point to an individual or a particular human group. This pointing capacity of identifiers is their indexicality. Just as our index fingers help us point to someone, our personal identifiers point. I use the term "index" inspired partly by the work of Charles Peirce ([1895] 1998), who argued that there were three types of signs: icons, symbols, and indexes. Icons share some quality with their object, as when a mathematician uses a curve as a resemblance to a mathematical formula. Symbols are signs that "have become associated with their meanings by usage," such as most words like "blue" or "happy" (§3). Indexes point to a specific object. They answer the important question "which one?," as when I share with someone as I walk my dog that I live down the block in the dark sienna house. "Which house?," my interlocutor asks; "the dark sienna house." This is an indexical statement. Had I been at a visual distance from the house, I perhaps would have said, "I live in that house," while I pointed to it, and "that" alongside my pointing finger would perform the role of index. Or, even better, perhaps all I would do is raise my hand and point. When it comes to humans, indexes specify a person or group of persons. Just as indexes in general answer the question "which one?," human indexes answer the question of "who?"

Albert Atkin (2005), a Peirce specialist, argues that throughout Peirce's work, he identified five crucial features of the index, and all but one can help us understand how anonymity depends on the indexical. Atkin writes:

> 1. Indices use some physical contiguity with their object to direct attention to that object. (163)

When I sign a letter, I use my name in a specific spot, typically the bottom, to indicate that I am the author. The reader uses that name, my name, to direct attention to me, the author, even if I am absent or even if they did not witness my signing of the letter. From the perspective of reader or viewer or user, an index signifies physical contiguity. The index, the trace, points toward an actor, the author, the agent. When Charlotte Brontë signed her books as Currer Bell, she used this indexical practice of presuming physical contiguity and forced attention toward a person, Currer Bell, whom the reader nonetheless did not know was fictive. We call anonymity in this case Brontë's manipulation of the "attention directing" capacity of the index.

> 2. Indices have their characteristics independently of interpretation. (163)

Indexes point regardless of whether an interpreter is there to understand the pointing or not. Take for instance a human footprint traced on mud. The footprint points to the physical contiguity of a human regardless of whether another human is there to understand this fact. This means also that even in the person's or observer's absence, the moment in which a person stepped on the mud and left the footprint, the footprint attests to the contiguity. Yet, because the footprint points to physical contiguity, a footprint can be falsified, thus pointing to a different body. The same is true of a signature (see previous paragraph) or a Social Security number. Insofar as these human indexes point to a human, they can be falsified or tricked. Because a person can be absent and still be referenced by an index, it is possible to deceive the interpretant. These first two properties of indexes make anonymity possible.

> 3. Indices refer to individuals. (164)

While Atkin here is referring to individual objects in the world, in this book indexes indeed refer to individual beings or individual categories of beings, as when an index refers to race or gender.

> 4. Indices assert nothing. (164)

Peirce is right in general, but this statement is wrong when it comes to human indexes. When human indexes are proper names, for instance, indexes indicate gender, often ethnicity, nationality, and even class. Human indexes such as names, but also races, genders, ethnicities, are propositional. In other words, some indexes definitely assert something. Some indexes also perform the role of propositions, statements that have truth effects. The name Paul Smith does not only force our attention to the individual Paul Smith but also toward males from English-speaking communities. Even a Social Security number expresses that the individual is registered with the federal government as legal resident. Those who steal these numbers, and, under the cover of anonymity, work in the United States, make use of this fact: SSNs imply legal residence and legal work status.

> 5. Indices do not resemble, nor do they share any law-like relation with, their objects. (164)

This means that human indexes do not share any phenomenological characteristics with the humans they point toward. Even a footprint's fidelity to the foot is dependent on the type of clay or mud and will never be faithful to the original. If this property of indexes did not exist, anonymity would be impossible. In fact, it is because we understand that human indexes do not resemble their humans that they can be used for deception. The name Paul Smith may suggest gender and ethno-linguistic precedence but does not resemble or stand, like an icon, for the individual named Paul Smith.

Peirce is useful in helping us understand the semiotic foundations of personal identifiers or human indexes, the term I often use. Importantly, his work is useful in helping us see that some fundamental characteristics of anonymity are rooted in the semiotic structure of indexical signs. That said, human indexes have particular properties that are different from other indexes. As I noted regarding number 4 ("Indices assert nothing"), human indexes often have social lives and dimensions that cannot be separated from the indexical. This was not new to Peirce. His work also recognized that icons, symbols, and indexes were sometimes different facets of the same sign or statement ([1895] 1998, §9). For this reason, a human index is no different from other signs that name a thing, such as the word *apple*. The word has indexical properties, but it also connotes meanings depending on context and culture. In Peirce terminology, the word *apple* is both index and symbol, and so is the name Paul Smith or Charlotte Brontë.

Human indexes behave like indexes in general but also have peculiarities such as their capacity to be propositional. Another peculiarity of some human indexes like names that makes them quite different from other words or signs is that they have what philosopher of language Saul Kripke (1980) calls semiotic rigidity. Names directly point toward the same object in all possible contexts. This means that personal names are significantly different from names in general. Let me illustrate the difference by reference to the work of Michel Foucault (1989), who in *The Order of Things* dedicates a large section to naming and does it from the perspective of poststructuralist thinking and from within the linguistic turn. He indicates that one of the primary functions of naming is to designate, to point, but soon naming becomes more; it is the vehicle to express that which is old and new: "[Names] become endowed, little by little, with poetic powers; their primary nominations become the starting-points for long metaphors; these metaphors become progressively more complicated, and are soon so far from their points of origin that it is difficult to recall them" (122). Yet, he is thinking about naming in general; thus, he takes for granted principles of Saussurean grammar, such as the arbitrary nature of the sign and the recognition that naming changes and different signs may be attached to one referent. One may call a horse *caballo* (in Spanish) or *hors* (Old English). However, personal names, human indexes in general, are extraordinary in that their capacity to designate is crucial and central to their function, in that they are not fully arbitrary, and in that they do not evolve. A name like Gwendolyn may change form over time, but it would be a mistake to say that a person who was named Gwendolyn in the eighteenth century should be renamed Jennifer today, even though Jennifer is considered a contemporary form of Gwendolyn. That body named Gwendolyn was attached to that name. Case closed. Personal names point to the same object in all possible contexts.

Kripke's semiotic rigidity connects to Peirce's principle of physical contiguity. Imagine a christening, the ceremony when parents, community, and a priest give a child their name. A public declaration with the body of the child present (physical contiguity) confers the name to the child, and this name is attached to that body, always (semiotic rigidity). Other rituals (legal, social, religious) may alter the name (e.g., marriage, sex change, migration), but in all of these cases, a community official attests to the physical contiguity of the body and the name, and a new rigid connection ensues. These properties of human indexes help us think and theorize the use of human indexes in history, and they are particularly useful in helping us think the semiotic trajectory by which personal identifiers identify and signify. For the purpose of anonymity, Kripke, Peirce, and Foucault help us start recognizing some of the most important semiotic and signifying properties that make identity dissociation possible and powerful.

Human indexes, personal identifiers, point to specific humans because they are embedded in specific hermeneutic traditions that help readers, interpretants, and users presume and understand when confronted by a human index attached to an action or a publication. What Peirce theorizes as indexical capacities, from the perspective of users, are hermeneutic rules, the basic guidelines individuals and institutions use to make sense of human indexes. They are the rules of interpretation. Human indexes, for instance, have guarantors that can prove a body and a name or a face are connected. A name has the guarantor of community or community official. The photograph has the inscribed image and capturing technology. Names do not resemble the individual. Someone named Apple does not look like an apple. Yet, some human indexes like photos are iconic enough that people believe they can identify the individual. But faces, unlike names, change, and they have a narrow temporality that gives them other properties. Facial indexicality fades through time. Names endure through history. Names are propositional and give us information about the individual, including gender, often ethnicity, and sometimes even class and race. So do faces.

Individuals and institutions that use anonymity are aware of these hermeneutic traditions and manipulate them in order to have the desired effect of anonymity. When anonymity is the result of individual or institutional actions, anonymity is a reflexive action that recognizes the hermeneutics of indexes. Emily Brontë used the hermeneutic convention of presuming a work of literature has an author, and that the author's name was typically displayed alongside the book title, to constitute her space of anonymity. The reader knew or inferred that the name Ellis Bell was the author's, not the place of publication or a random person. The reader also knew or inferred that Ellis was the given name and Bell was the family name as was standard at the time in England. Given the politics of publishing and gender at the time, Emily bid on the name Ellis being read as representing a man, and she did this because it was hermeneutically reasonable.

The first hermeneutic task of indexes is specification. Indexes point toward a person or a specific group. They identify a "one" (e.g., Benjamin Franklin) or "one group" (women) and are thus understood to be differentiators. Implicit in the indexical work of the name Benjamin Franklin is that one person was Benjamin Franklin and the rest of humans were not. A human index refers to a concrete or specific individual or group, and, for this reason, the first hermeneutic task of a human index is numerical.[5]

Concrete indexes, like names or addresses, specify an individual but also function as categorical indexes. Concrete and categorical indexes exist in a dialectical relationship to each other. They refer to two sides of the same coin in that all concrete indexes imply categorical belonging, and all categorical indexes imply an imagined concrete individual (as the archetype or epitome of that group). As I noted previously, when Emily uses Ellis Bell to publish, Ellis Bell points toward a single, in this case fictional, individual but also toward the category of *male* and even to the category of *English*. A house address (a concrete index) specifies where someone lives, but it also denotes and connotes wealth, class, and sometimes ethnicity. In places like Los Angeles, having an address in Boyle Heights, a mostly Latine neighborhood, categorizes the dwellers. Concrete indexes thus have a duality, and they do the work they do because they sometimes provide secrecy—Emily could remain anonymous—but also because they manipulate inferences related to categories. With Ellis Bell, the book would be judged differently than if Emily had left her name on the cover. When you introduce yourself as living in Boyle Heights, you are also inviting inferences about your class and ethnicity.

This means that a great many examples of identity dissociation depend partly on the secrecy provided by the manipulation of a concrete index and partly on the manipulation of categories. This includes forms of agentic anonymity, such as the anonymous publishing of novels by nineteenth-century female authors, but also the type of indexical dissociation inherent in a woman adopting or being forced to adopt a man's name after marriage. The married name specified a person but also the category of married woman, and, because of this category, the types of social, economic, biographical, and political rights that would legally and customarily be taken away (I expand on these issues pertaining to unnaming and renaming in Chapter 6).

Human categories are the essence of knowledge about humans, and they impact daily interactions as well as formal ways of knowledge in the human sciences. On a daily basis, we interact with each other, making inferences about the categories we seem to represent that shape these interactions. Without these categories, and the inferences they invite, the social world would be unmanageable. We would feel incapable of experiencing ontological security. Categories are crucial to being in the world, to making it predictable and thus understandable. They are the basis of order, and the reason human categories matter is that they help us understand the world as an ordered space. Human categories, expressed through categorical indexes such as race, gender, sexual orientation, class, ethnicity, nationality, age, and others, are often hierarchical, and they perform the role of placing bodies, individuals, and communities in specific social locations in harmony with their classifications.

In their seminal work on classifications, Geoffrey Bowker and Susan Star (1999) introduce us early to concerns pertaining to the growth of indexing and the forms of order and freedom these may produce:

> As we evolve the classifications of habit—grow common fingertips with respect to linkages and networks—we will be faced with some choices. How standardized will our indexes become? What forms of freedom of association (among people, texts and people, and texts) do we want to preserve and which are no longer useful? Who will decide these matters? (8)

The preservation of these freedoms includes the preservation of anonymity and, as others show, privacy, which have been common ways of sidestepping concrete identification in order to avoid categorical identification and classificatory systems. *The importance of these classificatory systems cannot be overstated: They are central to social order, and when social order needs changing, when we need social disorder or alternative order schemas, the ability to be anonymous incentivizes individuals and communities to participate in social change.*

The reason human indexes shape social order is that they make us accountable. It is because President Biden's face, voice, and name were associated with his speech that we made him accountable in a particular way for what he said. On the matter of COVID-19 vaccines, for instance, we expected him to be the best-informed person that he could be and to be truthful about what was truly best for the nation. He was held accountable to standards specific to his identity as a speaker. The same is true when I talk in front of my students or when a community leader talks in front of her constituents. Identity and identification make us accountable. Our human identifiers—our names, addresses, Social Security numbers, emails, and other personal markers—make us accountable to others, to the law, to our peers, and to each other. And accountability shapes our behavior, culture, and society. Our indexes give form to our social life and community obligations. Sometimes, accountability is touted and promoted by those who seek order, and order can be wonderful, as when we experience safety as we walk down a street, or when we know that we can rely on peaceful transitions of power after an election, or when we know that garbage collection will happen, for sure, on a specific day and time. But social order has a dark side, and it is from this troubled perspective that scholars like Helen Nissenbaum (1999) connect anonymity to accountability. Social order produces standards of normality that can be troubling and constricting, a normality that can marginalize individuals and hurt the social fabric, which is always more than rules (Lyon 2004). This is why anonymity is often socially useful. Anonymity can help establish alternative order structures to bypass negative standards of normality affecting individuals, including those who fear the stigma associated with the experience of domestic violence, mental problems, or the contraction of some illnesses like HIV. Anonymity has been a key strategy to at least ameliorate some negative effects of order by inviting people to seek help when needed instead of hiding for fear of being stigmatized.

Social order depends on social hierarchies, classifications, norms, and legal structures that are experienced as control, domination, and even subjugation by many groups and individuals. Social order and accountability can mean something quite different if you are wealthy or if you are poor, a man or a woman, heterosexual or queer, or White or nonwhite. Many people and many communities experience a social order that systematically forecloses spheres of action and expression, and to those who have experienced order and accountability in this negative way, anonymity has been a freeing technique. This is true today and has been throughout history. When a person's social location is marginal, but the person wishes the benefits associated with a more powerful, central, social location, individuals routinely work on their indexes to craft personas that may be welcomed in power centers. We change our dress codes, accents, biographies, and often even names to be read as belonging to the circles of power. We hybridize our identities and learn to speak (with) two tongues (Anzaldúa 2000).

It is because indexes make us accountable to states and to each other that anonymity has been understood as a technique for crafting a space of legal and social impunity. This is not simply important to dissidence. It is also important to other forms of illegality. We may act in public without suffering the consequences of our actions, as when an undocumented person uses someone else's SSN to get a job, when individuals use the dark web to acquire illicit drugs, or when an individual constructs a fake digital persona to harass another person.

Accountability exists in two interrelated registers: the register of obligations and the register of enumeration. This is why the term is common in the philosophy of ethics, but also in the discipline of accounting. These two registers are always already present when we talk about accountability. Someone, some "one," can be held accountable only if they are. A simple statement such as "Hector Amaya is the writer of this book" illustrates my point. Here, to name me is to make me accountable and to enumerate me, to count me. The act of naming me is the precondition for my words and my actions to be socially judged, to be tested by Kant's publicity condition (see Conclusion). For this reason, naming is, in a sense, a juridical statement for what I write that makes me responsible, an author, an owner. Lie or truth; blasphemy or prayer; what I write is mine, and I should be responsible for the consequences of my writing, of my actions, for I am the author, the owner of the copy and of the right. To name precedes obligation. Anonymity disqualifies it.

Anonymity, Techniques, and the Subaltern

The capacity indexes have to make us accountable, and thus the capacity of anonymity to make us free from or disrupt some systems of order, is not a capacity inherent in indexes as signs. Anonymity may manifest at the level of the signs, but anonymity's importance to humans, institutions, and groups is entwined with other social mechanisms and reasons. So, the question of "what is the best way of conceptualizing anonymity?" is more than a question about semiotics. The semiotic work of indexes constitutes the possibilities of identification and anonymity, which are two presentations of the same mechanism that I call *indexicalization*. Anonymity is the name we give to indexicalization when indexical dissociation is activated. This ontic generator, indexicalization, expresses itself, or presents itself, in the world in multiple ways (indexing, anonymity, privacy, classifications, categories), but it is defined by a limited set of techniques that allow for the play of indexing (identification) and identity.

To help us think about anonymity as indexicalization, I use two very different complementary analytic tools. I use the notion of "cultural techniques" to explain the more machinic and material aspects of anonymity. But this is not enough. Cultural techniques, I show later, are not designed to explain experience, subjects, and subjectivity, and, for this reason, I also use Anzaldúa's notion of nepantla, which is a framework designed to theorize how individuals experience and attend to identity challenges. Both are needed because anonymity is both subjective and objective; it happens within the subject and at the institutional level; it is manifested in individual actions and challenges but also in technical questions and solutions by institutions; it is crucial in the constitution of subjects by institutions and other structures; but it is also a powerful example of agency, power, and individual creativity.

The term "cultural technique" comes from German media theory, and Siegert (Siegert and Winthrop-Young 2015) defines it as the "operative chains that precede the media concepts they generate" (11). Instead of engaging with signification, cultural techniques focus on the material and technical operations that precede signification. For instance, a biography, a media concept that points toward a story based on a single life, follows the allocation of a name to a person, to a body. The media concept, biography, follows the technique, naming. An anonymously published novel is so only after the space of author is left blank (without a name) or occupied by a pseudonym, for instance, Ellis Bell. In other words, the cultural technique that is indexicalization can yield discursive effects (biography), which can be seen from different perspectives, including economics (publishing), power (patriarchy), politics, and epistemology (what is a biography but a set of knowledge claims anchored on a name and on a life?).

Just like identification, anonymity is an expression of the ontic generator that is indexicalization. The play of indexes allows for the play of identity and variations related to how indexes connect to or fail to connect to individuals or groups. Importantly, privacy is another presentation of indexicalization. Indexicalization is an inherent multiplicity that presents as anonymity, privacy, and identification, and even though this book does not deal centrally with privacy, it is important to note that privacy is a particular presentation of the identity options possible in indexicalization.

A productive way of thinking about indexicalization connects to a particular description of cultural techniques as method. Siegert (Siegert and Winthrop-Young 2015) writes:

> The analysis of cultural techniques observes and describes techniques involved in operationalizing distinctions in the real. They generate the

> forms in the shape of perceptible unities of distinctions. Operating a door by closing and opening it allows us to perform, observe, encode, address, and ultimately wire the difference between inside and outside. Concrete actions serve to distinguish them from earlier nondifferentiatedness. In more general terms, all cultural techniques are based on the transition from nondistinction to distinction and back. (14)

A material component, the door, generates the distinction in the realm of inside and outside and, at the same time, allows for the recognition, performance, and encoding of significant cultural distinctions.

When I claim that *indexicalization is a cultural technique*, I am claiming that indexicalization is, in a sense, like a door, as referenced by Siegert. Like a door, indexicalization mediates between two worlds, between two realms. Indexicalization is the space in-between, the moment of nondistinction that holds all the identitarian possibilities at once, just before a set of possibilities is chosen or manifested and the universe of nondistinct humans (and their possibilities) become indexed, sorted, categorized, classified, and made accountable. Indexicalization itself, the mediation, is shaped by power formations, social schemas, socio-technical systems, social needs, and individual needs.

I use cultural techniques not simply because Siegert provides the useful metaphor of the door. Cultural techniques, in Siegert's work and also in the work of others like Friedrich Kittler, Cornelia Vismann, and Thomas Macho, are an analytic framework that captures the complexity and importance of mediation, materiality, techniques, processes, and infrastructures in the constitution of the human. Kathrin Dünne and her coauthors (2020) phrase the importance of mediation and what this means to research in the following: "Formulated grammatically, thinking in terms of cultural techniques thus means thinking primarily in verbs. Hence, when cultural techniques take the place of the predicate, the roles of things (the object) and people (the subject) trade places: things become observable as acting subjects and humans become observable as objects" (6). It is thus not anonymity, but anonymizing; not categories, but categorizing; not order, but ordering; not count, but accounting. Indexicalization as a cultural technique thus alerts us to the mechanisms that carry out the anonymizing, ordering, categorizing, or accounting.

The term "indexicalization" may be mine, but it is inspired by Siegert's work on processes of documentation, registries, archives, and the myriad techniques that keep track of humans (e.g., Vismann's work on files) and that constitute human categories and human possibilities. Cultural techniques are thus different from other media and communication theorizations anchored on the importance of language, semiotic systems, and meaning. They alert us to technologies of inscription and the types of relationality that these technologies, in their materiality, procedural, and formulaic possibilities entail.

While this chapter starts with the indexical properties of personal identifiers and thus may seem anchored firmly on the importance of semiotic systems, I treat indexes in their more technical manifestations, their pointing, sorting, ordering, and accounting affordances that precede signification. Human indexes are thus not simply signs; they are archival mechanisms, filing systems that help us order the social world and that participate in the constitution of self and other. And because indexes are part of such a crucial subjective process of constituting self and other, indexicalization to the subject is more than techniques. Siegert (Siegert and Winthrop-Young 2015) believes that "the modern subject as an autobiographical animal" (84), but the autobiographical is more than a predictable narrative. *Anonymity enters people's lives when an autobiographical pathway has to change, in moments of rupture, when circumstances challenge our identity, when individuals need to reinvent themselves.*

As a queer, Latine person who grew up on the US/Mexico border, Anzaldúa experienced and theorized what it meant to exist in between worlds. Her theories of identity have influenced Latine studies, feminist theory, queer theory, and critical race theory, and her work constructed a framework to understand the challenges and possibilities of identity transformation. Toward the end of her career, she used the notion of nepantla to conceptualize these challenges. *Nepantla* is a Nahuatl word meaning "the in-between space" or the "between times." Spatio-temporal, the term allowed Anzaldúa to reference a space of nondifferentiation situated in between worlds and identity possibilities. In her work, nepantla explains what happens to identity, knowledge, and experience in transitional moments in life. Anzaldúa (2000) describes it as a "birthing stage where you feel like you're reconfiguring your identity and don't know where you are. You used to be this person, but now maybe you're different in some way. You're changing worlds and cultures and maybe classes, sexual preferences" (225–26). Transitions are not easy, and AnaLouise Keating (2006) reminds us that nepantla exacts a price from the subject:

> During nepantla, our worldviews and self-identities are shattered. Nepantla is painful, messy, confusing, and chaotic; it signals unexpected, uncontrollable shifts, transitions, and changes. Nepantla hurts!!!! But nepantla is also a time of self-reflection, choice, and potential growth—what Anzaldúa describes as opportunities to "see through" restrictive cultural and personal scripts. As I understand the term, then, nepantla includes both radical dis-identification and transformation. We dis-identify with existing beliefs, social structures, and models of identity; by so doing, we are able to transform these existing conditions. (9)

Although neither Keating nor Anzaldúa connects nepantla to anonymity, what they describe can help us understand the subjective side of indexical dissociation. After all, the processes of disidentification central to Anzaldúa's work are partly modulated through identity categories and identifiers. We can thus use nepantla to understand subjective challenges and possibilities while in the space in between, just before indexical dissociation is manifested. These challenges and possibilities have methodological and analytic lessons to the study of anonymity.

The first is the importance of engaging anonymity from the perspective of experience. Indexical dissociation should not be characterized or defined only by the role it plays in issues of structure, politics, or epistemology. Indexical dissociation matters to individuals, and it is adopted or experienced in diverse ways. Having your name removed and another name imposed on you as part of slave processes would be experienced very differently than changing your name in a migration process that you have wished or desired. In *Roots*, Alex Haley's famous novel about slavery, the central character Kunta Kinte yells repeatedly in desperation, "My name is Kunta Kinte!!," as a rejection of the forced removal of his name, a removal that stood for everything that, and everybody who, was taken from him. Haley is a descendant of Kinte, and though fictionalized, the story has biographical elements that remind us of the importance of indexical dissociation to slaves and how painful losing your name can be. By contrast, I was recently chatting with a colleague at my institution who was born in China but now uses an Anglicized name. I asked her why she changed it, and she mentioned practical reasons, and nothing was mentioned of negative feelings toward the change. She seemed to be at peace with the change and saw it transactionally. We experience indexical dissociation in particular ways.

As Diana Martínez (2022) argues, nepantla is also a reminder that the body matters. Processes of anonymity often highlight personal and embodied vulnerabilities (20). After all, indexes stand for embodied beings that exist under systems of order that can impose punishment on people who defy it. Kinte is clearly an example, one that forces us to reckon with the humanness of the index bearer, but many other processes of anonymity are equally important because they happen to embodied beings. Anzaldúa was a Brown, queer, Latine individual, and each of these identities was deeply shaped by her embodiment and the order systems that constrained her. She used the metaphor of birthing for a reason, to highlight both the embodied sense of identity reinvention or reshaping and the pain of going through it. As I noted previously, not every identity subversion or transformation is equally painful, but they all happen to bodies and we must attend to this reality if we are to understand anonymity.

Nepantla helps us see the importance of affect to anonymity. With this concept, Anzaldúa meant to capture the affective side of disassociation, because identity changes either come from pain or result in pain. I don't imagine that Emily Brontë adopted Ellis Bell as a pseudonym without some pain. Ellis Bell offered Emily Brontë sociocultural cover and economic gain *but* at the cost of her having to write under difficult conditions and then deny herself the sociocultural recognition of her literary accomplishments. If cultural techniques highlight the machine-like operations of indexicalization, nepantla is a reminder that autobiography (Siegert's term) and affect are entwined and that our indexes, which help us organize our biographies, are signs for which we have powerful feelings and signs that stand for part of our lives. And, when they need to be removed or changed, new indexes are reminders of biographical losses, a past that is gone or becomes hidden.

Nepantla may be painful, but it holds promise. In Anzaldúa, nepantla is an opportunity and a space for reinvention, and it can thus be a moment for reflexive agency. Indexical dissociation, while in transition, may be painful, but the pain holds the promise of a rebirth. Sarah de los Santos Upton (2019) adds that this "in-between stage [is] characterized by chaos and disorientation, where individuals experience dissociations, breakdowns, and buildups of their identity" (124). This liminal space makes possible, necessitates, and/or invites identity possibilities that conjure different realities to the subject. Some identity options open up; others are eliminated. But subjects on the border can tactically deploy some identity variations and hide others (Ortega 2016, 76). Part performance theory, part phenomenology, nepantla invites self-invention.

One of the most generative aspects of nepantla is that identity is theorized as essentially multiple and even fragmented. Robert M. Gutierrez-Perez (2012) explains: "Nepantla is a space where the appendages of your identity have been hacked from their joints and thrown into the sky. It is an in/between space where your imperative is to put yourself together, even if your ring finger must replace a toe or if you must hold your arm in its socket. In order to cultivate this healing space, we must invest ourselves in the pain, so we, as a community, can carry it together" (200). Gutierrez-Perez's vivid illustration reminds us that some identity transformations force biographical redefinitions, and in others, new elements of identity may be added, shifted, or abandoned. Migrants from Latin America, for instance, cross the border and become ethno-racial minorities, which upplays racial aspects of identity while sacrificing others like regional identities, which are typically important within a nation. In Mexico, I was a northerner from Sonora and carried with me stereotypes attached to other northerners. In the United States, I am a Brown Latine, and I had to reassemble my identity in order to make sense of the new meanings attached to me. I am at least partly aware of this, of what is left behind, what is imposed on me, and what is possible with my new identity assemblage.

Part cultural technique and part a nepantla *dispositif*, anonymity is the name we give to indexicalization when indexical dissociation is at stake. In anonymity, the ontic generator reverses, destabilizes, or breaks indexing, and it does it by dissociating the otherwise sorted, categorized, and properly addressed individual or group from their indexes. A woman author can pass as male. An index like Emily Brontë is substituted on the cover of the book by Ellis Bell, and the substitution engenders a particular type of literary criticism associated with masculinity because it hides the gender of the author. In other words, anonymity is a cultural technique and nepantla *dispositif* that works with indexes (Emily, Ellis) as they are inscribed on material means (book cover) in order to produce specific social, cultural, epistemological, or juridical relationships (criticism shaped by gender). But the anonymizing does not have only external manifestations. The anonymizing is part of an internal identity struggle at the level of the subject, the challenge of needing to exist in the in-between in order to bypass or make sense of identity constraints that burden and limit the individual.

There are at least three elements, three technologies, essential to anonymity: (1) *indexes*, semiotic technologies that point toward an individual or a group; (2) *technologies of inscription*, which record and process indexical materials; and (3) *relational technologies*, which connect indexes to intersubjectivity and interaction. The cultural technique or nepantla *dispositif* that is indexicalization is the reworking of these elemental materials, and all are essential to the outcome that is anonymity. Most examples of anonymity, such as the hiding of one's identity in 4chan or the organization Anonymous, are examples of the removal or disconnection of indexical materials. This removal, however, is not abstract. It happens on a material basis, a substratum, such as the digital record central to the imageboard 4chan, the printed word "Ellis Bell" on a publication. It is, therefore, because the indexical is inscribed that it can be removed. The indexical removal is meant to elicit or facilitate specific social and power relations, as in the example of Anonymous, which is one that uses anonymity in order to protect the integrity of the speech of its members.

The three elemental materials (indexes, technologies of inscription, and relational technologies) are themselves quite rich and require further examination and specification. They have particular histories, and their interrelations are also contingent and fluid. Indexes have types and affordances that I began sketching in the Introduction but continue exploring throughout the book. The next chapter explores inscription on the body, and Chapter 5 explores it in machines and forms. Every chapter, including this one, analyzes relational technologies and the ways power is essential to most cases of anonymity, if not all. Last, I began this chapter discussing the ontic effects of indexicalization and anonymity on the subject. In the next chapter, I take this a step further and interrogate their impact on human ontology.

Pointing is the a priori of sorting, ordering, and accounting, and, for this reason, in this chapter, I introduce the term "indexicalization" to theorize anonymity, which bypasses some forms of order and accountability in favor of others. Indexicalization is like a door or a borderland in between two human and subjective spaces: One is occupied by individuals with needs and social goals that are represented in social schemas and sociotechnical systems, and the other is occupied by a universe of individuals as possibilities. Indexicalization allows the side of human needs, human goals, and human schemas to operate over a universe of individuals that becomes, thanks to indexicalization, sorted, categorized, and properly addressed. To be human is to exist on both sides of the door, to categorize and be categorized, to have goals and be the target of someone else's goal, to be part of institutions and to be institutionalized. Simply, *indexicalization gives way to the dialectic of indexing and anonymity*, a basic duality in social life, and, for this reason, indexicalization is the cultural technique or nepantla *dispositif* that precedes the important tasks of sorting, categorizing, and identifying and their equally important opposites of unsorting, uncategorizing, and unidentifying.

The dialectic of indexing and anonymity is the basic component of the economy of anonymity. This dialectic precedes the distinction kin and foreign, self and other, and I and you. It gives form to the space of obligations, the world of contracts, rules, and norms, and it outlines the space of freedom, impunity, and revolution, which are also social recategorizations and resortings. Their complementarity is relevant to the type of lifeworlds and systems, using Habermas's terminology, that they help shape. But while the importance of identity and indexing is unquestioned, anonymity is often treated on the sidelines, as if the social could exist without it, as if the individual could experience life fully without it. Yet, what would happen in a world where we are accountable for all our actions? How can we change this world if full accountability is the norm? What would happen to us if our ascriptive characteristics, our birth categories, were our destiny? How could we alter what we are supposed to be without bypassing some social rules and order? And how can we bypass our destiny without first defying our identities, which are also our indexes? Using words common in Anzaldúa's work, we are all inner exiles.

Two

Anonymity and Ontology

We are all inner exiles, as Gloria Anzaldúa noted, which, I believe, implies that anonymity is ontologically important or, in other words, that indexical dissociation is of fundamental consequence to individuals and society. The case of Nex Benedict illustrates the state of inner exile that Anzaldúa refers to. Nex Benedict was an Indigenous teenager whose short life was marked by conflict associated with the indexes of nonbinary individuals:

> The death of a 16-year-old nonbinary student after an altercation in a high school girls' bathroom in Oklahoma has drawn national attention and outrage from gay and transgender rights groups that say the student had been bullied because of their gender identity. Nex Benedict, who often used the pronouns they and them and told relatives that they did not see themselves as strictly male or female, died in early February, one day after the altercation with three girls at Owasso High School. The medical examiner has ruled the death a suicide. (Edmonds and Hassan 2024)

In Nex Benedict's tragic case, indexes mattered, not only to them but to those who bullied them and to the State of Oklahoma. In 2022, Oklahoma became the first state to prohibit the use of nonbinary gender markers in birth certificates, and students are forbidden from using bathrooms that do not match their sex assigned at birth. Dean Spade (2015) reminds us of the importance of thinking "more broadly about how gender categories are enforced on all people in ways that have particularly dangerous outcomes for trans people. Such a shift requires us to examine how administrative norms or regularities create structured insecurity and (mal) distribute life chances across populations" (9). This chapter is inspired by cases like Benedict's and works like Spade's but asks the more general question of whether anonymity shapes ontology. The ontology question matters, particularly if we are concerned with changes in the economy of anonymity due to new socio-technical realities. Considering anonymity at the ontological level is a first step toward understanding how changes to the economy of anonymity may mean changes to the experience of being human, too. That, in my mind, is a huge deal. If anonymity is essential to the subject, if anonymity is part of a subject's interiority, then the economy of anonymity is not simply exteriority or epiphenomenal to the individual. If anonymity is part of human ontology, then the economy of anonymity partly determines being.

The question of anonymity and ontology is complex, but I believe that the best way to introduce the complexity and begin the process of inquiry is by first clearly defining the basic terms of engagement (anonymity and ontology) and their interrelation. I define anonymity here in the same way that I have in previous chapters, as indexical dissociation, with the caveat that indexical dissociation can have different meanings and connections to anonymity. Sometimes, removing our indexes anonymizes and is experienced as invisibility, as when Jane Austen uses indexical dissociation to publish, or alienation, as in the feelings experienced by the central character of Ralph Ellison's *Invisible Man*. Yet, the problem of indexical dissociation is magnified when we consider that, in other instances, the indexes that legally and socially identify us have anonymizing effects and can make us feel invisible, as in cases in which sexual assignation given at birth does not match the identity or reality of a person. In cases like Nex Benedict's, indexical dissociation is a step necessary to match identity with identifiers. Nex sought to expose their nonbinary identity by disavowing their binary ascription. And, for some time, Nex likely lived with the awareness that they existed with, at least, two sets of indexes: one, legal, public, social, that defined them wrongly; yet another set, one that they likely used to refer to themselves, was private and needed to move from private to public.

As argued throughout this book, we tend to use the term "anonymity" to describe three types of dissociation processes: agentic anonymity, which is a dissociation initiated by an individual wishing to bypass specific power arrangements; institutional anonymity, which involves practices that institutions and organizations use to bypass systems of power or to empower individuals to act without concern for retaliation or reproach; and contextual anonymity, which is an affective and epistemic response to the feeling of being invisible, unknown, or unremarkable. Given the three ways in which anonymity enters our lives, I believe that anonymity is experienced regularly, maybe even daily, by most, particularly those who live in big urban centers, those who use social media regularly, those who feel compelled to act in public but require impunity to do so, and those whose life transitions require them to adapt to a new world. Yet, understanding anonymity also depends on whether we understand identification or the way that indexes participate in the shaping of human experience. In this chapter, for this argument, I focus on natural language indexes such as personal names, race, and national status, and biological indexes like gender, race, sexes, and age. In the case of Nex Benedict, these indexes include the name Nex, the ethno-racial designation Indigenous, the age (a teen, a minor, a kid), the place of residence (Owasso, Oklahoma), and the pronouns (they/them, he, trans).

Ontology is an area of philosophy and critical theory that I will try to bring down to a few ideas pertinent to this analysis in the hope that this will clarify the aspects of ontology that are useful to the thinking of anonymity and identification. Let me point out first that ontology engages questions about "being," about things that exist in the world (Wrathall 2022). But ontological investigations do not engage only being. Heidegger makes an important distinction, which I use in this book, between ontology and ontic or, if you prefer, Being and being. Mariana Ortega (2016) explains the difference as follows: "In [Heidegger's] existential description of the human being, 'ontological' refers to ways of being, whereas 'ontic' refers to entities or particular facts regarding those entities" (10). Jan Slaby (2021) describes Heidegger's distinction as follows: "The ontic concerns concrete properties and characteristics of an entity, in contrast to the ontological which pertains to the specific *way* an entity of a certain kind *has* its characteristics" (542, italics in the original). The ontic is relatively easy to grasp because it is manifested in properties and characteristics of entities. "A human is a mammal." On the other hand, ontology depends on higher-level arguments that aim to show, in the words of Lynn Rudder Baker (2019), "an inventory of reality, of what genuinely exists without redundancy—for example, what objects, properties and kinds there really are" (4). The ontological question may thus be, What does it mean to be human?

In the following, I show that anonymity and indexicality are connected to human onticity and ontology. By human onticity, I mean the properties and characteristics of humans, such as the ability to use categories or categorical indexes and concrete indexes like personal names. I also show the grounds for entertaining the possibility that anonymity and indexicality are also ontological regarding humans, not only ontic. This may seem like a controversial position, but both Heidegger and Ortega regard ontic and ontological as connected and involved in a back and forth worth reflecting on. Finally, on this issue, I use the analytics of ontology as a way of understanding human beings as they are entangled with a world quickly changing, a motivation not too different from that of all the voices cited here.[1]

This query has several steps. The first section presents scholarship that argues for the connection of categories to ontology. I treat this connection as a philosophically settled issue and one that allows me to first state that categorical indexes have ontological capacities. That said, what is unsettled is whether categorical indexes have ontological capacities because they are about categories or because they are indexical. The following section tests the latter and argues that concrete indexes also have ontological properties. Thus, categorical indexes are ontological not because they are about categories but because they are indexical. If I am right, and both categorical and concrete indexes have ontological capacities, this means that indexical dissociation shapes ontology, an argument I discuss next. That is, if indexes are ontological, their dissociation must have ontological effects. There is one significant problem. Ontological arguments that rely on indexical association, or identity, tend to presume a unitary self. I argue, however, that indexical dissociation necessitates theories of selfhood that are not unitary. In the last section I argue, borrowing ideas from Latine philosophers Mariana Ortega (2016) and Gloria Anzaldúa (2000), for the notion of a multiplicitous self as a notion that fits the ontological possibilities of anonymity.

Ontology, Anonymity, and Categorical Indexes

Baker's (2019) definition of ontology as "an inventory of reality, of what genuinely exists without redundancy" (4) borrows from Aristotle, who begins his *Categories* with an argument central to this book and this chapter:

> When things have the name in common and the definition of being which corresponds to the name is the same, they are called *synonymous*. Thus, for example, both a man and an ox are animals. Each of these is called, by a common name, "animal," and the definition of being is also the same; for if one is to give the definition of each—what being an animal is for each of them—one will give the same definition. ([1963] 2002, 3)

Aristotle's ontology shows in the sentence that "a man and an ox *are* animals" (my italics). The ontological argument here is embedded in the most common of verbs: "to be," which in the sentence is "are," the verb that connects the ontology of ox to that of man as animals. Aristotle's ontology, like Baker's, is predicated on the idea of an inventory of things that exist in reality, and this inventory, like Aristotle makes clear, can be manifested only through categories that have names. Categorical indexes, thus, are as crucial to ontology as they are categories of the real. For one cannot have categories without indexes or a real that refuses to be categorized. So, in a very fundamental and uncontroversial way, categorical indexes are essential to ontology.

What makes indexes ontological is precisely the capacity human indexes have to point and make possible sorting, ordering, and accounting. Indexes are part of human ontology because they are crucial to the type of being that is the human. We are not simply "beings." We are beings with names, labels, social systems, responsibilities, and, I may add, technologies. This much is argued by philosophers and other scholars of social constructivism, social ontology, socio-technical approaches to classifications, and posthumanism. A common thread in these different ways of engaging human indexes is that categories comprise classificatory systems like gender and race that shape our lives in such a way that we *become* them. Categories and indexes are thus not only elements of ontology, as Aristotle would have us think. When it comes to humans, who are the entities that think, use, and experience the categories, categories and indexes also have ontological effects. They participate in the constitution of types of humans. Assigned the category of "boy," a child is embedded in social, cultural, political, and symbolic relationships that teach "him," guide him, shape him, discipline him, into becoming, indeed, a boy.

This position is consistent with social constructivism, which proposes that personal or impersonal agents (for instance, social structures, metaphors, culture, categories) produce reality as we understand it, including ourselves (Hacking 1986, 1999; Lakoff and Johnson 2003). Because social categories have the capacity to constitute being, social constructivism matches well with social ontology, which is a particular way of thinking about being that acknowledges the constitutive role of social reality, concepts, and categories in the formation of things (Baker 2019). In social ontology, being is real, but it is also understood as shaped by external forces. Socio-technical approaches to classification aim to understand the way classifications are crucial to human experience and forms of power, and for that reason, classificatory schemas, and the infrastructures that support them, are the center of social order (Bowker and Star 1999). And posthumanism proposes that humans are entwined with technology in such a fundamental fashion that one cannot speak of human ontology without acknowledging its technological foundation (Hayles 1999; Haraway 2016). Today, we may care about human indexes (data, personal identity, privacy, anonymity) because the computational turn has transformed indexicalization. But our concerns about indexes, categories, and names are as old as Western philosophy. That said, the computational turn is radically transforming human ontology, and, for this reason, the posthumanist argument is not the outlier but the reason for our current concerns.

Echoing positions common in social constructivism and social ontology, I am interested in the way categorical indexes constitute subject positions, ways of being that are particular and contextual but also quite real. That is, these categories are not simply in our minds or in our systems of knowledge. They are also in the world. Human ontology is dynamic because, Baker (2019) notes, ontology is always in and with time and thus specific to a context and a moment in history. The inventory of things that is reality changes through time, and different moments in history will shape a specific inventory of things and specific ontological possibilities.

Time changes and shapes human ontology, but the reason for change is not that time is something like a substance external to things. The reason time changes human ontology is that time is *with* the real and changes it, creating different contexts for different possibilities of existence. Humans must think these different possibilities and do so with, among other things, categories and names. In turn, categories and names that explain human possibilities constitute them.

Ian Hacking (1986) calls this process of co-constitution dynamic nominalism.[2] Categories about humans, he posits, have the capacity to constitute being, but being exists independent from categories and categories themselves reflect types of being. It would be a mistake to claim, for example, that mental illnesses did not exist before these illnesses were named and classified as such. Dynamic nominalism proposes that "numerous kinds of human beings and human acts come into being hand in hand with our invention of the categories labeling them" (236). With this concept, Hacking is trying to do what one may call an ontology of the human that recognizes that human characteristics are always in contexts that are historicized and narrated and that defining humans is not the a priori of human types. Human differences exist whether we name them or not, Aristotle notwithstanding, but these differences acquire different properties when they are named, and it is these properties that social constructivists and scholars of classifications try to explain. In defense of dynamic nominalism, Hacking adds that it is the only type of nominalism "that can even gesture at an account of how common names and the named could so tidily fit together" (236). Dynamic nominalism thus explains the centrality of indexicalization to ontology as well as to theories of social power. It also bridges the gaps between social constructivism, social ontology, and studies of classification.

If Baker and Hacking are right, then dynamism can take at least two forms. If being should always be considered in time, in history (Baker), and if the being of humans is often constituted by the dynamism of names and human reality (Hacking), then historical changes surrounding humans throughout a lifetime may be manifested in name/categorical changes that have ontological capacities. One finds quick evidence in support of this proposition in the general names we use to designate humans by age through a lifetime: baby, child, teenager, adult, and senior. These are designations that become essential to our being in time, but some, like the notion of teenager, did not exist long ago. Ben Cosgrove, in an article for *Time* magazine (2013), writes:

> Historians and social critics differ on the specifics of the timeline, but most cultural observers agree that the strange and fascinating creature known as the American teenager—as we now understand the species—came into being sometime in the early 1940s. This is not to say that for millennia human beings had somehow passed from childhood to adulthood without enduring the squalls of adolescence. But the modern notion of the teen years as a recognized, quantifiable life stage, complete with its own fashions, behavior, vernacular and arcane rituals, simply did not exist until the post-Depression era.

Cosgrove's article then goes on to show the ontic capacities and characteristics of the category as well as their newness. At the moment of this writing, I have an eleven-year-old son who, I believe, is about to embark on the ontic transformation that is teenage-hood. My son is aware of the same, and we are all beginning to adapt to a change that we believe will be not only superficial but substantive.

If the process of becoming that is life defines us, and we define ourselves with categorical indexes, then the essence of being is historicity manifested partly through indexes, indexical association, *and* indexical dissociation. Human onticity is living *in* history and *writing oneself into history*. The world shapes and changes the individual, but the individual changes the world, and our ideas and emotions about normality are shepherded by history alongside our technologies, which may become our capacities.[3] We are not being but becoming, and becoming is a time-oriented ontology that depends on technologies of change, including, I argue, anonymity.

If being is becoming, anonymity, understood as indexical dissociation, enters the flow of life not only as a social potential, as latency, but as an ontic reality. We change throughout life, and our indexes change not simply because we choose (agentic anonymity) or because institutions force us (Cosgrove's article shows how *Time* magazine played an important role in the creation of the American teenager). *Our indexes also change because they need to change.*

Our indexes mark life transitions, and when life changes, new indexes make past indexes invisible, which is another way of saying that our past may and, perhaps, should feel anonymous. A famous phrase in Corinthians 13:11 in the Bible speaks to the double dynamism of history and nominalism: "When I was a child, I talked like a child, I thought like a child, I reasoned like a child; when I became a man, I did away with childish things." The power this phrase has held over time is partly a deep awareness that the essence of our being is becoming, which was important to religions predicated on the idea of conversion. But part of the power rests on the words "I did away with childish things" and the awareness that to become is to unbecome; to call oneself an adult is to do away with childish things. One does not simply face change; one must face it.

There is a second way in which the particular dynamism of human ontology creates ontological complexities. While age categories like child, teenager, and adult have unquestionable ontic power, the issue of whether individuals fundamentally change through time remains. Typically, when a child becomes a teenager, we think that a single individual has changed. That is, the teenager and the child are not two different individuals, even though substantive physical, psychological, and sociocultural changes have altered the individual. We presume identity continuity even when accounting for these dramatic changes. This is why I used the term "ontic," not "ontological," to describe this process. But am I right? Or, do changes as those exemplified by age and other temporal markers at one point become ontological? What about other temporally affected ontological states like migration, marriage, severe illness, transsexuality, or dementia? Do these become ontological at some point?

In *Persons and Bodies* (2000), Baker engages the possibility that humans, or persons, which is the term that Baker prefers, have temporal dynamism and complexities not accounted for by social ontologists like Hacking. Baker proposes that identity continuity is best understood as fulfilling the criteria of a first-person perspective: "So, person P1 at *t1* is the same person as person P2 at *t2* if and only if P1 and P2 have the same first-person perspective" (132). She gives a more phenomenological explanation of her postulate in the following:

> Every morning when I wake up, I know that I am still existing—without consulting my mirror, my memory, or anything else. I can tell. Perhaps I even have a dramatic experience that I might express by exclaiming, "I'm alive! I'm alive!" . . . The subject of the experience of realizing that she is still alive is either I, or it is not I. If it is not I, then I cannot be aware (without being told) that such an experience is being had. And if it is I, then I know without being told that I am the subject of that experience. (136–37)

In this illustration, Baker shows that our first-person perspective precedes a personal evaluation ("my mirror, my memories") that would judge changes in order to bring them in harmony with the sense of individuality and oneness that the first-person perspective provides. Like a particular type of consciousness, the first-person perspective is an awareness of oneself that needs no mediation ("without being told"). But once mediated with mirrors, judgments, evaluations, and memories, the first-person perspective becomes the "I" that stabilizes the self through changes and that encourages an experience of continuity even though we age, we may migrate, we may become prisoners, or we may become unhoused.

Unlike that first fraction of a second in which the first-person perspective is unmediated, most things pertaining to humans need mediation, language, names, and categories. This includes changes that occur through life, and we use categorical indexes, which have ontic capacities, to make sense of them. But we also use concrete indexes like personal names, nicknames, titles, honorifics, to mark important life processes. In Mexico, I was known as Héctor German Amaya González, but I can see that man only askance, refracted. It is not an affectation but a historization and recognition that my self, which is always in the present, and my subjectivity have essentially changed through the process of migrating away from Mexico. The first-person perspective, the "I," allows me to experience continuity, but not to claim it. The claim is self-narration. Something continues and holds some aspects of my person together, every refraction, but many things have changed. My indexes are manifestations of these changes. When I claim that Hector Amaya marks the new self, in a new country, with a new set of linguistic rules, I am also claiming that the index Hector Amaya dissociates me from Héctor German Amaya González and that man's onticity. That man was not a migrant. I am. Just like man dissociates from childhood, my migrant name dissociates me from my premigration name. I do not present any longer to the world as my Mexican self, and that part of my self becomes unnamed and unmarked history. Those who interact with me in my new world as Hector Amaya know only a portion of me marked by the time I left Mexico. The rest remains more or less anonymous, invisible, and sometimes painfully inconsequential. Inspired by Baker (ontology in time) and by Heidegger (onticity), I am interested in thinking about humans as becoming, and, in this way of thinking, dynamic nominalism cannot exist without indexical dissociation, anonymity. In becoming, dynamic nominalism begets anonymity. To help me in the thinking of humans as becoming, I direct my attention to Latina philosophers, including Anzaldúa, Mariana Ortega, and Jackie Martinez.

Ontology, Anonymity, and Concrete Indexes

Arguing for the importance of concrete indexes to onticity or ontology is not the norm. In social constructivism, social ontology, and studies of classifications, the norm is to focus on the ontic capacities of categories. But I believe that indexicalization does not simply organize humans into groups. Indexicalization is also crucial to individuation, and this insight is important to questions of onticity and ontology. Just as individuals are always part of groups, the fact that human groups are composed of individuals is highly consequential to the type of groups we have. This perspective is old. It is consistent with Aristotle's perspective, who understood the individual entities (a person) that composed a category (humanity) as the primary substance. Individuals, he reasoned, can exist without categories, but categories cannot exist without individuals ([1963] 2002, 2b4). Ergo, a first and primary ontology is related to the individual as individual.

Yet, unlike the Aristotelian tradition, which includes Baker, I am interested in the indexes that identify individuals, and my interest is dual: it is partly about the oneness of the individual, oneness that is marked by concrete indexes; but it is also about the fact that indexes, particularly natural language indexes, signify. The issue of signification is consequential to onticity, for if natural language categories are ontic, they are so because they signify, and through their signification and meaning, they enter culture and life as viable ways of being. The category woman has ontological capacities because it means a host of ideas that are expressed culturally and through social, political, and legal practices, not simply because the category woman places a boundary around a set of bodies.

This matters to the study of anonymity. Agentic anonymity is carried out because individuals reflect on the meaning and consequences of having indexes in their lives. Individuals know that indexes make them accountable to others and the law, and when they choose to bypass these order systems, they often use anonymity to do so. One may use a pseudonym to post a hateful comment on social media; one may create a fake email address to "shop" at a place that the individual prefers to keep secret; one may use VPN technology to do something illegal like buying narcotics on the dark web; or one may use BitTorrent to download copyrighted material without legal repercussions. In all of these cases, individuals used anonymity reflexively, aware of the social and legal work of indexes.

There is one more way in which an emphasis on concrete indexes adds to the literature. The dynamic nominalism that Hacking introduces in the context of human categories has effects on ontology. Human ontology, Hacking and others argue, is partly the product of the human categories we use. I believe this insight applies also to individuals in their relation to concrete indexes. Consider first that humans are the only type of ontological objects that can potentially have a record of all of their members, all eight billion, thanks to concrete indexes and technologies of indexical inscription. Our ontological present (following Baker's advice to always attend to ontology in time), shaped by socio-technological factors like datafication and surveillance, cannot be understood without the awareness that we are an ontic entity that can claim to have a catalogue of each of its members as individuals, with particular concrete indexes. Our uniqueness is phenomenologically subjective *and* epistemologically objective. We feel unique and believe we can prove we are so. In the current socio-technical present, our uniqueness is not a liberal, individualistic, theory of ontology. Our uniqueness is a social fact, using Durkheim's term, and we have the catalogues provided by tax records, birth records, SSN records, census records, the data sets to prove it.[4]

Our uniqueness is not important only because it is epistemologically objective. Our uniqueness is manifested partly by the subtle and complex relations of correspondence between indexes, individuals, and identity. My body seems male, and, for that reason, it represents maleness to most. But I use the term "seems" to suggest that this evaluation (my body's maleness) is a calculation based on a mostly visual appraisal of a body wrapped in dress, a dressed body that hides or accentuates different aspects of my physiognomy. The evaluation is more than the evaluation of my body; its evaluation too theorizes the meaning of my dress and the way the dress covers or uncovers, suggests or hides. Yet, we know that it is also possible to represent maleness without experiencing oneself or defining oneself as male. Our bodies are not simply presence. They also re-present, and hence represent the absent, or those others who make up the category who may or may not be my gender kin. I may see in my body maleness that I reject; I may see in my body femaleness that I wished others could see. These representations may be accurate (people may infer rightly that I identify as male) or an appearance (people may presume maleness on an individual who identifies as nonbinary or female). In examples like this, anonymity lingers like a specter, and individuals who have spent time hiding their identities (the metaphor of the closet comes to mind) have existed with a degree of anonymity not because they lack a name or categorical identifiers but because there is a disconnection between their indexes and their selves.

The stakes of evaluative judgments about bodies can be significant, and these stakes can be glimpsed in the case surrounding Herculine Barbin. Adélaïde Herculine Barbin was born intersex on November 8, 1838. Raised as a woman and living indexed by the name "Alexina" until her twenties, Barbin was reassigned as male and renamed "Abel" after a doctor "discovered" that she had been misassigned, a move that Lauren Guilmette (2017) describes as "casting h/er out of all previously known institutional relations and social bonds" (3). That their life would be tragic and end in suicide is theorized by Foucault in relation to the Western obsession with "true sex" in the introduction to *Herculine Barbin* (1980) and also done so by others, including Judith Butler, who, in *Gender Trouble* (1990), argues that Foucault indulges in romanticism when he writes about the time prior to the doctor's visit when Barbin could live with a sort of ambiguity.

Whether Butler or Foucault is right is not important here. What is relevant is the fact that these arguments are partly carried out by reference to indexes; they are about the proper connection of a concrete index (Alexina or Herculine) to a categorical index (woman) and the discovery that dissociated the person who was Alexina from those indexes, her name, her nickname(s), and her sex. The sexual reassignment that followed the doctor's visit prompted a renaming (from Herculine or Alexina to Abel) that fitted the new sex (man) ascribed to the person. It is worth repeating that the shift and names and sexual assignation damaged Barbin's social relations and constituted one of the bases for the tragic ending. In this case, it is proper to use the term "anonymity" to describe and qualify this indexical dissociation, for, as in other cases of anonymity as in slavery, the indexical removal and substitution constituted the basis of a misrecognition that expelled the subject (Barbin) from the world they previously lived in. Though neither Foucault nor Butler uses the term "anonymity" to describe the identity challenges engendered by the disconnection between sex, indexes, and the social that Barbin experienced throughout their life, I read their life as illustrative of the affective reaction to the discord between self, index, and the social—the three dimensions crucial to making Barbin's body legible to themselves and others.

Today, more than a century and a half after Barbin's suicide, their case seems oddly familiar. I began with the quotation regarding Benedict's suicide to draw this connection. In the United States, gender and sexual norms have changed dramatically in the last decade, particularly among the young. In many places around the United States, including California and the elementary school that my son attended, many kids and young people accept gender fluidity as a given, without judgment. In a growing number of locations and institutions, to declare oneself queer or nonbinary seems so normal that it is almost unremarked. To be trans is, however, more controversial, and even in these "progressive" locales, there is often the need to share this only with those whom you trust. Such caution becomes overwhelming in other conservative locations and neighborhoods. Not every place is like Los Angeles or, within LA, like my neighborhood, and youth culture, politics, and hate are also quotidian ways of enforcing old-fashioned gender and sex rules. The current gender and sexual landscapes seem like a minefield created by the normalization of the idea of gender fluidity, on the one hand, in some locations and publics and the huge and often violent backlash against it, on the other. Powerful well-funded forces among major political groups like the Republican Party seek to undermine and even punish what many consider sexual progress.

Powerful religious leaders have also participated in spreading hate and condemnation toward gender and sexual minorities, with particular scorn for nonbinary and trans persons. As in Barbin's time, politics and religion set the stage for how persons experience sex and gender.

The resulting social landscape makes today not too different from Barbin's time. Nonbinary, intersex, and trans persons are some of the human groups with the highest risk of engaging in suicidal thoughts or of committing suicide. And, like for Barbin, part of the angst and difficulties experienced by nonbinary, intersex, and trans persons has to do with constricting categorical indexes (the availability of options beyond male and female), with the legal provisions that support them, and with whether persons can legally change their names to match their identity. As DeChants et al. (2022) have documented,

> For many transgender and nonbinary people, using identification documents that do not match their gender identity and/or expression can disclose their identity to other people and expose them to harassment and violence. When using documents not concordant with their gender identity or expression, 40% of transgender adults report harassment and 15% report being asked to leave a business or public accommodation. The stress of having one's gender identity non-consensually disclosed and the possibility of harassment and violence contribute to minority stress among transgender and nonbinary individuals. This minority stress is, in turn, associated with mental health disparities, including elevated risk of anxiety, depression, and suicidality. (5016)

The beating preceding the suicide of Nex Benedict began partly because Benedict was using a girl's bathroom. And though it is still unclear whether this was a deciding factor in the beating, nonbinary and trans persons report huge levels of anxiety and conflict because of such issues. Other research has corroborated and added to what DeChants et al. argue. Researchers have shown that being able to legally change a name and sex designation leads to higher rates of employment for transgender Black persons, higher income, and stable housing (Hill et al. 2018, 30). Unsurprisingly, these indexical changes were also connected to increased well-being and fewer suicidal thoughts. If being is ontology, these cases help us see that categorical and concrete indexes are not simply ontic. In these cases, indexes are ontological, and so is indexical dissociation.

Latine Feminist Ontology, Anonymity, and the In-Between

Previously I discussed Baker's (2000) theories on the ontology of human persons, and I want to use her arguments to probe further on cases referring to indexical dissociation due to sexual identity. Baker believes that the first-person perspective allows persons to have identity continuity, and she goes to great lengths to show how this happens. Anzaldúa (2000) would perhaps agree that identity continuity is crucial to life. She writes:

> Identity is sort of like a river. It's one and it's flowing and it's a process. By giving different names to different parts of a single mountain range or different parts of a river, we're doing that entity a disservice. We are fragmenting it. I'm struggling with how to name without cutting up.... I was trying to do that with the *new mestiza*. I was trying to get away from just thinking in terms of blood—you know, the *mestiza* as being of mixed blood. The *new mestiza* is a mixture of all these identities and has the ability, the flexibility, the malleability, the amorphous quality of being able to stretch, and to go this way and that way, add new labels or names which would mix with the others and they would also be malleable. But it's hard to articulate. I am trying to find metaphors—like the mountain range, the river, the *mestiza*—but they're not quite what I want. (132–33)

Echoing the classic imagery of Heraclitus (500 BC), who used the idea of the river to propose an ontology of becoming, Anzaldúa uses the river also to illustrate the unity of being in becoming, while Baker uses the first-person perspective to account for oneness through life. The first-person perspective is, Baker posits, an interior perspective that becomes the ground for first-person pronouns that allow one to think oneself as oneself "(e.g., 'I am happy')" and that allows us "to attribute to ourselves first-person reference (e.g., 'I wonder whether I'll be happy in ten years')."

This last form "shows that the speaker has a concept of herself as herself. The first-person perspective opens up a distinction between thinking of oneself in the first person (not just having thoughts expressible by 'I' but conceiving of oneself as having such thoughts) and thinking of oneself in the third person. Once someone can make this distinction, she can think of herself as a subject in a world of things different from herself" (91–92). Baker also argues that a capacity needed by someone to exhibit first-person perspective is being "in an environment . . . conducive to the development and maintenance of a first-person perspective" (92). The examples she uses to illustrate the possibility that some environments may not be conducive to a first-person perspective include a person in a coma, which may not allow for the perspective to be active, but it is a state that allows, at least theoretically, the maintenance of such perspective.

An important peculiarity of human persons, Baker adds, is that humans have bodies that become the object of their first-person references. This is clear because human persons can think their bodies without needing a name or a third-person pronoun like she/he/they. When one's leg hurts, one can think "I am in pain" without the need for third-person reference. What makes one's body one's own is that a person can think of and refer to this body "from the inside," and this particular body "expresses intentional states and character traits that are" the person's (94).

Like any other thinker's, Baker's theories are made possible and limited by the examples she uses to think the world and by her metaphors. This is particularly important in the more analytic side of philosophy, for each concept such as the notion of a first-person perspective is only as good as it is applicable to the real, which is full of concrete possibilities that may prove the concept right or wrong. Alas, in Baker's intellectual locale, literary metaphors are not encouraged, and thus her concepts are the dry metaphor of science. Baker tests these concepts judiciously, even with extreme examples, sometimes outrageous thought experiments, that include the possibility that persons may be transferred into machines, or dead bodies, or bodies that include mechanical body parts, or persons that may not be human-like gods and other possibilities. Not unlike Anzaldúa, who tests the idea of river, mountain range, or the *mestiza*, Baker prods reality, imagining the thing she imagines has boundaries that capture all possible individual cases. She does this because she is interested in whether her ideas pass the harshest tests. That is her methodology of analysis, which is common in philosophy. The same can be said of Anzaldúa, who, however, exists in the world of truth as imagined by the more literary humanities, which has different epistemological traditions and safeguards.

These safeguards make a difference. Baker may use extreme imaginary examples, but she does not analyze what I would consider are contemporary crucial problems to the idea of identity continuity *in the world*, which are the problems Anzaldúa dwells in. These include challenges to identity brought about by sexual and gender dynamics, by migration, race, and ableness. These types of examples are absent in Baker, and thus, she does not question the possibility that some environments may present challenges to the development and maintenance of first-person perspectives or that some bodies or forms of embodiment may not express a person's interiority, at least not throughout a lifetime. This type of shortcoming is not unique to Baker. Jacqueline Martinez (2014) would place judgment on Baker's engagement with the questions of ontology as the easy privilege of White feminists: "[White feminists] can . . . take their intersubjective position for granted and thereby make their own sense of the world into a total world, even while making claims to the contrary" (229). The reason for the shortcomings aside, I want to test Baker's ideas against examples like those in this chapter, examples that push the idea of identity continuity to the limit, and examples that are partly manifested in questions of indexical dissociation.

Like others, I have found in Anzaldúa's ideas compelling theories of the world, a world defined from the margins inward, a subaltern world, the opposite direction from most. Her words taught me more about identity than many hefty books did. She has inspired me for roughly the same reasons Anzaldúa has inspired philosopher Mariana Ortega (2016), who criticizes Heidegger on the same grounds that I criticize Baker:

> While Heidegger painstakingly explains major ontological, existential characteristics of a self that is *thrown*, he unfortunately does not explain the specific ontic situations that are of concern for the self that is "there" and that dwells in the world. His primary interest remains in fundamental ontology, in finding general ontological characteristics of human beings, even if it is an ontology that is always connected to the ontic or specific characteristics of humans. Anzaldúa and other Latina feminists, however, underscore the ontic, the specific material characteristics and conditions of human beings. Latina feminists concentrate on the particular power relations informing specific economic, cultural, and societal "theres." (53)

Ortega, inspired by the writings of Anzaldúa, but also Maria Lugones and Martinez, introduces the concept of "multiplicitous self," a theory of selfhood and human onticity that accounts for life experiences unaccounted for by Baker or Heidegger. Ortega's "total world" (using Martinez's words) includes and indeed starts at the margins with analytic problems rooted in lives lived "in-between," at borders demarcating powerful ontic categories. She quotes Anzaldúa to tell us about these marginal beings that exist between categorical borders that in her work are the center. Anzaldúa calls these subaltern beings *los atravesados*, "the squint-eyed, the perverse, the queer, the troublesome, the mongrel, the mulato, the half-breed, the half dead; in short, those who cross over, pass over, or go through the confines of the 'normal'" (qtd. in Ortega 2016, 3). Each of the categories referenced by Anzaldúa and Ortega call attention to multiplicity, or, rather, oneness as multiplicity (18).

In almost all ways, Ortega's multiplicitous self seeks to explain questions that are the same or similar to those by other thinkers, from Aristotle to Heidegger to Baker, who seek to explain the particular type of being that is the human or, as Baker would prefer, a human person. These include questions of identity, experience, perception, and what Baker calls identity continuity, which Ortega refers to, in the Heideggerian tradition, as existential continuity. What sets her ideas apart is that she, like other Latine philosophers, wants to explain humans in a world that is not experienced like a single world but as a plurality, humans that live between worlds, social enclaves that demand specific and discrete forms of being, experiencing, behaving, and feeling. These border crossers, *los atravesados*, share some challenges, though clearly not all. It is quite different to be queer than to be mulatto or mestiza. Yet, there are also commonalities that become ground for theorizations of human persons who have to adapt to being multiple, because their worlds are many. This adaptation is not perfect or without grief:

> Even though all of us are multiplicitous, some multiplicitous selves—those who are multicultural, queer, border dwellers, and whom Anzaldúa names *los atravesados*—experience more of what she describes as "psychic restlessness" and "intimate terrorism" due to their marginalization and oppression. That is, these selves' multiplicity is sharper, sometimes piercing, thus leading to a sense of alienation and *Unheimlichkeit,* or uncanniness, that makes their lives more vulnerable to injustice. (Ortega 2016, 51)

In some times, in some places, these identities are grounds for extreme marginalization, and, in the words of Lugones, these persons are treated as "pliable, foldable," "file-awayable, classifiable," or disposable (Lugones qtd. in Ortega 2016, 97).

The examples I have referenced earlier, Benedict and Barbin, illustrate sharp, even piercing, multiplicities that can lead to self-alienation, as Ortega argues, and that force the individual to consider changes to indexicality, to the terms, names, and pronouns that define them, and that constitute forms of relationality inclusive of the types of embodiment particularities that individuals may present. In these cases, the maintenance of the first-person perspective includes working on the "I," as Baker remembers, but also refiguring the indexical mechanisms by which a person can operate in the social and prefigure the third-person perspective.

The problem in Baker is not the first moment of waking up every morning in which one realizes one is alive. I am with her up to that point. The problem is the instant after, when a person reflects on themselves as embodied beings in a world in which embodiment is subject to social evaluation, challenges, and perhaps opportunities. To cisgender individuals, sexual and gender majorities, this instant is unlikely to raise concerns. But to trans, intersex, and/or nonbinary individuals, this is nepantla, an in-between, or, in Hortense Spillers's words, the vestibular (2003, 232). This is a moment of reflexivity as referenced in other types of research. In the health literature, for instance, as in the work of Ilan Meyer (1995, 2003), sexual minorities "experience a conflict between their identity and the institutionalized values of heteronormative society . . . thus making sexual minorities more susceptible to negative life events. . . . Negative life events, their anticipation, and the internalization of their meaning lead to negative population-level mental health outcomes (e.g., anxiety, depression, suicidality) and negative life events (e.g., housing insecurity; food insecurity) for this community" (Johnson et al. 2022, 119). Understanding oneself from the third-person perspective anticipates negative and positive interactions that determine tactical and strategic decisions about oneself. Among the strategic long-term decisions are adopting new pronouns, as in the case of Benedict, or processing a legal name and legal sex change, measures that in Barbin's case were imposed by medical/legal apparatuses but that are common among trans people today.

These indexical dissociations have a great impact on a person's life. Spade (2015) notes the following challenges:

> For trans people, administrative gender classification and the problems it creates for those who are difficult to classify or are misclassified is a major vector of violence and diminished life chances and life spans. Trans people's gender classification problems are concentrated in three general realms: identity documentation, sex-segregated facilities, and access to health care. (77)

Vulnerable populations and trans, nonbinary, and intersex persons often are at risk of losing access to state benefits like health care, shelter, and unemployment if there are mismatches between documents (driver's licenses, birth certificates, public benefit cards, passports, immigration documents) and/or identities. In places like the United States, government agencies and states have particular policies to track gender classifications that can create inconsistencies that add administrative vulnerability to already vulnerable persons.

> The wide range of policies and practices means that many people, depending on where they live and what kind of medical evidence they can produce, cannot get any records or ID corrected, or can only have their gender changed with some agencies but not with others. So, for example, one person born in New York and living in New York might have a birth certificate she cannot change from "M" to "F" because she has not had genital surgery; a driver's license that correctly reflects "F" because she got a doctor's letter; Social Security records that say "M" because she cannot produce evidence of surgery; a name change order that shows her new feminine name; and a Medicaid card that reads "F" because the agency had no official policy and the clerk felt the name change order and driver's license were sufficient. (Spade 2015, 79)

If, as Bernhard Siegert (2015) argues, the modern subject is "an autobiographical animal" (84), biographical discrepancies like the ones noted by Spade and experienced by Benedict and Barbin fundamentally erode the ability of individuals to exist in a modernity shaped by bureaucracies.

I began this section with Anzaldúa's theorization of identity. She says, "Identity is sort of like a river. It's one and it's flowing and it's a process. By giving different names to different parts of a single mountain range or different parts of a river, we're doing that entity a disservice. We are fragmenting it" (Anzaldúa 2000, 132–33). But fragmentation and multiplicity are unavoidable the second one reflects on the identity negotiations the day is about to bring or on the way our selves may be fragmented in documents, by documents, and the indexes and onticities they host. In Anzaldúa, the dialectic of the one and the many, the one and the multiple self, the one and the fragmented, changing self, cannot be resolved. They are in a perpetual state of tension characterized in the metaphor by the fluidity of the water and the relative immobility of the riverbank. Naming, indexes, are fictions in the sense that they capture an instant of a moving, changing self, but they are nonetheless necessary fictions, the fundamental chaptering of the autobiographical animal's story.

Previously I mentioned that Ortega (2016) criticizes Heidegger for failing to anticipate specific ontic situations that may undermine his visions of ontology. Ortega would likely consider the situations by Benedict and Barbin the real test of ontological theory. Would Heidegger's pass? In Heidegger, the problems faced by Benedict and Barbin may be ontic, not ontological. These problems may be related to being with a small "b," not Being. But Anzaldúa may remind us that other types of subjects also exist in situations of multiplicity and fragmentations, those whom she calls *los atravesados*. These subjects are not mental experiments of the type that Baker uses to test her theories. They are embodied beings with *general problems of multiplicity and fragmentation* who have to struggle with the first-person perspective, the possibility of alienation, vulnerabilities, bureaucratic misalignments, and autobiographical incoherence. These subjects face forms of invisibility, anonymity, misrecognition, and miscategorization that trouble the subject's sense of self, that force movement and change. Indeed, if categories have ontic capacities, if names shape life, they most fundamentally misshape it. Life is a struggle because indexes have ontic capacities, but we cannot go without indexes (Anzaldúa's painful realization), and thus we need to change them, give them some of the fluidity that life has, even if the process by definition means more anonymizing, more forgetting.

At what point does the particular become the general or the ontic the ontological? Ortega notes that Heidegger seems more concerned with fundamental ontology and "general ontological characteristics of human beings" than with the ontic and specific. But she is perhaps too generous. Heidegger moved ontology closer to life when he defined self as *being-in-the-world*, a self in the making, a self that moves forward (like a river?), but as Ortega (2016) hints, he considers this projecting forward of the self only partly reflexive (52). For Anzaldúa and the subjects she thinks about, the future is a problem that the self must attend to through reflection; survival is at stake. This can be seen simply as a difference of emphasis. Heidegger does consider being-in-the-world as partly reflexive, but Anzaldúa invests more in reflexivity. And this difference hints at a more fundamental difference between Heidegger, an individual whose future was not full of deadly possibilities and vulnerabilities, and another whose life was defined by struggle. Ultimately, it is about defining what is general to the human and what is particular.

I use these examples, including Barbin's, to illustrate the importance of indexes to anonymity, but to also illustrate that these issues and questions are not simply shaped by categorical indexicality or their classificatory power. Concrete indexes are organizing tools for the subject, who uses them in conjunction or alongside categorical indexes to make sense of the self and other. They are the linguistic and social side of the first-person perspective. Concrete indexes such as Herculine or Alexina are part of the phenomenology of indexicality. They are the terms Barbin used to organize life and experiences, and he conceived them as singular, as belonging to that of an individual, her/himself marked by uniqueness, what romantically we term human, a subject not an object, a biological entity whose coherence was shaped also by science, law, and their social contexts. When betrayed by medicine and law, Barbin's biological markers made her a peculiar object of knowledge and of ridicule. Perhaps Barbin felt expelled from the realm of subjects, social actors, to the realm of objects, the passive recipients of scientific scrutiny and social calculation. Guilmette (2017), commenting on Barbin's last months, writes: "Subjected to scandalous rumors and consigned to 'that half of the human race which is called the stronger sex' (HB 89), Barbin had to leave all previously familiar sites of community for the anonymity of Paris, where they sought work unsuccessfully as a man and lived in poverty and isolation" (5). Guilmette cites Margaret McLaren, who added a note and a puzzle: "When Herculine was a woman, she was too strong, too gawky, too tall, too masculine. But when she was a man, she was too soft, too weak, too feminine. But her body and appearance were the same" (McLaren qtd. in Guilmette 2017, 5). Their body and appearance may have been the same, but, McLaren implies, they were resignified in the sexual reassignation and they stopped having the meaning Barbin was accustomed to.

It is tempting to think about biological indexes as a "real" given support by natural sciences, but Barbin's case reminds us that all indexes, including biological traces, exist also in the realm of discourse and are subject to cultural, social, and legal constraints and theorizations. They do not simply "present" the individual: They "represent" (as per Foucault or Butler), and this representation may change in context, or it may change over time, as when Barbin was obligated to live under the categorical index of male. Strictly speaking, most indexes represent absences, but the play of presence and absence is perhaps always in a state of deferral, what Jacques Derrida (1982), in referring to the trace, defines as *différance*: an endless dynamic of returns and differentiations that move toward an original referent that never shows. Barbin's name, composed of a few letters, represented them; the gender assigned to her represented her and, later, changed, and the new indexes represented them. In this reassignment, we, the outsiders to their life, were no closer to knowing them. The certainty of science could not make them present, a feat that is never possible through indexes. *Différance* is endemic to indexes, and what *différance* highlights is, among other things, the centrality of absences, and of the play of absences, to life.

As much as I enjoy the power of Derrida to describe identity and the relationship between signs and the real, I prefer the lyrical complexity dressed as simplicity that Anzaldúa brings to her ideas on identity. The river metaphor troubles metaphysics in ways that even Derrida does not. *Différance* is dynamic, but the dynamism is marked by attending to the stages. Applying *différance* to identity is like attending to the movement that is evident when you look at the riverbank. Yes, one can never fully attend to identity, for identity has already changed. But Baker and Anzaldúa are right about identity, as are Heidegger, Aristotle, and Heraclitus. The flow of the river, the first-person perspective, and existential continuity are primary ontology. That feeling of flowing down in time and space defines us. But this primary ontology is incomplete without attending to the changing nature of being human, the becoming that is our nature. And this becoming cannot exist without recognizing that the self is multiplicitous and fragmented, able to hold us together in different worlds, but on the condition that it can change and be multiple.

Three

The Myth of Anonymous Publicity

The previous chapter argues that anonymity gives form to the subject. This chapter explores anonymity in the social by returning to an idea introduced at the very beginning of the book. In the Introduction, I noted that surveillance and datafication matter because we believe, implicitly or explicitly, that anonymity and privacy matter to individuals and societies. When we conjure imageries of absolutism reliant on hypersurveillance, as Orwell does in *1984*, we are arguing that there is something essentially valuable and powerful about being anonymous to the eye of power. This value and power are particularly important to subalterns who, by definition, *need* social change, but it is equally important to anyone wishing or hoping for change. As the specter of authoritarianism and absolutism looms powerful on the horizon of the West, anonymity will become increasingly important, just as it is already in places like China. As stated before, from the perspective of subalterns and those wishing to participate in civic actions, it is anonymity, not privacy, that holds the promise and possibility of political and social change, and it is anonymity, not privacy, that defines the value and worth of studies of surveillance and datafication.

This is far from saying that anonymity is the solution to social change. Clearly, to many, in most cases in the West, activism, access to the public sphere, social organizing, allyship, open debate, and electoral politics tend to be sufficient to bring about change. But not every change can be brought about in this way if you are a subaltern. In general, the closer we are to authoritarianism, the closer we are to violence and the farther we are from open politics. In these contexts, anonymity matters. From a subaltern perspective, the state routinely looks as if it is an authoritarian and violent state and, for this reason, to subalterns, anonymity has always mattered.

Yet, anonymity is no magic bullet. While the connection between anonymity and freedom is a preferred connection, one that has been described at length by many and one that is implied in almost every study of surveillance, this connection is also mythical, and, for this reason, it tends to hide its historicity and its contradictions. The economy of anonymity is not simply a reflection of anonymity's use value or anonymity as a thing of the real. The economy of anonymity depends also on anonymity's mythical status, which fuels particular uses of anonymity and hides others. The myth of anonymity partly enlivens important sectors of the economy of anonymity, particularly those characterized by agentic anonymity and its connections to formal politics. The myth, however, is dangerous not simply because it hides anonymity's historicity and contradictions. The myth is also dangerous because it leads to risky miscalculations.

This chapter analyzes the myth of anonymity by returning to a case I developed in my previous book.[1] The case revolves around one person, whom I have known as Lucy for the last few years. Lucy is a pseudonym adopted by a blogger who, with a friend who took care of the technical side, created and maintained a popular website in Mexico from 2010 to 2013. The site, named *El Blog del Narco* (*EBDN*), published and distributed photos, videos, and articles about the violence in Mexico at a time when Mexican journalists were forced to self-censor to stay alive. Although anonymity was essential for Lucy and her survival, her case doesn't represent all acts of anonymity, nor do I use it as an exemplar to prescribe anonymity as a solution or a weapon, as will become evident in the following pages. Nevertheless, Lucy's life and its particular conditions give us insights into the myths giving meaning to anonymity. My evidence comes from the blog *EBDN*, from Lucy's words, a book that she published in 2013, and a blog also published in 2013 after she closed *EBDN*. I use her words as evidence of negotiations with material and technological conditions, as well as evidence that the concepts that Lucy used to justify her actions were projections of material and technological a priori.

Before the words, we have her actions, and what Lucy did in and with her blog was public and anonymous, and it is these two terms, "publicity" and "anonymity," that provided the basis for her actions and her words. But a complication immediately ensues when we put anonymity and publicity together to create the composite concept "anonymous publicity." From the perspective of day-to-day uses of anonymity, the concept anonymous publicity makes sense. As I noted in the Introduction, anonymity is always about public acts or statements. But this is not the whole story.

From the conventional conceptual historiography of publicity theory, the concept anonymous publicity is an oxymoron, a contradiction. This conventional historiography defines publicity as openness, and anonymity is the contrary.[2] I expand on this later, but here let me note that one may be tempted to dismiss this perspective: After all, Lucy and most people who commented on her blog did not see anonymous publicity as a contradiction. Yet, there is evidence that her anonymous public practices were discursively framed in ways using language loaded with the normative and conventional promises of publicity theory, the very intellectual, conceptual, and discursive milieu that engenders anonymous publicity as a contradiction. Because of this, I do not think we can dismiss these contradictions. If discourse sets the universe of possibilities for actions, contradictory discourses constitute a treacherous terrain for action. This chapter argues that the reasons anonymous publicity presents itself as a contradiction in publicity theory help explain, at least partly, what happened to the blog and to Lucy. And these reasons, I show, are evident when anonymity and publicity are treated as cultural techniques defined by their relationship to materiality.

By engaging publicity theory with the notion of cultural techniques, I am turning one of Bernhard Siegert's ideas backward. In the introduction to *Cultural Techniques: Grids, Filters, Doors, and Other Articulations of the Real*, Siegert (2015) writes a narrative about the emergence of cultural techniques based on the tension between materialities and publicity. He historicizes the rise of German media theory as a rejection of traditional media studies' concerns with the political potential of the public sphere. Siegert presents Jürgen Habermas's work on the subject as a "fictional construct bequeathed to us by Enlightenment thought" (4). I agree. Yet, unlike Siegert, who uses ideas about publicity as examples of hopeless enthusiasm, I want to dig deeper into these connections. For, while it is true that the overemphasis on public sphere theory has limited the intellectual and philosophical reach of media studies, the public sphere is also a thing of the real, and, as Siegert helps us see, the real matters. To Lucy, the stage on which she has to perform her civic deeds is real. Siegert writes: "[The] analysis of cultural techniques observes and describes techniques involved in operationalizing distinctions in the real. They generate the forms in the shape of perceptible unities of distinctions. . . . Concrete actions serve to distinguish them from earlier nondifferentiatedness. In more general terms, all cultural techniques are based on the transition from nondistinction to distinction and back" (14). So, rather than turning my back on publicity, I engage it as a thing of a real structured by anonymity and indexicalization. *I believe publicity is a posteriori to indexicalization.* Importantly, it is a posteriori that is part of the cycle of indexical distinction and nondistinction that Siegert alludes to in the quote.

The following section introduces, historicizes, and explains Lucy's case. The rest of the chapter is dedicated to the conceptual and historiographic hypothesis that links anonymous publicity to myth, materiality, and cultural techniques. The argument has the following sequence: First I show that publicity is conventionally defined in relationship to openness, and I treat openness as a material and social determinant that privileges visibility and self-disclosure. Second, I show that less conventional definitions of publicity, those that connect publicity to collectivity, allow for the possibility of anonymous publicity. In this conceptual space, anonymity is paired with invisibility, secrecy, and opacity, which are media concepts based on materiality. The pairing is not without consequences. It generates contradictions that can be ironed out only with the use of myth or ideology. In Lucy's case, the myth of heroicity paved the way to the dangerous actions that shaped Lucy's life as a blogger and afterward. The last section analyzes what trust is in anonymous publicity. Can one trust and be trusted when speaking anonymously? I argue that the answer to this question is crucial to a redefinition of anonymous publicity as a socio-technical practice.

Lucy

Civic duties are a type of public morality, one that is meant to give answers to the question, "How shall I act?" Civic duties are felt as internal compulsions, as obligations toward oneself and toward others. Lucy declared that she did what she did because it was her civic duty, and this civic duty was given meaning and shape by three contexts. Two were immediate: the context of violence in Mexico and the socio-technical context. The third one is as old as the Enlightenment and is embedded in the very ways of thinking about politics and citizenship. Immediate contexts often offer the tactical possibilities (what can I do at this moment to address this problem?), while intellectual traditions or ideologies provide the strategic logic (of all the possibilities for action, which one fits better with ideas of the good life or society?).

Lucy's actions were performed in the immediate context of the massive escalation of violence that Mexico experienced beginning in December 2006, when new President Calderón took power and violence in Mexico exploded. Some blame President Calderón for breaking the tense peace between the government and drug criminal organizations (DCOs) when he ran on the platform of security, a platform that placed him in a collision course with DCOs. The "drug war," if we are to call it that, began with military interventions in states like Michoacán and continues today in a large portion of the Mexican territory, with particularly bloody consequences in states bordering the United States: Sinaloa, Michoacán, and Veracruz. Today, the violence has continued, even if headlines in Mexico and abroad are no longer representing it with the same intensity. For an expansion on the history and evolution of drug violence in Mexico, see *Trafficking* (Amaya 2020).

Calling the violence in Mexico a "drug war" is, in some senses, a misnomer. Wars tend to offer some clarity as to who is a friend, who is an enemy, and on whose side our alliances should be. But in Mexico, there have been no clear two sides. DCOs are peopled by common Mexicans, sometimes by our neighbors, sometimes by our friends or relatives. Government forces are also not always representing the interests of the population, nor are they carrying out their violent engagement with DCOs with clear protocols of war. Human rights violations, for instance, have exponentially grown, and neither the police nor the military has risen to the occasion. To complicate matters even more, corruption among political and the state security apparatus has made it ever more difficult to know for sure who works for DCOs and who does not. Caught in the middle are the great majority of Mexicans who suffer the consequences of the violence and of the erosion of their security.

A second immediate context was socio-technical, in particular the widespread adoption of internet technologies and the world wide web, which provided new communicational possibilities to social actors like Lucy to make sense of and even respond to the violence. As I note in *Trafficking*, these technologies were crucial to the DCOs as basic communication and were used by cartels to communicate with competing DCOs, with the state, with media organizations, and with the citizenry. Digital communicational technologies like the internet, social media platforms, digital news, and the blogosphere also constituted the cultural, informational, and political context that Mexicans used to learn about, debate, and respond to the violence.

The immediacy, scale, and duration of the massive violence have fueled new and old doubts about the trajectory of Mexico as a nation. Mexican citizens have experienced the violence as a crisis of politics, a crisis of the state, and a crisis of journalism, and these types of crises cannot be simply solved with state actions. They necessitate a new way of doing politics, community, and social obligations. To many Mexicans, these crises require a reengagement with democracy and liberalism, crucial intellectual traditions that we have come to associate with Enlightenment thought, even if, in the Mexican context, these traditions are often localized, made to fit the problems of neocolonialism and technological and economic dependency on the Global North.

The immediate violent and socio-technical contexts and the wide and deeper context of crises that challenged Mexican democracy converged on a third context: the principles and Enlightenment ideas of publicity, the communicational anchor of political communities structured around the principles of deliberation. In our political cultures and in our political theories, publicity is not a by-product of democracy and liberalism. It is the ground on which they are built. It is because we can come together and debate in the public sphere that we can bring to life a democracy that represents the complexity of our societies. Entwined as they are, publicity and democracy are the rich grounds on which politics flourish. For this reason, crises that pertain to politics are often first manifested in the public sphere. And Mexico's massive violence was no exception.

The violence shaped and twisted Mexico's political life, and it also shaped and twisted Mexico's public sphere, and this was most evident in the way journalism had to adapt. More violence meant more reporting on the violence, and this was something that DCOs opposed and tried to influence by threatening, assaulting, and killing journalists and attacking media outlets. Twisted and misshapen, the Mexican public sphere grew weaker when it was most needed. Self-censorship became normal and even rational, which created a communication gap in regions dominated by cartels. Citizens in these regions, thus, experienced the ontological insecurity of violence and the added ontological insecurity of lacking the means to understand the violence, the means to avoid it, and perhaps even to respond to it. The erosion of the Mexican public sphere due to the self-censorship of the press had thus significant repercussions on the citizenry, and it is hardly surprising that some answered the question "How shall I act?" by trying to remedy this erosion.

The violent context causing the erosion of the public sphere placed barriers on anybody trying to enrich it, which is why some of the most successful actors in the Mexican public sphere were those who resorted to anonymity. This socio-technical affordance of digital culture provided some protection to civic actors hoping to address the violence in public channels. During the years following, we witnessed the rise of a small but increasingly influential anonymous blogosphere and social media, including Lucy's blog. Some blogs have had either brief publication runs or amateurish designs and never had a chance to grow. But a few of the blogs significantly impacted the Mexican and global public sphere, and none was more influential than *EBDN*.[3] I use the term "*EBDN*" as if I were designating a singular blog, but there have been several blogs with similar names and even similar origins. Several of the domains originated in May 2008, with the same internet provider (who.godaddy.com) connected to Monterrey, Mexico, and to the same email address in Nuevo León, suggesting that they were owned by a single person or organization. It is, however, unclear who managed or authored these early blogs or even whether they were managed or authored by the same person or persons since 2008. Today, there is still at least one blog with a similar name, but the heyday of *EBDN* is in the past.

Lucy's digital anonymity was a calculation that she could avoid the likelihood of punishment in a violent environment where other media were harassed and attacked for their reporting. Her goal was to use anonymity to bypass the forces of censorship that were silencing traditional journalistic sources. These forces, she argued, included government and organized crime efforts to stop news organizations from reporting or pressure them to report the bare minimum. In her view, the government censors by underreporting or hiding the chaos that regions in Mexico were experiencing.

The risks were immediately evident. *EBDN* was under attack from the beginning.[4] Often, Lucy stated, these attacks were cyberattacks from the Mexican government. "We change where we live every month. We've been in basements. It's very difficult. We hide our equipment in different places. If the authorities get close we run" (Lucy qtd. in Carroll, "They Stole Our Dreams," 2013). As the killing of bloggers in 2011 and the ongoing threat and attacks demonstrate, Lucy's concerns were not just paranoia. Clearly, the DCOs and some members of the Mexican state were going to great lengths to control the public sphere and to force, through the most brutal coercion, silence over clamor. In an interview in 2013, Lucy wrote about being highly traumatized by these events as they dramatically reminded her of the precariousness of her situation.[5] In the introduction of her 2013 book, *Dying for the Truth: Undercover Inside the Mexican Drug War*, published in Spanish and English, where she narrates a year in the life of the blog, Lucy recalls how in the four days prior to the writing of the introduction to the book, she and her partner had received nine different photos of killings with messages written on top of the message: "you are next *EBDN*." Violence seemed to be always near, even if anonymity permitted this violence to stay at arm's length.

Lucy's blog included a red top banner with the name Blog del Narco. The banner's bottom edge was a second, interactive banner that was the main navigation tool. The buttons in this second narrow banner changed over time. Sometimes, they included a "History" button that took you to blog entries organized by date. Sometimes, the banner included a geographical logic, and buttons would take you to specific Mexican states like "Sinaloa" or "Michoacan." Importantly, this banner always had a "Videos" button that took you to a section that included hundreds of thumbnails that allowed you to stream videos of the violence. These included videos of crime scenes but also executions of all sorts: decapitations, dismemberments, and executions with pistols that would show a person as they were shot, typically in the head. Another button took you to "Photos," and these were curated with the same logic as the videos. Both the videos and photos allowed for comments, and some comment sections were long debates about the event and the reason for the crime. A side banner included a search option, but also advertising. Over the years, *EBDN* and other anonymous blogs collected the most violent archive in the visual history of humanity, in my opinion unparalleled to this day. Yet, even though pain, shock, and even trauma could not be avoided when interacting with the videos, news, and photographs found in *EBDN*, they became some of the most famous citizen journalism sites in and from Mexico.

The main portion of the page was occupied by written articles describing or commenting on violent events. Anonymous, but dated, these news or blog pieces were reports of violence or arrests or, less commonly, policy decisions or political scandals that may affect the way the state was fighting organized crime. Anonymity allowed *EBDN* to hide the authorship of these pieces and to hide the fact that often they were plagiarized news pieces from traditional media. According to *Fronteras*, a news internet portal, *EBDN* plagiarized news pieces from *Proceso*, *Reforma*, *El Norte*, and *Cambio*. *Proceso* made similar claims. But the plagiarism did not go in only one direction. Jorge Tirzo (2013), codirector of the *Revista Mexicana de Comunicación*, showed that many traditional news organizations also plagiarized from *EBDN*.

There were substantial differences between what *EBDN* did and what *EBDN* meant to different publics. To Mexican intellectuals like Tirzo, even with its weaknesses, the blog was a positive example of what is possible with the participatory potential of the web, which includes the ability to crowdsource content, publish at low costs, and perform collaborative curation of material. These positive characteristics were the most beneficial to society because *EBDN* published about narco-trafficking at a time when news self-censorship was increasingly common. Tirzo's position was echoed by others within and outside of Mexico. The reasons are complex, but they fit within a framework that valued *EBDN* for the same reasons that we value the best of journalism—the people have the right to know what is going on in their neighborhood, cities, and states, and whoever does the job of disseminating truthful information to people is playing a valuable role in society. Insofar as *EBDN* played this role—even if this was not the only role it played—*EBDN* deserved respect for the good it provided for society. Yet, these were not the only reasons that made *EBDN* unique among blogs publishing about the narco wars. *EBDN*'s willingness to post graphic visual and video material submitted by users and its ongoing proximity to violence paved the way for its huge following from 2010 to 2013. This proximity to violence also prompted its closing.

Although the first of the sites associated with *EBDN* appeared in 2008, it wasn't until the site *Blog del Narco* (blogdelnarco.com) appeared in 2010 that the blog began gaining users by the millions. The former 2008 site was allegedly published by El Historiador, another anonymous blogger, while the latter 2010 site was written and published by Lucy and an assistant or webmaster. The sites coexisted, but it was Lucy's site that created the largest traffic and caught the imagination of many. At its highest points, in October 2011, Lucy's site ranked forty-seventh as the most-visited site in Mexico and sixth among news websites, coming in behind only *El Universal*, *Milenio*, *El Norte*, *Reforma*, and *CNN*. Viewership fluctuated greatly depending on the events published, but *EBDN* remained important in Mexico up until Lucy's site ceased publishing new material in 2013. The reasons had to do with violence.

On September 13, 2011, the bodies of a young woman and a man who had collaborated with *EBDN* and other social media (Twitter, in particular) appeared hanging from a bridge in Nuevo Laredo, Tamaulipas. The woman was hung from her hands and feet, like a pig in a roast. She was tortured, seminude, and disemboweled. The man was hung by his side, pierced through his hands, and with a cut on his side so deep that you could see the bones. On the bridge and around their bodies were yellow posters, referred to as "narcomantas," which stated: "This is going to happen to all of those posting funny things on the Internet. You better fucking pay attention. I'm about to get you." These two victims had tweeted and blogged about drug violence and participated in sites like *EBDN*. The narcomanta was signed by the Zetas, a violent splinter cartel that has tried to control Nuevo Laredo for some time now. Eleven days later, the body of journalist and blogger María Elizabeth Macías was found, decapitated, also in Nuevo Laredo, with the signature of Los Zetas. According to the narcomanta displayed by the body, Macias was killed not simply because of her news reporting but also because of her comments on blogs and Twitter. Lucy reports that, on top of her body, the killers left "keyboards, a mouse, and other computer parts strewn across her body, as well as a sign that mentioned [*EBDN*] again" (Blog del Narco 2013, xi). Crimes against other bloggers and reporters continued shaping the reception and production of *EBDN*, and they were unquestionably one of the reasons why Lucy stopped her site in 2013.

How to think about anonymity in Lucy's blog in the violent, sociotechnical, and Enlightenment contexts? Why did she publish a blog when she knew the materials would likely put her in confrontation with the state and the DCOs? I have asked myself these questions many times, but I now see them as the wrong questions, because implicit in these questions is an answer rooted in a psychology available to us through her words and a definition of agency anchored in the humanism of the Enlightenment. I want to instead focus on the fact that anonymity is a cultural technique and, like Friedrich Kittler (1990, 1999) helps us see, discourse is not the a priori of technology. Using the method of cultural techniques means re-centering the material and technological and placing these as the a priori of being. In anonymity, material and technological factors shape the discourses that define it and the media concepts that surround it. Anonymity, indexical dissociation, cannot even be conceived without understanding how indexes work in the social and whether they can be removed or substituted. Lucy's actions and words are thus more than evidence of her state of mind. They are also evidence of her material and technological conditions. Lucy depended on the capacity of digital technologies to shield identities, and the blog was anonymous while it lasted. This dependency is the material and technological a priori, but because anonymity is entwined with discourse, there are also discursive precedents that gave shape and meaning to the possibility of acting in the social by using anonymity. In Lucy's case, the discourse around her use of anonymity points toward concepts such as civics, heroicity, and duty.

Lucy repeatedly couched her actions in the language of civic duty. She claimed that she is a young woman in her mid-twenties who created *EBDN* as a way of filling the information gap in cities like Monterrey, where violence was huge and reporting was scarce. Single, without children, and a patriot, Lucy repeatedly noted that her actions also had the goal of correcting the global perception of Mexicans as corrupt, uneducated, and violent. Lucy describes herself sometimes as a journalist and, in other instances, simply as someone with "experience gathering information" (Blog del Narco 2013, 3). It is unclear whether she ever was trained as a journalist or worked as one in a news organization. Regardless, she framed her blogging practices as "citizen journalism." Besides Lucy herself, others like David Sasaki (2010) and Andrés Monroy-Hernández and Luis Daniel Palacios (2014) call *EBDN* "citizen journalism." Citizen journalism is used to designate the reporting and civic work of individuals not associated with news institutions. The work of citizen journalists is thus "free" in the sense that it is unpaid, and it is also free in the sense that it is voluntary, highlighting the fact that bloggers feel that their work is akin to their civic duty.

Lucy's words and actions are closely connected to a cluster of media concepts that include the public sphere, publicity, civics, duty, and even heroism. In this case, however, all of these concepts are associated with or operated under the aegis of anonymity, and it is thus worth asking how anonymity transforms these concepts and what this transformation tells us about Lucy's case, but also about the socio-technical conditions giving form to the events. The next section shows that the most substantive connections between publicity and anonymity are founded on the material genealogy of publicity theory. This material genealogy is the historical antecedent to Lucy's words and actions, one that explains how materiality and technology became the a priori to Lucy's case.

Anonymous Publicity

The idea of anonymous publicity circulates broadly in the cultural sphere, and it is embraced and acted upon all the time. What Lucy did is, in many ways, not different from becoming a TikTok performer who uses a nickname to hide their identity or a YouTube influencer who adopts a pseudonym to build a wall between their private life and their public performances. But, in significant ways, what Lucy did was quite different. Hers was a civic action, not a commercial performance, and the meaning and type of anonymous publicity in her case were, thus, different. This civic action was inspired by political discourses and promises that defined democratic and liberal politics during and after the Enlightenment, and it is this Enlightenment genealogy that shaped the meaning of the practice.

However, there is a contradiction central to the civic notion of anonymous publicity. Anonymity is about secrecy, opacity, and invisibility. It is about doing something in public but hiding who you are. Contrariwise, publicity is tied conventionally to openness, light, and self-disclosure. Put these two notions together and we have a contradiction, which is a poor guide for understanding and even rationalizing actions, options, and consequences.

Contradictions in life are not rare, and, indeed, whole philosophies like Hegelian dialectics have been based on contradiction. But in the case of anonymous publicity, the contradiction is not temporal (and temporality is crucial to dialectics) or part of a process toward synthesis. Anonymous publicity can be read as a contradiction so essential that it belongs to the type of contradictions foundational to logic. It is what is defined as a logical contradiction, which occurs when a proposition conflicts with itself or when statement A and its denial, statement non-A, come together. If anonymity is about secrecy, opacity, and invisibility, and publicity is about openness, anonymous publicity is a logical contradiction. That is, unless one or both terms are wrongly defined. I believe an explanation, but not a resolution, to this logical contradiction is possible by analyzing the conceptual history of publicity and by more clearly linking publicity and anonymity to materiality.

Publicity is understood normatively as crucial to democratic deliberation and expressive freedoms. It is a communicative act meant to foster understanding and perhaps even consensus. I engage it differently. I treat publicity as a media concept that is rooted in materiality, technology, and the cultural technique of indexicalization. In so doing, I am not rejecting publicity's conventional normativity but treating it as a posteriori to what is a more foundational conceptualization of publicity as materiality. I am able to do this partly because the definition of publicity as materiality is already part of publicity's conceptual history. But in this conceptual history, from the seminal work *The Human Condition* by Hannah Arendt to the influential work of Jürgen Habermas's *The Structural Transformation of the Public Sphere*, materiality is established but then treated as secondary to the communicational and relational possibilities publicity engenders. Publicity's root in materiality is evident when we consider that one of the most significant connotations of publicity is openness. If it is public, then it is meant to be seen, open, without walls, like a play performed in a Greek agora, which, not coincidentally, is the model many use to spatially and materially "think" the concept of publicness and the realm in which publicness is performed, the public sphere. It is certainly the way Arendt uses public, and it is ultimately true in Habermas's. In both cases, that which is public is that which is in the open. In Arendt and Habermas, openness is spatial (it implies copresence) and indexical (it implies self-disclosure).

What does the normative element of openness imply in terms of publicness? If the public spheres are materially open, publicness, the way of being in the public realm, includes or implies the normative idea that to be public, one must be willing to place oneself in the open for everyone to see and identify. Publicness thus tends to be conceived as a spatially reflexive action, as a willingness and perhaps even a desire to make oneself visible, to identify oneself as an individual willing to embrace all the vulnerabilities associated with copresence. In a very real sense, this view of publicity works only when individuals have assurances of their safety, when individuals can trust those around them. One is willing to make oneself vulnerable when there is a reasonable expectation of relative safety. People debating in coffee houses, an example used by Habermas, trusted that disagreement would not end in physical harm. Clearly, self-disclosure, allowing others to know who you are, is a luxury that many, including Lucy, did not have, which means that this normative idea of publicity is restricted to the few who have access to the material and relational outcomes that Habermas so powerfully evokes. It also means that the modernity that Habermas so craftily sketches is perhaps nothing more than a social world limited to the few and not the many.

A different genealogy of publicity connects better to Lucy's case and to the way publicity works in most contexts, cases, and times.[6] This genealogy is not about openness but about secrecy, and it is found not in Habermas but in the work of Reinhart Koselleck (1988). In *Critique and Crisis*, Koselleck argues for the importance of secrecy to the rise of publicness. Like Habermas, Koselleck uses historical arguments (he may call his arguments a "conceptual history") to theorize the rise of society and of publicity. Unlike Habermas, Koselleck believes that secret societies, in general, hold clues as to how publicity and society emerged in most European states.

In Koselleck, the move from feudalism to enlightened forms of state organization could not happen without new forms of social consent that could substitute religious and monarchic forms of legitimization. These forms of consent appeared in secret societies, which allowed for the forms of institutionalized political plurality, spaces where politics was held to moral standards and morality became a political good. These secret publics, the Masons, the Illuminati, the Cosmopolitans, and others, appeared because of the same cultural and technological conditions that had in the sixteenth century fueled religious plurality: the multiplication of discourse made easier by the printing press, the rise of the mercantilist classes, and the emergence of printing in vernacular forms. These material and technological forces were the conditions of possibility for political pluralism and moral criticism and for the new post-feudal citizen. "The citizens," Koselleck writes, "lacked executive power, but they possessed and retained the mental power to pass moral judgments" (1988, 55). The ability to exercise this power and judgment depended on new material social organizations: Secret societies constituted communities without hierarchy that shared moral principles and techniques. These lodges attracted the new classes of people that were acquiring economic and social capital (e.g., mercantile classes, professionals, and even bureaucrats) and that, nonetheless, had no power to shape politics. In the absolutist state, these groups needed material spaces to come together, spaces that could allow them to share views about society and the state in relative anonymity. These secret societies were thus places that fostered criticism and even political dissent. Secrecy was required, for in the absolutist state, dissent was dangerous to the dissenter.

Koselleck's work is a useful reminder that the value of material opacity, secrecy, and privacy in contemporary political cultures is rooted in these early experiences and material organizations. There is a through line between secret societies and Lucy, one that depends on an understanding of publicity entwined with materiality and secrecy. Historical examples connecting Koselleck to anonymous publicity abound, even though techniques of secrecy in public required anonymity (public acts but hidden identity), not only privacy (private acts with no witnesses). Famous members of the Masons, for instance, included George Washington, Benjamin

Franklin, James Otis, and Paul Revere. Some historians have argued that as many as twenty-one signatories of the Declaration of Independence were Masons (Feuerherd 2017). When Thomas Paine (who, by the way, was not a Mason) anonymously published and distributed *Common Sense* in 1776, he was simply following the protocols of survival and political morality of absolutism, the same that the Masons had adopted. The uses of disguises by the Sons of Liberty in the American colonies or, in England, the Blacks, did the same. Since early modernity all the way to the present, anonymity has been associated with dissent and revolution. Pen names and pseudonyms have been normal to critical discourse; even the US Constitution was published anonymously early on. Michael Kimaid (2015) notes, "Many editorial pieces in the seventeenth- and eighteenth-century English Atlantic were written under the guise of pen names, and pen names were vital to the public discourse of the American Revolution" (76). Benjamin Franklin went as far as suggesting that the colonies ought to be narrated through anonymous and pseudonymous writings. Recognizing these practices in relationship to moral and legal impunity, Franklin added that pseudonyms "enabled men of honor to behave dishonourably" (qtd. in Kimaid 2015, 76).

Similar practices of anonymity were used in Mexico's War of Independence. In the important months preceding the armed rebellion of 1810, anonymous fliers, broadsides, graffiti, and cartoons were found often in important public spaces across New Spain and definitely in the capital, Mexico City. Timothy Henderson (2009) adds: "The government did its best to assert its control . . . issuing harrowing decrees threatening harsh consequences for any who would 'alter the peace and fidelity of the Kingdom.' The Inquisition set up a force of detectives to chase down malefactors; hand-operated printing presses were outlawed; and rewards were offered for information leading to the arrest of dissidents" (50). The monarchy thus issued laws, harnessed the judicial power of the inquisition, and tried to monopolize the technologies that were affording the very possibility of discursive and political pluralism, namely, the printing press. As in other nation-states born out of revolution, anonymity in Mexico was grafted deep in the Mexican political imaginary. In the decades that followed, anonymity in Mexico and the United States became a mythical concept associated with heroic narratives central to the birth of these nations.

When Lucy and her partner embraced anonymous publicity, they joined a distinguished group of thinkers, intellectuals, and political actors. Because of her gender, Lucy joined another powerful group. During the eighteenth and nineteenth centuries, anonymous publicity had also enabled women to act in public, at a distance, often under the guise of another name. Since the eighteenth century, women routinely used pen names to be able to have a public or literary identity, and they relied on deception to be able to participate in the public sphere. These include Ellis Bell (Emily Jane Brontë), Currer Bell (Charlotte Brontë), Lucas Male (Mary Harrison Kingsley), George Sand (Amantine-Lucile-Aurore Dupin), Vernon Lee (Violet Paget), George Eliot (Mary Ann Evans), Ouida (Maria Louise Ramé), G. Noel Hatton (Mona Alison Caird), Ralph Iron (Olive Schreiner), A. S. Byatt (Antonia Susan Drabble), E. L. James (Erika Leonard) and, of course, J. K. Rowling or Robert Galbraith (Joanne Rowling). Anonymity, secrecy, and opacity were thus not only central to the play of politics in revolutionary nations but also central to those wishing to push back against the absolutist power of patriarchy over women.

Lucy's anonymous contribution as well as her pride to finally reveal herself as a woman in interviews in early 2013, connect back to these traditions against politics and patriarchy. She believed that her actions were citizen resistance against oppression; hence, she understood her work as a sacrifice performed for the good of the collective. On July 8, 2013, in one of her last posts, Lucy writes full of desperation and insight: "I initiated the Blog del Narco and my luck changed. What about if I had done nothing? What if I had been a Mexican indifferent to reality? What if I had remained quiet? What if I had decided to remain with my eyes covered?"[7] She saw the digital realm as a space where secrets needed to be revealed, shown to all, and where revealing these secrets would help those endangered by the violence, where her words and activities would make a difference in society. Later she states that she does not tolerate lies or secrets: "I wanted people to learn the reality of what was going on in Mexico" ("quería que la gente conociera la realidad de lo que estaba ocurriendo en México"). She saw her blog as a way of participating in civil society, a type of civic relationality, and as a way of doing politics with a small "p." And the same perspective was shared by a segment of the international community that complimented *EBDN*'s work, who admired the style of civics the blog represented. The admiration was rooted not only in what *EBDN* did but in the fact that her civic work was extremely dangerous. The comments sections were vicious places. Lucy and her partner received hundreds of threats to their lives. And they took these risks, nonetheless, and justified them as duty, as needed political action, as pushing back against corruption and oppression. She wanted people to know the reality of her city and used anonymity as a reasonable measure to protect herself in public.

Lucy's actions and words were overdetermined by the histories of secret societies and the women who published anonymously for centuries, which show that Enlightenment political ideals depended on, and connected to, indexical practices and materiality. What complicates Lucy's actions and words is also what differentiates them from the world of the Masons, Paine, the Brontë sisters, and Franklin. Lucy's world is shaped by the fracturing of materialities characteristic of the digital era. Our social lives exist in flesh and in the digital realm; our digital lives leave traces that point toward our embodied selves. We are persons in all these realms, and our actions have unpredictable consequences, as none of us can clearly mark material, spatial, and temporal boundaries. If I am right and the media concept of publicity is a projection of material and technological a priori, then Lucy's anonymous publicity had to be unstable, fractured, and contradictory.

A material engagement with publicity and anonymity is a crucial step toward eliminating the logical contradiction inherent in a normative interpretation of the concept "anonymous publicity." This material engagement suggests that secrecy was part of publicity from its onset, and this is evident in the importance of the walls that allowed individuals to share, like equals, concerns about society. In Habermas, this material history is understood as openness, and his work used coffee houses (walled spaces) and salons (walled spaces) as examples of spaces that invited open self-disclosure. Habermas writes less about the fact that these spaces were also enclosures, and, just like the agora in Athens was enclosed behind the walls of the city (Benhabib 1993), the social interactions within the enclosure could also be characterized as secret, behind walls. One can argue that all these seminal scholars, Arendt, Habermas, and Koselleck, agree on the importance of materiality and secrecy to publicity and that the only difference between Koselleck and the Arendtian and Habermasian positions is that Koselleck starts with the walls, not with dialogue and communication that the walls made possible.

Koselleck's analytic move, however, is significant, for it means that to Koselleck, and to me, the walls are the a priori of publicity. The walls and their materiality are a boundary that separates the population at large from the intimate space of publicity. The boundary thus constitutes two types of people: those who can be trusted even in disagreement and those who cannot be trusted. The walls are a sorting mechanism, the cultural technique at the root of the media concept that we have come to associate, thanks to Habermas, with publicity. Importantly, the walls work on the principle of indexicalization: They rely on identity and self-disclosure; they sort, filter, and categorize; and they also activate particular relational techniques, some that Habermas perhaps mythologizes. I am referring to the willingness to enter into dialogue, perhaps even rational dialogue, with others in order to come together and, as a public, together become powerful actors in the polis.

Two practices anchored on materiality and indexicality come together in the term "anonymous publicity." Publicity is based on open dialogue, debate, reason, and self-disclosure. Publicity operates under a sorting logic that presumes that everyone who listens can be trusted, even in disagreement. Publicity is built on trust. Anonymity, on the other hand, attempts to reduce risk and vulnerability with indexical dissociation. Anonymity is not based on the principle of direct dialogue but on the idea of revealing truths, like Lucy suggested. Anonymity operates on a sorting logic that separates those who can be trusted from those who cannot. *Anonymity is built on mistrust.* When the practices and discourses of anonymous publicity conjoin, they form logical contradictions that can be ironed out only with ideology or mythologies. They do not disappear but are hidden. The contradictions include the idea that revealing truths can constitute publics in a similar way that debate, dialogue, and critique can. They also include the troubling idea that sorting listeners or users in terms of trust or mistrust does not matter if one hides the identity of the speaker or, if you prefer, that a type of mistrusting trust can exist. Last, the contradiction particular to Lucy's case has to do with materiality itself, with the idea that a secret publicity anchored on the notion of physical walls (e.g., the publicity of the Masons) could be replicated with digital walls. The contradiction here is in the equation of digital walls with solidity and true opacity, which are the crucial properties of brick-and-mortar walls and enclosures. Digital walls are socio-technical constructs. Though digitation is material, nothing in digitation is based on the properties of solidity and true opacity. A digital wall, unlike a brick-and-mortar wall, is conceptual: the outcome of software, algorithms, protocols that can be fooled, tricked, malfunction, and mistakenly shared. Digital walls are not walls.

Heroicity

The contradictions at the heart of anonymous publicity can be deadly. If the social context is pushing someone to consider anonymous publicity as the only way of acting or else, the social context is too dangerous. Few contexts have been more dangerous than Mexico after 2007, but even this context was not enough to dissuade Lucy, her partner, and many others from remaining hidden, silent, on the sidelines of the so-called drug war. Observers admired and continue admiring these digital masked warriors, and, to these observers, anonymity was more than a protective measure. Anonymity was awarded value and gave meaning to actions like Lucy's. Anonymity was part mythology, evidence of a dangerous context and the courage it took to confront it. Anonymous publicity was made heroic.

The tragedy is that there is evidence that Lucy herself believed this myth. Her story does not end with her promotion to civic hero by some in the international community. On May 5, 2013, only weeks after Lucy's series of interviews in March and April revealed her work to the public, her colleague, the webmaster who helped with the technical side of the website, called her one last time and simply uttered the word "run" (Carroll, "Blog del Narco," 2013). No one heard from Lucy's colleague again. After hiding for a few days, Lucy fled first to the United States and then to Spain. A few days later, she used Skype to contact Carroll, the writer who had previously interviewed her for *The Guardian*, and revealed her state of panic and loneliness. Her last post in *EBDN* was May 3, claiming that she did not have intentions to resume. She was staying in a boarding house with enough money to last a few months but was otherwise without contacts and almost without identity in a country not her own. Carroll writes: "Her biggest fear is she will see her colleague appear on a video of the type that frequently appeared on their blog: battered, interrogated, gazing into the camera, knowing a terrible fate awaits." Her stay in Spain did not improve. She writes in her new blog: "Sí, ha sido un gran error venir a España. Yo sé, España es un gran país, pero lamentablemente no me había percatado de las buenas relaciones que tiene con Felipe Calderón Hinojosa. Acepto que ha sido un error" (Yes, it was a big mistake to come to Spain. I know, Spain is a great country, but sadly I wasn't aware of the great relationships it has with Felipe Calderón Hinojosa. I accept that it was a mistake [translation by the author]).

On June 5, 2013, Lucy started a personal blog (http://blogdelucy.com) in which she wrote about her race to survive. This short-lived blog is available in the Internet Archive. Her first entry is about the publication of the book *Dying for the Truth* (Blog del Narco 2013). Her second one, on June 6, is about her race to survive away from Mexico. Sometimes thankful to all who had reached out and spoken to her encouragingly through email and Twitter (#blogdelnarco and later #elblogdelucy), sometimes morose, Lucy spoke of her struggles, hunger, the sense of betrayal she had to live with, her dreadful opinions about the Mexican political system, in particular the executive power held by President Calderón.

In July 2013, she published an angry letter asking the international community to help her leave Spain. She seemed aware that her journalistic quest was understood through a different register than the work of other famous new media political stars; she argued that she had not received any help because "I am Mexican, and not Cuban like Yoani Sánchez, or US-American like Edward Snowden." Sánchez, the creator of the famous human rights blog *Generation Y*, has dedicated her life to shedding light on Cuba's internal dissonance, including Cuba's poor human rights record, the challenges to freedom that Cubans routinely experience on the island, and the small corruptions involved in having to live waiting for daily basic necessities, from electricity to bread. Her blog is a trusted source of political commentary and criticism, and she is broadly recognized and respected around the world, particularly after *Time* magazine (the international version) placed her on the cover in 2008 and named her one of the most influential people. Her fame has allowed her to go on fundraising trips to different locations, including Mexico (October 2013), where she received strong monetary support to continue her work. Lucy herself declared her support for Sánchez's work, yet their experiences as female Latin American bloggers could not be more different (Corsa 2008). The year after Lucy disappeared, Sánchez's blog became an independent digital newspaper (*14ymedio.com*) in Cuba, further adding weight to her words and views on Cuban society and politics.

Unlike bloggers Lucy and Sánchez, Snowden came to fame as a whistleblower, a computer professional who leaked classified information from the US National Security Agency in 2013. Among other things, his leaks revealed the illicit manner in which the NSA spied on other nations, including allies like Germany and Brazil. Although these leaks were highly controversial, Snowden became a hero to many for his willingness to break US law, arguably for the well-being of others and for the principles of good government and just international relations. Like Lucy, his life after the leaks in 2013 required ongoing hiding and relative isolation (Burrough et al. 2014). The key difference is that he may fear jail; Lucy feared death.

On July 22, 2013, a request for funds to get out of Spain was issued by or on behalf of Lucy in the crowdfunding site Kapipal (http://kapipal.com). According to the site, she was able to collect close to 500 euros or, if you prefer, a pittance. Was Lucy correct? Was the international community's apathy a type of racism or anti-Mexicanism? I do not think so. I believe that Lucy presumed that the nature of her sacrifices, the risks she had to take to publish the blog, and the fact that her actions filled a civic and public need made her case equivalent to those of Sánchez and Snowden. And, from the perspective of her deeds, she was right. But her anonymity made her case different, and this difference shaped the public reception of her blog and the type of relationality her public actions activated.

In *The Human Condition* (1958), Hannah Arendt gives us clues to understand the relational outcomes that may be expected with anonymous publicity. Arendt discusses what Seyla Benhabib (1993) later referred to as "the agonistic public realm," and, in this discussion, Arendt reflects on Greek oral traditions and what these tell us about publicity. She is inspired by Homer's heroes, Ulysses, Achilles, Paris, and Hector, to name a few, who come to us through the web of sociality made possible by oral stories. Reflecting on the relevance of such narratives, Arendt focuses on the nature and pairing of action and speech. The actions that distinguish those who deserve to be in public, those actions that single out an individual and that make them worthy of admiration and respect, are actions always followed by or explained by speech. It is through action and speech that individuals reveal their uniqueness and their identity, their difference, vis-à-vis the world. *Actions without words lose their subject.* Reflecting on the hero of these narratives, she writes: "The action he begins is humanly disclosed by the word, and though his deed can be perceived in its brute physical appearance without verbal accompaniment, it becomes relevant only through the spoken word in which he identifies himself as the actor, announcing what he does, has done, and intends to do" (179). It is the spoken word that characterizes the entrance into the public realm, and it is only through words that actors can leave behind a lasting influence in social relationships. Through speech, actors reveal their "life stories," and through self-disclosure, social actors can become protagonists on the web of social stories, the monuments and histories that surround the hero and that inscribe the hero in memory.

Arendt's notion of agonistic publicity (Benhabib's term) is based on orality, materiality, and copresence. The courageous act of self-disclosure central to publicity was courageous not because showing oneself in public may mean harm and perhaps death. In Arendt's work, "courage and even boldness are already present in leaving one's private hiding place and showing who one is, in disclosing and exposing one's self" (1958, 186). In many ways, Hector, Lucy, Sánchez, and Snowden are the same. They were willing to take enormous risks on behalf of the collective, but Hector, Sánchez, and Snowden left their "private hiding place" and showed their identities. This tactic constituted a type of relationality in which publics were able to connect their actions to their identities. Their bodies and/or their concrete indexes connected actions to their bodies and to their histories, to their families, and to their social networks.

Arendt (1958) acknowledges that in war situations, anonymity is often required to act in public. But anonymous publicity in warring contexts is, for her, "mere talk," incapable of revealing the "who" and hence incapable of transcending the moment. This "mere talk," as she would label Lucy's public intervention, cannot be memorialized because it is only through the courageous act of self-disclosure that a public act becomes story (180). Exceptions exist but are rare. To my knowledge, in Mexico's recent history, only the leader of the Zapatista Army of National Liberation (EZLN) was able to briefly maintain anonymity while becoming an iconic hero in Mexico and around the world. Subcomandante Marcos, the pseudonym he used for years, became one of the leaders and a spokesperson for the Zapatista Indigenous uprising that transformed Mexico from the 1980s to the 1990s. Iconized in visual records by the black ski mask and pipe he often used, Subcomandante Marcos was anonymous for only roughly thirteen months: from January 1994, when he revealed his leadership role and became a darling of the Mexican and international press, to February 1995, when Mexico's President Ernesto Zedillo revealed the identity of the already iconic leader (De la Grange and Rico 1999, 76–83). Rafael Sebastián Guillén Vicente, the university professor–turned–guerrilla leader, became an icon of the Mexican left, a public intellectual who used the persona of Subcomandante Marcos for many more years to elicit the effect of a heroicity linked to anonymity, even though after 1995, we knew who he really was.

Can an anonymous public hero exist in the digital realm? Not if the hero needs something back from the people or from institutions. Members of Anonymous, the famous organization of hackers that uses digital snooping as a way of doing activism, can expect to be treated as heroes only while they inhabit the masked persona they are known for. Their anonymity has not stopped their vulnerability. Members of Anonymous in Veracruz, Mexico, experienced such vulnerability in 2011 after launching OpCartel, an operation that targeted Los Zetas, one of the most violent Mexican cartels. The operation was quickly stopped when one of Anonymous's members was kidnapped by the cartel, and Los Zetas threatened the family of the kidnapped person and promised to kill ten members of Anonymous if they dared to reveal the information the hackers had gathered about the criminal organization (Naone 2011). When the heroic act cannot even be performed and police cannot or prefer not to protect, hacktivists cannot be called digital heroes. Similar to members of Anonymous, Lucy's public role could not be truly open; her heroicity, if that is what we need to call it, could not be attached to her identity as in the case of Snowden or Sánchez; she could not trust some of the visitors to *EBDN*, and, as she powerfully narrates, her day-to-day activities were carried out by hiding, in fear, by tricking the trusted systems, by moving from location to location, and by never revealing who she was or where she was.

The case at hand reveals the prescience of Arendt's words. Lucy's actions, her blogging, her writing, and her willingness to publish others' work are quickly becoming erased from memory and were already insufficient in 2013 to incite a significant response, as the painful failure to crowdfund her escape using Kapipal revealed. It is likely that this lack of response to Lucy was rooted in the type of mediation she used and her anonymity, which became the production tactic and emblem of the danger in which she existed. Her heroic persona was linked to her need for anonymity, and digital technologies provided the techniques to establish this anonymity. In the process of embracing anonymity, however, her actions lost the ability to transcend the moment, to become "story," and, if Arendt is right, her deeds and words will likely be forgotten.

I want to restate what should be clear by now. Deeds are not enough, according to Arendt. Deeds and words are also not enough. Deeds, words, and self-disclosure are the three elements that Arendt proposes are necessary for public actions to be inscribed in memory. Even though the threats to Lucy's life have been more certain and terrifying than the risks taken by Sánchez or Snowden, Lucy's quest did not fit the parameters of heroic stardom that have become the norm in internet celebrity culture. Sánchez herself has reflected that the fame of her blog gave her relative protection from Cuba's government. It is likely that Snowden felt the same. In a sense, they have been both relatively protected by fame and by their willingness to openly reveal their identities alongside their deeds. They could trust, relatively speaking, that their public actions would not be met with violence. Yet, what is trust in anonymous publicity?

Reciprocity of Trust

In a very basic sense, Lucy's case is all about trust or lack of. Her civic, identitarian, technological, and material decisions pointed toward her need to build or produce trust in a context that made it extremely difficult, using tools that helped build trust but also undermined it. The massive violent crisis in Mexico and the very complexities and ambiguities of digital technologies undermined trust in general and the systems that may produce it. This section examines the connections between trust and anonymous publicity, and I want to start by noting the complexity of the concept of trust itself. Trust can be understood as an affective orientation toward others and toward the future. Trust is partly a feeling, one that connects affect to reason and past to future. It is partly an assessment of our felt ability to understand our surroundings and to predict what others will do and what will happen if a specific course of action is chosen. Trust is thus affective but also epistemological, for trust is partly how we feel about our capacity to predict.

Reciprocity of trust is always a precondition in publicity theory, even if it is often unacknowledged. This is the clearest in oral, face-to-face communication where speaker and listener must trust their safety to be honest, to enter into dialogue, and to disagree with each other. In face-to-face communication, speakers need to have at least two types of trust. They must trust that they know who the other speaker/listener is, even if they disagree with them, and they must trust the other's behavior during the disagreement. In debate or face-to-face communication, trust is meant to produce safety, which, not coincidentally, is the Old Norse etymological origin of the word: *treysta* meant "to make safe" (Garmonsway 1928, 144). Trust is the outcome of or the feeling that faith provides, the confidence that allows us to disagree without fear. In Spanish, which did not benefit from the Old Norse precedent, trust translates simply as *confianza*: the belief that everything will be fine, particularly if we exchange words in very specific, predetermined, and recognizable ways. Trust during disagreement is not an outcome that can be taken for granted but can more or less be predicted in some specific institutionalized contexts, when it belongs to a social system, to a *habitus*. In particular, feeling safe even in disagreement is part of the modern *habitus*, and this element of sociality has a particular history that can be traced as the rise of "civility" and "politeness" in public settings (Bourdieu 1990; Seligman 1997, 65).[8] We trust we can disagree with each other without needing violence if we feel we are in a context with people who are civil, who are polite. The relation to publicity is not coincidental but foundational. The term "civility" itself and the behaviors it implies are rooted in the Latin *civitas*, the same root of "citizen," which, in turn, comes from the Greek *polites*, which refers to a member of the *polis* (Smith 2002, 106). Civility and politeness thus meant more than good manners; they referred to the personal characteristics needed to be part of a democracy, which include debating without violence. Civility and politeness are trusting systems in copresent debate. They refer to pre-agreed upon protocols of interaction that allow us to communicate without fear of reprisal.

All forms of technological mediation, from writing to digital interactions, undermine trust, for they allow for communication without copresence. Some, like writing and broadcasting, separate speaker/writer (speaker from here on) from listener/audience/reader (audience from here on). If in copresence a speaker is always also a listener, one-way communication technologies like writing and broadcasting (telegraph, radio, television) constitute two types of subjects, subject positions, and identities, that of a speaker and that of an audience. Reciprocity of trust becomes a problem. There is a spatial and, often, a temporal gap that separates writer from reader, speaker from audience. This means that all forms of technological mediation have had to develop practices and techniques that reestablish trust, and we can call these practices and techniques "trusted systems." In writing, trusted systems were meant to connect, like copresence, writer and reader, and were about establishing identity, authorship, and vulnerability. Peter Seligman (1997) forwards a useful definition of trust that serves our purposes well: Trust is an "institutionalized model of generalized exchange" (106). *Trusted systems are not about agreement but about recognition*. I don't have to agree with what a writer wrote, but I trust I know who I am disagreeing with.

Trusted systems are needed in publicness, for debate, and they are even more needed when face-to-face open communication is impossible and the trusting effects of openness, honesty, and self-disclosure are necessary. This is particularly true in contemporary societies, which tend to be complex social arrangements that bring together dissimilar populations. More than ever, today's democracies depend on systems of cohesion, which can be the result only of debating about our differences. Yet, mediated communication is a general model of exchange that seems to privilege intellectual harmony, not debate. Readers, listeners, or viewers who find something that they disagree with do not have an ethical duty, which is part of face-to-face interaction, to engage the other's ideas or argument. They can simply stop reading, listening, or viewing. The echo-chamber effect that many have written about regarding US media is partly a technological problem and partly a problem of socialization, a way of avoiding intellectual disagreement in exchange for the easy exchange of ideas with those who agree with you. Face-to-face is great for sustaining community, but it can be more socially meaningful in debates and thus in pluralistic societies.

This is partly why Habermas's *Structural Transformation* (1989) tracks the rise and decline of the public sphere, from publicness to what he calls the "re-feudalization" of the public sphere, in terms of an erosion of face-to-face sociability, the rise of the power of public opinion, and the eventual substitution of public opinion for public relations, a market-driven way of being social and political (135). Trust in the highly technologically mediated modernity that he means to study is not gone but thinned down or difficult to attain. We must consider that the trust needed to hold a system of agreement together is a minor thing compared to the robust trust needed to hold a system of disagreement together (Putnam 1995). In disagreement, impoliteness and lack of civility can quickly become violent. Absent the power of copresence to invoke an ethical relation of trust between self and other, the self may quickly normalize impoliteness and incivility (Peters 1999; Dahlgren 1995).

Reinserting trust in communication is thus partly about reinserting recognition and nonviolent protocols of behavior, which should safeguard debate during disagreement. Recognition is required in order to know whether those who speak and those who listen are indeed who they claim to be. Clearly, in writing and in broadcasting, full recognition is impossible, as writing and broadcasting insert temporal and spatial barriers between sender and receiver. Digital environments are a bit better at reconstituting trust. In the blogosphere, recognition starts with the blogger, who must disclose who they are or, at the very least, engage in the crafting of a unique and trustworthy authorial voice. Lucy established first an anonymous identity, and over the course of the three years, her identity was recognizable through her authorial voice, the consistency with which she wrote, curated, and produced the blog. Later, in 2013, she adopted the pseudonym Lucy, and for the last few months of *EBDN*, she was known to those following her case with that particular concrete index.

Anonymity and pseudonymity depend on attestation, a person or a system that can corroborate the standing of the person sharing information. For instance, Carroll, when he got the request from Lucy to talk after she left Mexico, asked Lucy to prove that she was who she claimed to be by showing him that she was in control of the *EBDN* site. Lucy did it. Thanks to the magic of digital communication, Lucy changed the site in the way Carroll requested, and by doing this technological, material gesture, Lucy acquired what lawyers may call "standing." With this gesture, mediated by keyboards, servers, optical fiber, and other technologies, Lucy proved that she had the authorial identity to make the claims she would. Lucy's authorial standing was entwined with the technologies she used and their materiality.

What did Carroll actually trust when he asked Lucy to prove that she was who she claimed to be? Carroll trusted liveness, the capacity of digital technologies to convey embodied presence. Liveness replicates copresence just as authorial identity stands for self-disclosure. Both mechanisms allow users to understand whose work they are using (reading or viewing). The feeling of liveness is relatively easily achieved in new media technologies, which are quite adept at replicating a sense of embodied copresence and thus at generating this aspect of trust. Chatting through the web allows you to almost see how a finger on the other side of the world, perhaps one in a "help" station in India or Brazil, just pressed the letter "q," giving you a feeling of their embodied presence. This gesture is not just "natural." It is a specific socio-technical translation made possible by the hardware and software design. Someone had to build the sensing mechanism (keyboard or cursor), and someone had to code what we recognize as liveness. Chatting, for instance, often registers the other's presence by showing blinking dots while they are typing even before we can see their words. I remember the first time I encountered the blinking dots. I simply did not know what they meant, but, over time, I came to understand that I needed to interpret the blinking dots as a machine gesture that was meant to translate the presence of the other's body.

Temporal immediacy replicates copresent, face-to-face communication. It was easy for Lucy to convey trust while she updated her blog daily, and her ongoing embodied labor could be felt. Authorial identity was assumed. Users no doubt felt that only Lucy (or whoever anonymous entity they imagined as the author) could be in charge of the changes. This assumption about authorship is partly the result of the ubiquity of trusted systems and the users' awareness of their existence.

Trusted systems are key to establishing authorial identity in the digital realm and central to digital indexicalization. Most users of digital media have to interact with at least some of these systems on a regular basis. Using the world wide web, for instance, requires emblems, logos, signatures, secret codes, URLs, keychains, and passwords to give and receive assurances about identity. In fact, to attest to the staggering number of unknown elements in digital communication environments, most computer communication uses multiple trusted systems simultaneously. I wrote this passage at a coffee shop using a computer that is accessible to me only because it requires a password to log in. My computer relies on security software to identify new malware, Trojans, and computer viruses that could harm my computer. I access and back up my files on "the cloud," so I had to use a password to access the coffee shop's wireless system, which uses my URL as part of the trusted systems it depends on. The cloud system I use requires a "digital certificate," a high-tech identity marker that assures the cloud that I am who I am or, if you prefer, that my computer is "who" my computer says it is. These trusted systems use security protocols, cryptography, and hardware security systems to assure that the book you are reading is written by me, that it is safe, backed up, and that nobody can steal my ideas so that you can eventually read them. Digital identities and communication cannot exist without these. Trust would otherwise be as impossible as proving authorial identity.

While retaining their individual anonymity, Lucy and her partner used these systems of trust, too. They were part of the risk equation. They registered and bought space for their website from a legitimate internet service provider (ISP) (http://godaddy.com) using a "signature," in this case, a real email address originating in Monterrey, Mexico. They used a series of pertinent passwords to enter their DNS provider's website and modify the *EBDN* website. In fact, these basic trusting systems allowed Lucy to prove to Carroll (*The Guardian*'s journalist) that she was indeed who she claimed to be. Significantly, this proof was modifying the website and, thus, Lucy's proof was at the level of the embodied labor of publisher, not author. These trusted systems are partly assurances about the embodied location of the author, and, thus, they create a paradox for bloggers like Lucy.

The paradox of digital trusted systems is that the systems that establish authorial identity (IP addresses, ISPs, and the passwords connecting these two) are the systems used to construct anonymity. Indexical dissociation is predictable in this way. It is the inverse of indexical association and thus necessitates the same elements. Lucy and her partner used these trusted systems to protect themselves from dangerous users, but the digital walls proved to be insufficient, for the same trusted systems tethered the blog to their bodies, and liveness made this tether ongoing. As long as they kept updating the blog, they were physically connected to it. The digital walls meant to protect Lucy's identity and location could be used to find them, as the disappearance of Lucy and her partner proved.

Lucy's digital anonymity eventually failed, as tricking digital trusted systems is much harder than most realize. Yet, while it worked, her anonymity allowed thousands of contributors and commentators to share their experiences and views about and with drug violence in Mexico. She was trusted, even if this trust was not universal, but whatever trust she gathered through her role as a blogger withered away once her reporting stopped. Trust in her necessitated a different type of maintenance than the trust of other public persons, other *heroes*, whose identities are entwined with their heroic actions. Unless Snowden or Sánchez betrays through action the spirit of their extraordinary acts of publicity, our admiration for them will remain attached to their life stories and their bodies, the very emblems of the risk they took for their communities. Without ongoing activity, without exposing her life to danger, the elements of liveness that Lucy could deliver, Lucy's pleas quickly became alienating, those of an unknown other, one that will likely be forgotten.

All technologically mediated forms of communication have in common that they all bypass an important element of face-to-face communication, one central to publicness. In the copresent debate and sharing that we associate with the idealized forms of publicness, openness is possible because of reciprocity of trust (Papacharissi 2010, 122). Idealized forms of publicness, such as Arendt's, rely on the trust of two, the speaker and the listener, the writer and the reader, the singer and the audience, the anchorperson and the viewer. Walter Cronkite, the beloved CBS anchorperson, was live and trusted but not present. Almost always his body was hidden from those who, in rage, may have listened and wanted to respond, those who wished to disagree with him, and would have even harmed him in anger. Many trusted him, but he didn't need to trust viewers. Reciprocity of trust was not required. Broadcasting and other forms of distant communication cannot fully reconstruct publicness. We call them public persons, but these anchors benefit greatly from the opacity permitted by media technologies and the institutions that safeguard them.

I interviewed international journalists working in Mexico a few years ago, and they all shared with me that they felt safer writing about the violence than their Mexican counterparts. They felt that their nationalities (most were US citizens) and news organizations (*The New York Times* or similar publications) gave them a level of protection that many of their Mexican colleagues did not have. This meant that they could write more freely and were sometimes given access by the DCOs that Mexican journalists did not often have. As I mentioned before, Seligman (1997) defines trust as an "institutionalized model of generalized exchange" (106), and the international journalists benefit from their institutionalized identity, which elicited specific protocols of interaction from readers.

Bloggers like Lucy and her partner, however, lacked that institutionalized identity. They published alone, and this fact added to their vulnerability. Like Cronkite or the international journalists working on Mexico, Lucy wanted to be trusted but could not fully trust some of the users of *EBDN*; she actually feared them, as she repeatedly stated when referring to the hundreds of threats by state forces and DCOs she and her partner received. She did not have a powerful news institution shielding her from danger, or cops ready on the dial to protect her in case of need. Instead, she relied on the peculiar, contradictory affordances of new media technologies to generate trust through liveness, and anonymity through digital opacity. These two affordances, however, are complexly intertwined, raising the possibility that certain types of publicity in digital realms will never fully work in contexts of violence.

Mark Coeckelbergh (2013) dedicates a book to exploring the complex ways in which technology has opened up new conceptions of risk and vulnerability. His account of these issues is meant to clarify a type of phenomenology co-constituted with technology, technological possibilities, and the new risks and vulnerabilities associated with both. Early, he introduces the concept of "being-at-risk" as an ontological ground, one that places vulnerability as a precedent to experience. Technology, he posits, is used routinely to "decrease our vulnerability." Technology is our "vulnerability guardian" (4), a vivid description that seems to encapsulate the reasons Lucy and her partner trusted internet technologies to protect them from the Mexican state and DCOs. For some time, the technologies allowed them to perform their public roles in absence, without directly risking their bodies. The technologies also allowed them to hide their identities, and they were able to do what they did anonymously for years. And the technologies allowed them also to have some mobility and to change places if they felt a location was compromised. Mobile and designed to foster anonymity, the suite of technologies of absence, which mediated between the bloggers and the world, seemed to guard them against risk. But Lucy and her partner failed to recognize the difficulty of achieving true anonymity in an environment constructed primarily to capture data traces. They failed to fully grasp the systemic and relentless nature with which internet technologies are nothing else than data-generating machines dressed as keyboards, cursors, CPUs, software, platforms, apps, phones, and touchscreens.

Perhaps Coeckelbergh is right about most technologies, but I wonder if the clarity with which he places technology as a guardian of vulnerability accounts only for technologies with a clear ontic proposition, one related to a technology's identity in terms of primary use by target users. To these users, internet technologies mean things related to discourses shaped by advertising, user talk, and experience. In 2013, the year that Lucy and her partner disappeared, GoDaddy, the internet provider that housed their blog, advertised during the Super Bowl (February 3) with a twenty-eight-second commercial that portrayed a young female announcer stating matter-of-factly that "there are two sides to GoDaddy's small business suit. The first is sexy, like supermodel Bar Refaeili," who is seated in a tight pink dress on the left of the announcer, who continues: "The second is smart, like Walter, IT guy," and Walter is represented by a young, White, slightly chubby man distractedly using a laptop who then turns at the same time that Refaeli turns to engage in a sloppy kiss. Humorous, memorable, the ad presents GoDaddy as the perfect union of sexy and smart, and the services it offers, internet hosting and mediating between small businesses and advertisers, are by extension defined in the same way. Weeks after the ad played during the biggest ad event in the United States, the Super Bowl, Lucy's partner disappeared, and she had to run for her life.

Technologies that mediate between humans and the digital realm do not fit Coeckelbergh's description as guardians of vulnerability; they typically are two-faced technologies that lip-sync the words of the advertisers of utility while commonly hiding features of their design, which are put together not for one type of user but for several. Data tracking affects the end user and provides, for instance, the grounds for personalization. But data-tracking technologies are chiefly designed to allow businesses and states, another category of users, to have the data they need, and it is in this cornucopia of data production, collection, and trade that users like you and me, Lucy and her partner, will be the most exposed to harm, risk, and danger. Unquestionably, Lucy's vulnerability was crafted and magnified by the nature of the technologies she used, by the ability of these technologies to foster trust without warrant.

This chapter shows that the economy of anonymity relies partly on a mythical understanding of anonymity's political and agentic capacities. This myth has made certain types of anonymity hypervisible to the detriment of others, and the reason is perhaps obvious. The myth of anonymity connects anonymity to heroicity and to counterhegemony. It is a myth about rebellion, one found in narratives of national origin and patriotism. But it is a myth that causes dangerous miscalculations, like Lucy's, and one that participates in the erasure of other important aspects of anonymity, including those defined by institutional and contextual anonymity. The previous chapter, for instance, shows that the economy of anonymity partly shapes human ontology. The next one shows anonymity as a partly hidden yet necessary figure in social theories dependent on trust and warrants. The economy of anonymity does not only manifest in the subject or in the social. The economy of anonymity touches social epistemology, particularly after modernity. Anonymity is the often-hidden aspect of being that social epistemology must resolve in order to theorize order and trust.

Four

Trust Among Anonymous Strangers

In some fundamental dimensions, we live surrounded by anonymous strangers. In the United States, 80 percent of residents live in cities, racial diversity is increasingly the norm, immigrants account for 15 percent of the population, and internal migrations are so common that in places like Los Angeles, my city, to be a native Angeleno is a rarity. Anonymous strangers surround us, surround me. In this book, I have defined anonymity as indexical dissociation and have shown that nobody is 100 percent anonymous, not even the stranger. I have also argued that concrete indexes are essential to the biographical, which is why most uses of anonymity are concerned with dissociation from concrete indexes and the biographical, a lack that defines the stranger. Who is the stranger but the one without name or biography? Categorical indexes, on the other hand, are part of every human interaction, including those with strangers, because we are always represented by categories like gender, race, nationality, age, and so on. The anonymous stranger is thus defined by categorical indexes that mark the distance between them and us, which is why Georg Simmel (1971) refers to the stranger as the foreigner, the racial other, the poor, and "sundry 'inner enemies.'" All these individuals become anonymous strangers when they lack the specificity of biography and they present to us as types, as Simmel notes. And, because they are nothing more than types, anonymous strangers present particular challenges when we interact with them, and the most evident is the inability to truly know them and thus the inability to predict what these anonymous strangers will do, how will they react to particular actions, words, or situations. How can we feel safe when surrounded by anonymous strangers?

The importance of Simmel's questions at the turn of the twentieth century point toward new social forces shaping the economy of anonymity. Urbanism and social mobility had centered anonymity in everyday life. Before modernity, industrialization, mercantilism, and colonialism, social life was given shape by recognition, but the world surrounding Simmel was given form by anonymity. But if Simmel lived in a time in which the economy of anonymity was radically changing, we are experiencing another radical reshaping of this economy. One century after Simmel, new technologies like the internet, video games, and social platforms have constituted digital social realms in which we interact with and as anonymous strangers constantly, by design, but not in the logic of the open urban space central to Simmel's work. As Wendy Chun (2021) argues, the vast "expanse of cyberspace" has become "the domesticated landscape of well-policed gated 'neighborhoods'" (xx). Personalization, which Chun relates to eugenics and racial segregation, has taken over our digital social interactions, and the principle of *homophily*, discussed at length by Chun, substituted the ethical quandaries crucial in our interactions with the stranger. Increasingly, in digital domains, we are no longer surrounded by anonymous strangers but by the anonymous kin, a collection of beings and digital selves that shape our lives, tastes, and preferences without ever fully knowing them or identifying them. What does this transition mean to social life and experience? How is the economy of anonymity changing?

This chapter traces a line between social theories anchored on the principle of prediction and trust in complex social environments. This line of thinking begins centuries before Simmel with Thomas Hobbes's *Leviathan*, runs through Simmel, Giddens, and scholars of the digital like Shoshana Zuboff, Nick Couldry, and Ulises Mejias all the way to Chun. This line shows the importance of the economy of anonymity to social theories invested in questions of trust, warrants, and order. It begins at the onset of modernity with ideas of the anonymous citizen inherent in notions of the social contract, moves to questions about the anonymous stranger, which connects Simmel to Giddens, and resurfaces again in the age of datafication and homophily.

I do not use contractarianism as a theory of the state but as a way of thinking about safety, trust, and order that places anonymity at its center. I argue that contractarianism defines the social as an assembly of anonymous strangers, and, as a political and social theory, contractarianism is a way of theorizing an economy of anonymity. Given that our political understandings of society are often rooted, implicitly, on contractarian ideas, one can argue that we also see the social with anonymity in mind, as an a priori. I find this political cultural understanding of society in Simmel's theories of trust and also in Giddens's theories of ontological security, which explain trust in social dynamics that are horizontal, between individuals and between individuals and institutions. The through line is the question of safety, trust, and order in heterogeneous post-traditional societies in which individuals interact regularly with anonymous others. These questions carry through the digital and are central to the work of Zuboff, Chun, Couldry, and Mejias. So, I ask, How do these scholars and theories address contractarianism and anonymity? In this chapter I analyze this through line and present a subaltern critique of contractarianism that answers the question, How can individuals build trust in others when these others are anonymous strangers who are no longer ruled by religion, tradition, and kinship?

The Problem of Trust in an Unpredictable World

On the surface, questions of social trust and order seem unproblematic. Most of us, most of the time, find ways of living with anonymous strangers. We follow rules of civility and politeness and use visual, cultural, and social cues to reduce uncertainty when interacting with others. Yet, that we have solved the problem of social life with strangers does not mean that we always feel safe. When we step outside our routines, our neighborhoods, our friend group, our city or nation, the question of safety may quickly rush back in. Because, ultimately, the anonymous stranger challenges what Anthony Giddens would call a person's "ontological security."

Giddens introduced this concept in a 1991 influential book titled *Modernity and Self-Identity*, where he elaborated a theory of selfhood attentive to the challenges of modernity. Among the influential ideas central to the book, he conceptualized ontological security, an effect of practical consciousness as humans attend to their surroundings and, reflexively, are able to decipher the best course of action, time and time again. He points out that crises challenge ontological security, but trust in, among other things, "the reliability of persons," allows individuals to move forward (38). Trust and ontological security are temporal management and epistemic techniques. They depend on the past to assess the present and act in ways that can be predicted by the person in the future. *But how can the anonymous stranger be trusted?*

There are no easy answers to this question, one that most of us face routinely. On the one hand, most anonymous strangers behave just like the rest, which allows us to presume them reliable to a degree. But Simmel notes also that in the presence of the anonymous stranger, we perceive these humans not as individuals but as types, as categories. And it is telling that in the brief list of strangers he mentions, the immigrant, the racial other, the poor, and our inner enemies are the types of humans that stand for the archetype of the stranger. By producing this list of strangers, Simmel reveals to us his positionality, which means that his argument is grounded in the concerns and realities as experienced by White, European, wealthy natives. Simmel (1971) even uses arguments that align with nativism when he writes: "The stranger is by nature no 'owner of soil'—soil not only in the physical, but also in the figurative sense of a life-substance which is fixed, if not in a point in space, at least in an ideal point of the social environment" (1). As if soil defined the kin and their trustworthiness, the stranger is here defined by what they lack. *Later I call this homophily through property, which is common in all contractarianism*. That Simmel has a positionality has to be acknowledged, but his positionality does not mean that his ideas are wrong. We all have standpoints. But epistemological positionality should instruct us to apply ideas carefully, which is what I plan to do here.

That Simmel was writing this famous essay in 1905 should come as no surprise. At the end of the nineteenth century and beginning of the twentieth, many in the West were concerned with the changing conditions of life under urbanization, mobility, internal migrations from the rural to the urban, the erosion of traditionalism and other social ties (kinship, religion, aristocratic class rule) that made life predictable in the past. When Simmel was writing about the stranger, others were writing about the anonymous crowd, the unruly masses, and the effects of propaganda on these new social groups and actors in a burgeoning century that would shortly see the popularization of cinema and the rise of radio to add to the power of the press. So many changes to social life required new ways of thinking about it. And, importantly, for theories of social order, which rely on the ability to predict the behavior of others, the social and technological changes typically meant that prediction and trust had to be retheorized.

Giddens is not a classic contractarian, but he cared about one issue central to Hobbes and other contractarian theorists of society: the problem of being and feeling safe in the modern world. Giddens's argument is partly a theorization of what modernity is and the type of subject modernity engenders. From a historical perspective, Giddens's argument has new and old elements: "Modernity is a post-traditional order, in which the question, 'How shall I live?' has to be answered in day-to-day decisions about how to behave, what to wear and what to eat—and many other things—as well as interpreted within the temporal unfolding of self-identity" (1991, 14). In the increasingly urbanized world that has characterized modernity, beginning with industrialism in Western Europe all the way to the present, the question "How shall I live?" is complicated by the number of anonymous strangers that surround us. How can anyone know how to act with and around anonymous strangers? Because of this uncertainty, because modernity is a post-traditional order system, Giddens notes that doubt is "a pervasive feature of modern critical reason" (3).

In Giddens's work, individuals attend to environments of doubt and risk by way of habits, what Giddens sometimes calls the "'natural attitude' in everyday life," and by the development of trust, which Giddens theorizes extensively (36). Habits and trust, the core of much ontological security, are not simply about the past. They are future making. Giddens notes that "under conditions of modernity, the future is continually drawn into the present by means of the reflexive organisation of knowledge environments" (3). These knowledge environments are partly embedded in technology, which means that the issue of ontological security is not simply, as Giddens sometimes implies, the result of our psychologies or our knowledges. Just like habits record the past to shape the future, technologies do the same. Technologies, from the coffee cup to the coffee maker, are material, technical, and instrumental objects that synthetize past answers to the material possibilities of life. Answers to the question "How shall I live?" are always partly technological, for it is with and because of technology that we can make actionable some of our desires, decisions, or impulses. Ontological security should not be over-psychologized. Ontological security should always be understood as partly psycho-epistemological, which is one of Giddens's contributions, and partly technological, which is my point. Indeed, knowledge environments are inconceivable without technology. Epistemology is not a thing of reason. It is also material and technological.

Indexicalization and identity are always part of order, and this includes post-traditional social order. Indexes that refer to humans represent difference and particularity, the two coordinates essential to signification, human categories, and the possibility of engaging the heterogeneity that defines the social in modernity. Indexes are not simply useful to theorists of order, sociologists, demographers, criminologists, economists, anthropologists, epidemiologists, pedagogists, and so on. Indexes make the phenomenal world legible. As Simmel argues, the stranger becomes somehow predictable by making it possible to identify oneself and others based on differences and particularities, thus allowing for the genesis of the social grammar that we use to make sense of the world, those who exist in it, and oneself. This grammar is indexical, but also spatial and temporal. Because the barista is on time, following the rules of Starbucks, I may encounter her to ask for my morning coffee and she may ask me the question "name?"

Two random individuals confront one another, coinciding in time and space, with stable identities anchored on particular indexes. One is a customer; the other, a service worker; one is behind the cash register; one is in front. She asks for a name, I say "Darth Vader," and Cindy, whose name I can see on her name tag on her uniform, smiles and yells, "A latte for Darth Vader!" Order is locative and is partly explained by indexicalization, the identity of a person, their credentials, the position a person has in institutions, which define their relation to others and determines their capacity to configure surroundings. In anonymity, I wait three minutes for my morning ritual.

In a modernity characterized by complex social environments and human difference, we leave the predictability of home routinely and find ourselves in situations in which trust has to be placed on something very different from familiarity. Borrowing from Ervin Goffman, Giddens (1991) uses an anecdote meant to show the trust inherent in "civil indifference," which is indifference based on anonymity and contractarianism:

> Civil indifference represents an implicit contract of mutual acknowledgement and protection drawn up by participants in the public settings of modern social life. A person encountering another on the street shows by a controlled glance that the other is worthy of respect, and then by adjusting the gaze that he or she is not a threat to the other; and that other person does the same. In many traditional contexts where the boundaries between those who are "familiars" and those who are "strangers" is sharp, people do not possess rituals of civil indifference. They may either avoid the gaze of the other altogether, or stare in a way that would seem rude or threatening in a modern social environment. (47)

Here, two social contexts, one described as "modern social life" and the other as "traditional contexts," are compared to highlight different elements of civility that we have come to expect in modernity, with a way of structuring order in traditional societies. While identity, indexicalization, shapes interactions in traditional societies, the relatively anonymous interaction between individuals in modern contexts is regulated by "an implicit contract of mutual acknowledgement and protection," a social contract that Goffman and Giddens place at the core of trust interactions in modernity. The way of separating traditional societies from modernity is not new, nor is the reliance on contractarianism to explain modern forms of order. Here I want to highlight the fact that both are rooted in particular notions of anonymity that can help explain order, trust, and prediction in increasingly complex social environments. Prediction in post-traditional societies becomes the most urgent and difficult problem to resolve because the individual is no longer imagined as bound by tradition and convention. Instead, the unit of analysis in post-traditional predictive orders is the anonymous stranger, an individual that, as Simmel suggested, cannot be known as individual but needs to be known as a type, a category, and, even then, cannot fully be trusted or known.

Goffman and Giddens implied a particular historiography to explain civil indifference. Before the arrival of modernity, Giddens suggests, individuals belonged to communities ruled by tradition and economic structures that brought certain fixity and, thus, predictability, to life. The future was not fully opaque; it was controlled. Individuals were confined by tradition, religion, family obligations, and societal expectations.

The feudal township or tribal enclave is the prehistory of homophily, the term that later social scientists would identify as central to the idea of prediction in a complex society. In these traditional, homophilic environments, a name, the basic unit of social grammar, indexed our kinship, gender, ethnicity, race, and nation. A name made particular what categorical indexes like gender, township, or race were making general. The vignette used by Giddens implies that in traditional societies recognition, not anonymity, structured social relations. But traditional societies have been eroding or disappearing since the beginning of modernity, with colonialism and industrialization, and something had to take the place of fixity to retheorize order.[1] Anonymous contractarianism, alluded to by Giddens, has been a common answer to how order and trust could be promoted in the increasingly dynamic social structures that we call modernity, a social order fueled by colonialism and mercantilism.

Starting with Thomas Hobbes's *Leviathan*, modern contractarian theories of order have been central to explaining social order, and this lineage includes John Locke, Jean-Jacques Rousseau, and, more recently, John Rawls. These theorists have in common that they conceive of a social order benefiting from the shared interest in justice, articulated often as preserving one's life and/or one's property. An anonymous social contract is used metaphorically as the binding artifact between individuals and between individuals and the sovereign/state, and this contract thus becomes the basis of intersubjectivity and politics. In this conceptualization, anonymity is essential. It is anonymous individuals (as in "anyone") that bound together constitute the sovereign's power, and perhaps nowhere is this clearer than in the cover to the original publication of *Leviathan* (see Figure 1). In this illustration, the giant is built by hundreds of nameless individuals that give Leviathan its body and its power.

This frontispiece illustrates one of Hobbes's key points:

> A multitude of men are made one person, when they are by one man, or one person, represented; so that it be done with the consent of every one of that multitude in particular. For it is the unity of the representer, not the unity of the represented, that maketh the person one. . . . And if the representative consist of many men, the voyce of the greater number, must be considered as the voyce of them all. (2005, pt. 1, chap. 16)

Anonymity here is implicit. What makes social contractarianism original is that individuals, without knowing each other, without the biographical that would produce predictability, would together nonetheless be able to form a type of power that could secure their safety and well-being. This is the primer of the modern citizen in contractarianism, one that constructs a category of being based on the social contract and based on a sameness that would later be criticized by feminism and critical race theorists, among others.

Anonymous contractarianism had several advantages that made it appealing to theorists from Hobbes onward. It helped early theorists imagine order in contexts in which pluralism was becoming the norm (Hobbes), and it helped later theorists like Locke insert economic changes as neces-

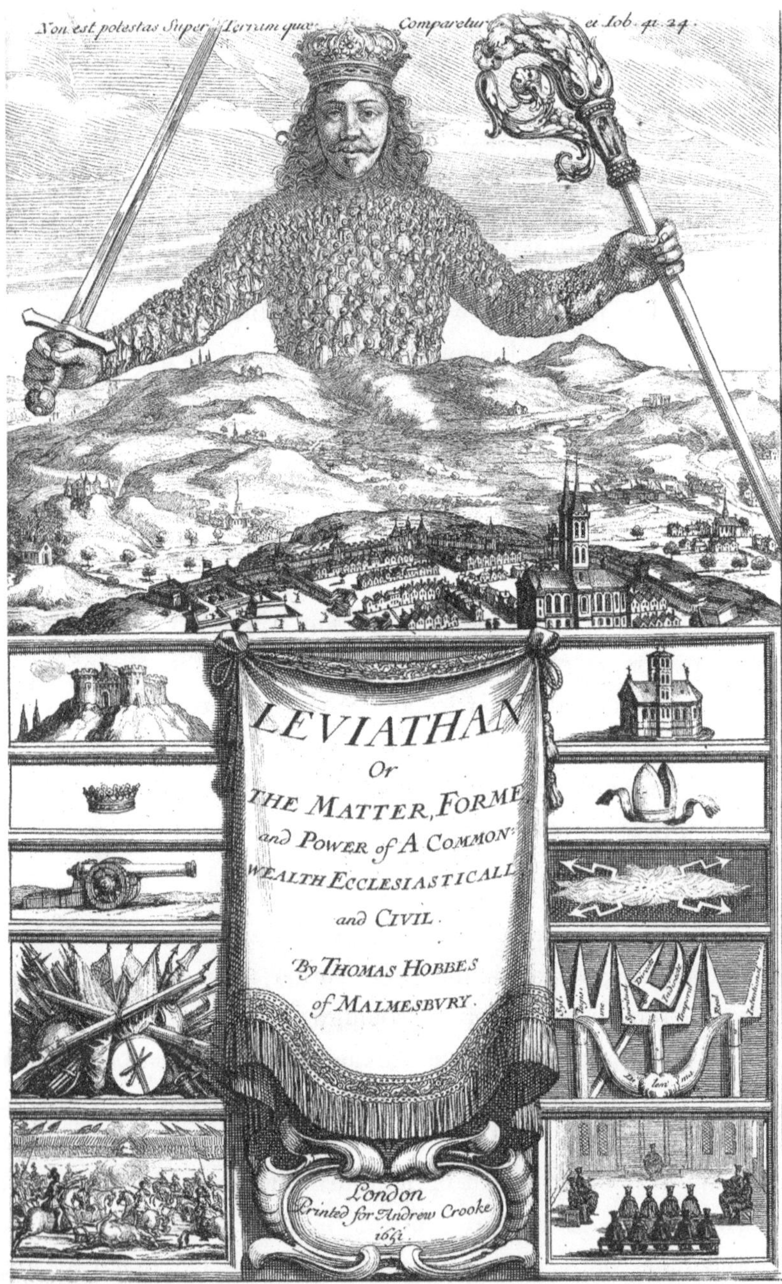

FIGURE 1. Frontispiece of *Leviathan* engraved by Abraham Bosse, with input from Thomas Hobbes, the author. British Library. Creative Commons CC0 1.0 Universal Public Domain Dedication

sary ingredients to any theory of social order. In Locke, and since, anonymous contractarian theories became connected to property and changes in the property regime brought about by the demise of feudalism, and the rise of colonialism and mercantilism inspired new ideas about social order. And, while neither Giddens nor Goffman acknowledges the connection between contractarianism and property, this connection has existed for a long time. Indeed, Hobbes did plenty of borrowing, and his *Leviathan* partly reactivated principles found in ancient Greek life and philosophy, including in Aristotle's *Nicomachean Ethics*, where private property is central to facilitating key citizen virtues, including generosity and restraint, and, anticipating Hobbes, property is also key to order. Aristotle writes of an order anchored in respect for private property: "Others, however, keep their hands off the property of other people from fear, thinking that it is not easy for one person to take another's property without their taking his; so they are content neither to take nor to give" (Aristotle 2014, 64). Ancient Roman law continued this understanding of order, making property the core structural force of civil society through a complex legal code of property and rights (Pagden 1990, 15). As did the Greeks and Romans, Hobbes and Locke placed property at the center of order and as a key ingredient of the type of peaceful and predictable coexistence that Giddens will later call ontological security. *Contractarianism changed the geometry of homophily by placing property between individuals and the sovereign above.* Recognition ceases to be the core of homophily and social trust. In an evolving modernity increasingly characterized by difference and urbanization, social trust and predictability could be constructed with anonymous social interactions if and only if individuals abided by a social contract grounded on property and, Simmel (1971) would later argue, money. Simmel noted that money allowed for anonymous strangers to be trusted, integrated into social life thanks to the mediating power of money, which made a world of property dynamic and predictable. Simmel goes as far as arguing that marginal individuals and communities, like emancipated Roman slaves, Jews, and foreigners, gravitated toward money transactions *because* money stood for social relationships they often lacked (221–25). A contractarianism of political agreements, property, law, and money could constitute order out of heterogeneity that would yield ontological security. Modern economy, one may infer, is also partly an economy of anonymity.

While appealing to those wishing to explain the relative peace and order characteristic of some Western societies, contractarianism has inherent flaws subject to criticism from a subaltern perspective. One such critique connects to contractarianism's reliance on property, propriety, and politeness. A second is a critique of contractarianism's assumptions of, and dependence on, equality and freedom.

A subaltern critique of property starts not with Hobbes but Locke, who better reflects on this evolving order. From early 1700s, for instance, England became a geography defined by enclosed parcels, spaces structured by law, culture, proto-liberal politics, and colonialism.[2] These different elements were at play in discussions about the nation-state in Locke's *Second Treatise of Civil Government*, in which he laid down ideas about property alongside basic ideas about labor (Greer 2012, 366–67). Locke, a champion of private property, the commodification of labor, and colonialism, used the open and, he believed, wasteful common spaces of the Americas as warning tales about the poverty that would ensue if England were to revert back to the commons. Private property, he believed, was socially responsible, for it produced the personal incentives to enhance productivity, and thus it was the legal tool by which a state could meet and exceed its needs.

In Locke, the order principle is constituted through a web of contracts that make property the legal avatar for order and safety. Ours, Carol Rose (1994) would argue, is a property regime. The centrality of property, thus, cannot be understood in isolation from the transition of Europe to capitalism and to colonialism. Property was the spatial logic behind the legitimation of the state as a sovereign territory, and law would become the conceptual mechanism to theorize violence and order. Yet, it is important to remember that, like most political and legal concepts, property was defined in alterity, in relation to the colonial other, the barbarians knocking at the door. When confronted with this history, the truism "My home is my kingdom" takes on a new meaning.

These are lessons of citizenship. Since the Romans, as Anthony Pagden (1990) reminds us, "civil society was, by definition, a society based upon property, and property relations were what constituted the basis for all exchanges between truly civil men" (15). Hobbes reactivated this Roman principle, which is also found in Locke. Since, order between citizens has been correlated to the ability of citizens to rely on a legal system that would help them protect their private property. Echoing Locke, James Madison famously wrote this principle of modern governmentality in 1792: "Government is instituted to protect property of every sort; as well that which lies in the various rights of individuals, as that which the term particularly expresses. This being the end of government, that alone is a *just* government, which *impartially* secures to every man, whatever is his *own*" (Madison 1962, 267).

In the centuries following Hobbes and Locke, the concept of property, which was originally tied to land, expanded to include all material things that could be owned and traded, increasingly including a wider array of immaterial things such as financially conceived yet intangible commodities and, as Madison would have it, rights needed for an individual's freedom in the public sphere, such as reputation and others. Cheryl Harris (1993) has even convincingly shown that even whiteness was treated as property in this juridical tradition: "In ways so embedded that it is rarely apparent, the set of assumptions, privileges, and benefits that accompany the status of being white have become a valuable asset that whites sought to protect and that those who passed sought to attain—by fraud if necessary. Whites have come to expect and rely on these benefits and over time these expectations have been affirmed, legitimated, and protected by the law" (1713). From land to the things needed to function freely in the public sphere, even whiteness, property has become the logic of life and the central technique to secure order.

But not everyone has had access to land or property broadly speaking. Slavery, settler colonialism, and coverture are systems of order based on the fundamental unequal access to property and to rights. Unsurprisingly, the histories of propriety and politeness are deeply racist and sexist. For good or bad, we see the material world through the eyes of property and understand the negative consequences that may befall us if we don't "respect" (to use Goffman's term) the property rights of anonymous others.

This is mine; that is yours. In fact, one may even argue that the reference to respect in Goffman's explanation of civil indifference is respect for the other's personal space and the other's self-ownership. Anonymous contractarian theories are a social technology meant to allow prediction in a world increasingly filled by anonymous others.

That the anonymous contractarian principle is found from Hobbes to Giddens (even if in the latter is only in limited form) attests to its importance and the steady role anonymity has played in social life and the theorization of the social and the political. The world of contracts imagined by Hobbes is a world of anonymity, for a promise of order that depends on an anonymous contract is a promise of the nonviolent interaction of two specific strangers or parties agreeing over property rights, over labor, or over obligations. The key promise of this anonymous contract is peace through order, a powerful normative idea that we reproduce in the saying "Good fences make good neighbors," which is an enduring argument to the orderly power of contracts, for fences stand for contracts and the indexical and property regime that contracts necessitate. *In contractarianism, our kinship is our property, and it is our attachment to our property that makes us and others predictable.*

Contractarianism is a political theory but also a theory about the rise of a contingent type of modern subjectivity, one that is always raced, classed, gendered, sexed, and abled. The evolution of property regimes from feudalism to modernity also provided the basis for different identity formations, ways of being subject, and basic notions of selfhood. The modern subject, partly the result of property, political aspirations, and social desires, is also the product of internalized forms of indexicalization. We think and feel with indexes; we treat each other attending to indexes, our own indexes and "their" indexes. Indexicalization is key to predictability, to any sense of ontological security, and, consequently, of ontological insecurity. Giddens (1991) connects these issues from the perspective of self-identity:

> Self-identity is not a distinctive trait, or even a collection of traits, possessed by the individual. It is *the self as reflexively understood by the person*

> *in terms of her or his biography.* Identity here still presumes continuity across time and space: but self-identity is such continuity as interpreted reflexively by the agent. This includes the cognitive component of personhood. To be a "person" is not just to be a reflexive actor, but to have a concept of a person (as applied both to the self and others). What a "person" is understood to be certainly varies across cultures, although there are elements of such a notion that are common to all cultures. The capacity to use "I" in shifting contexts, characteristic of every known culture, is the most elemental feature of reflexive conceptions of personhood. (53)

What Giddens calls "the capacity to use 'I'" is indexicalization, for the "I" is deeply connected to the diverse indexes we use to define ourselves, to our names, to our gender, or to our place of origin. The organizing property of the "I" is, however, shaped by concepts of "personhood," and here I am arguing that the idea of personhood in modernity is linked to property and to an intersubjectivity shaped by anonymous contractarianism.

The modern subject and modern intersubjectivity are crafted by the same chisel. They are the result of widely shared values about human relations and the hidden rules that normalize some transgressions and immorality. These values and their transgressions are partly tied to property. Scholars like Carol Rose and Gregory Alexander, among others, connect property to propriety and self-ownership, two key ingredients of the type of human an enlightened modernity meant to bring to life. On this, Rose notes: "That 'property' was the mainstay of 'propriety' was a quite common understanding before the seventeenth and eighteenth centuries. This understanding continued, albeit in abated form, even after the great revolutions at the end of the eighteenth century" (1994, 58). In the British-influenced American context, this view continued under American "republicanism," a political vision central to the formation of the early republic at the end of the nineteenth century, one that bound property to authority and self-rule. Democratic equality, rules of propriety, and what today perhaps we call politeness, were circumscribed by a republicanism that bounded these values to property and the humans that had it. It did not matter that the majority (married women, slaves, children, the mentally ill) could not access property (62). A bounded equality gave way to bounded propriety, bounded politeness, values that profoundly shaped and stratified society.

Today, it is quite normal to claim the value of politeness toward anonymous strangers and to expect politeness in return. The social performances that Giddens and Goffman refer to as contractual are precisely the result of cultures of politeness and reciprocity. We teach those lessons to our kids as some of the basic rules of living in our pluralistic communities, surrounded by strangers, some of the basic virtues that allow for coexistence in complex and diverse societies. But rules of politeness today are of course more complex. The echoes of republicanism are still strong. To many people, impoliteness, radical indifference, and even violence are appropriate toward those who are deemed inferior or inconsequential, and it is thus not unusual to suffer impoliteness regularly, particularly if your ascriptive (by birth) characteristics are given meaning by hierarchical systems such as patriarchy, racism, or nativism.

This aspect of modern subjectivity and intersubjectivity is reproduced systematically, and it has proven difficult to change. It is questionable whether Giddens or Goffman could have written those ideas about human politeness implicit in civil indifference if they had written from the perspective of, for instance, a racial minority. It is doubtful whether Simmel would have written about the stranger in the way he did after reading Ralph Ellison's (1989) *Invisible Man*. Let me illustrate why. In this book, Ellison uses the voice of a nameless central character to paint a very different picture of civil indifference than the one grafted by Giddens by way of Goffman, a type of stranger quite different from Simmel's:

> I am an invisible man. No, I am not a spook like those who haunted Edgar Allan Poe; nor am I one of your Hollywood-movie ectoplasms. I am a man of substance, of flesh and bone, fiber and liquids—and I might even be said to possess a mind. I am invisible, understand, simply because people refuse to see me. Like the bodiless heads you see sometimes in circus sideshows, it is as though I have been surrounded

> by mirrors of hard, distorting glass. When they approach me they see only my surroundings, themselves, or figments of their imagination—indeed, everything and anything except me. . . . It is sometimes advantageous to be unseen, although it is most often rather wearing on the nerves. Then too, you're constantly being bumped against by those of poor vision. Or again, you often doubt if you really exist. (1)

The indifference the book describes is radical and uncivil; if we are to understand this description as one of a stranger, this type of stranger does not fit Simmel's theories. The invisible man does not experience his invisibility and anonymity as a testament to what is common with those who ignore him; it is more foundationally different. Ellison's protagonist believes he is perceived ontologically different and thus as representing a difference that cannot be bridged, calculated, or trusted. A subaltern critique of contractarianism starts with this insight.

Yet, Simmel is right in that even issues of radical difference like the ones described by Ellison are navigated through and with categorical, not concrete, indexes. It is indeed telling that Goffman called civil indifference a type of interaction rooted in recognition, for one is indifferent to only that which is recognized as normal, unthreatening, or unimportant. There is a certain comfortable anonymity at the center of this civil indifference. I walk by someone whom I haven't met; they walk by me. We control our glance to show respect and adjust our gaze to make sure our stare is not threatening. The reward is to be treated in the same way, with respect, unthreateningly. But the fact that we are anonymous to the other person does not mean in this case that we are not indexed. On the contrary. This interaction is possible because categorical indexes and context worked together to structure an encounter fitting the parameters of normal. Civil indifference is a particular type of relational technique rooted in normalcy and propriety. Goffman and Giddens perhaps make the mistake of calling this type of interaction "modern" and presume that exceptions will be found in traditional societies. Exceptions are everywhere in modernity, and these are very obvious when indexed as an ascribed minority or subaltern.

There is a tension at the heart of contractarianism that was evident in Hobbes, but it is clearer in Jean-Jacques Rousseau all the way to Goffman and Giddens. Contractarianism presumes a fundamental equality that then translates into citizen and legal equality. There is one contract; and there is one community of individuals who are the signatories. In Hobbes, the preservation of the contract is through fear; in Rousseau, preservation is through freedom, expression, and self-determination. But in both cases, the contract is between an individual and civil society imagined as one homophilic community made of anonymous citizens.

Yet, as I argued previously, from the perspective of subalterns, the equality at the heart of contractarianism is at best a project, not a reality. This is why scholars like Carole Pateman (1979, 1988) and Charles Mills (1997) have crafted powerful subaltern critiques meant to show contractarianism as an inaccurate and even dangerous theory of society and the political. From a feminist perspective, Carole Pateman has convincingly criticized contractarianism and insisted that the presumption of "individual" "voluntarism" at its heart (we voluntarily enter as individuals into a social contract) is fundamentally patriarchal. In *The Problem of Political Obligation* (1979), she questions voluntarism; in *The Sexual Contract* (1988), she questions the very notion of the individual at the center of stories of right.

Pateman (1979) argues that contractarianism has always hidden the dimension of sexual subjection at the core of the social and that contractarianism works only because of this repression.

> The story of the sexual contract is also about the genesis of political right, and explains why exercise of the right is legitimate—but this story is about political right as patriarchal right or sex-right, the power that men exercise over women. The missing half of the story tells how a specifically modern form of patriarchy is established. The new civil society created through the original contract is a patriarchal social order. (10)

The core of Pateman's critique is the impossibility of equality within the social contract. Entering the social contract as equal presupposes an individual freedom that women have never enjoyed. It is impossible to enter a contract from a position of subjection and absurd to assume that anyone would enter a contract that would replicate, produce, and even justify their own subjection. The fundamental social geometry of the social contract, which requires the a priori of equality, is a horizontality that is never met.

Inspired by Pateman, Mills (1997) alerts us to the existence of a "racial contract," which fosters radical and systemic inequalities between the races, a contract meant to protect a fundamental difference between Whites and nonwhites in the United States: "[The social contract] is not a contract between everybody ('we the people') but between just the people who count, the people who really are people ('we the white people'). So it is a Racial Contract" (3). Mills argues that this racial contract is epistemological, political, and moral. Epistemologically, the racial contract begins with the constitution of human categories that will produce the differentiation between White and nonwhite, which will then be applied to the formal and informal "meta-agreements" that establish who is human and who is not (11). Politically, the racial contract transforms individuals into citizens, but not in opposition to the state of nature. The distinction of White and nonwhite requires that the state of nature remains as part of the social, albeit in the very hearts and minds of the nonwhites (13). The political, brought to existence by the White settler community, will exist in a perpetual state of distinction and struggle against the apolitical or pre-political, the state of nature that exists in the "savage" nonwhite residents. Morally, the social contract codifies existing morality to law, including feudal notions of substantive equality and inequality among peoples. The racial contract then restricts the fundamental freedom and equality of moral individuals to Whites, objectively separating the realm of moral obligations, where equality prevails, from nonwhites, who are neither equal nor free and whose nature cannot foster the moral goals and virtues of White morality.

The subaltern position that Pateman and Mills foreground gives further validity to the importance of anonymity in contractarianism, for, as I have argued throughout the book, slavery and coverture, two types of subjugation at the heart of the feminist and critical race theory critiques, are grounded partly in erasing the biographical in favor of the categorical. As I discuss in Chapter 6, coverture and slavery used forced unnaming and renaming as techniques of oppression. And, as I argue here, the biographical matters, which is why Dr. Martin Luther King Jr. used the biographical to illustrate his theory of justice in the famous "I Have a Dream" speech delivered on August 28, 1963, in Washington, DC: "I have a dream that my four little children will one day live in a nation where they will not be judged by the color of their skin but by the content of their character." Dr. King acknowledged and presented the stark difference between those whom we treat in relation to their concreteness, their biographies, and those whom we treat as types, with prejudice. How will my son Javier be treated? Will he be treated, as I feel I often am, as just another anonymous stranger, or will he be treated by the content of his character?

At the heart of contractarianism lie a few fables: That one can theorize safety and trust from the safest position, a majoritarian, hegemonic position that corresponds to the position of the White, educated, cisgender male. That citizenship is available, equally, to all. That trust is equally possible and safety equally available. A subaltern critique exposes these fallacies and notes that the question of "How shall I live?" is quite important but means very different things to different people. To Giddens, it is a question about social actions. To Simmel, it is a question about ethics and objectivity. When the subaltern, when the anonymous stranger is the one asking, the question becomes something else. It becomes, "How shall I stay alive?" or "How can I have respect and access to the privileges of citizenship and justice?" or "How can I stop being seen and treated as a stranger?"

Post-traditional Order with the Digital

Order in post-traditional societies is changing even more because computational technologies have introduced new possibilities to attend to the future. Sarah Brayne (2021) starts her book *Predict and Surveil* with a brief anecdote about a body found somewhere in Los Angeles County. The book's central concern is the way policing is transforming due to the systematic use of data and algorithmic and predictive logic. Sergeant Michaels, she narrates, informs her from the comfort of a desk that they are lucky: An automatic license plate reader recorded traffic nearby where the body was dumped, and, by correlating with time of death, they were quickly able to reduce the universe of indexes, human specific data traces, to three license plates. One of these, which Michaels quickly focused on, was from Compton, and correlating the identity of the car owner with what is called CalGang, he was able to determine that the car owner belonged to a gang at war with the victim's gang. Case solved. Past, present, and future were determined by data indexes associated with actions, places, and social networks, which were brought together and consequentially theorized to produce dramatic effects on someone's life. The case was also solved because social actions presumed to be anonymous, such as driving, were not. Whether the person arrested was culpable or not, the person arrested seemed to hold on to the idea that driving could be done anonymously in a city like Los Angeles. This was a miscalculation or misunderstanding.

The computational system used by the Los Angeles Police Department (LAPD) is called Palantir Gotham, a sophisticated platform that brings together an array of data sources, including state and government databases such as LAPD data, the Crime Analysis Mapping System, the sex offenders' registry, and many others. Palantir also includes an array of private data sources like LexisNexis, which has "84 billion public records from 10,000 diverse data sources, including 330 million unique cell phone numbers, 1.5 billion bankruptcy records, 77 million business contract records, 11.3 billion name and address combinations, 6.6 billion motor vehicle registrations, and 6.5 billion personal property records." Although the LAPD stopped using Palantir in 2020 after community pushback, predictive policing is here to stay. And public anonymity is transformed. We are surveilled everywhere. Palantir may have ended, at least temporarily, its relation with LAPD, but that same year, Palantir had secured federal government contracts totaling $1.5 billion, including contracts with the Pentagon, the Department of Justice, the Department of Homeland Security, and Immigration and Customs Enforcement (ICE) (Ongweso 2020).

What it promises is order. Archive after archive, in the hands of companies like Palantir, the past is shaping the future.

In 1991, when Giddens wrote his book on ontological security in modernity, knowledge environments were partly computational, but they were computational in a different way than predictive policing is computational today. Within years of Giddens publishing this book, datafication changed due to computational technologies that used myriad sources captured by automated human-computer interactions. In policing, 1991 is quite different from 2021. Law enforcement agencies used technologies such as fingerprint databases and photographic databases (which began in the nineteenth century) alongside crime databases to help theorize and predict criminal activity. In 1994, Brayne (2021) writes, New York City established COMPTSAT, the most sophisticated computational policing tool at the time, which collected crime data in real time, mapped it, and analyzed it in preparation for weekly meetings where trends are discussed and strategies devised. COMPSTAT spread through US cities in the 1990s and 2000s, but the difference between COMPSTAT and Palantir is significant. Individual lives were affected by COMPSTAT by way of broad effects, things like over-policing or under-policing areas, or, if you had had encounters with the law and your name ended up in one of the many law enforcement databases. But most US citizens were not directly considered within COMPSTAT as targets of policing. With Palantir, every US resident is a target of policing calculation. We are all suspects, but some of us are more suspect than others. The subaltern perspective would address the ways predictive policing systems target US residents unequally. This includes the deployment of automated license plate readers (ALDRs) or acoustic gunshot detection systems (AGDs) in urban areas rather than in more affluent suburban ones.

Brayne's analysis of policing in a datafied society alerts us to the fact that police forces use data purchased from corporate data brokers like LexisNexis. As critics of datafication and privacy help us see, the bulk of this data was not collected in a way that alerted individuals to its potential uses (Makulilo 2020; Rubinstein et al. 2014; Rubinstein 2018; Holbrook 2019). While Palantir and LexisNexis claim that these are legal uses of personal data, it is unlikely that the contracts regulating data extraction were clear enough to users to interpret their actions as consent (Radin). The increasingly common use of private data sets to meet public goals is evidence of new ways of exerting and imagining control over populations and of the way digital indexes have become a new type of commodity that is reshifting our understanding of power and the relations between capitalism, the state, and the individual.

Datafication refers to the way computer technologies have transformed humans into data or digital indexes, a process that is ubiquitous and has constituted the possibility of almost constant surveillance by corporations, tech companies, and governments (Couldry and Mejias 2019). In Shoshana Zuboff's work (2019), datafication and surveillance have transformed capitalism and are transforming the humans that live in datafied societies. According to Zuboff, "surveillance capitalism," the term she gives to this new form of economic power, is a multidimensional concept that explains a new social order rooted in the intersection of digitation and economics, one that changes fundamental dimensions of sociality, politics, and human nature. Surveillance capitalism is

> 1. A new economic order that claims human experience as free raw material for hidden commercial practices of extraction, prediction, and sales; 2. A parasitic economic logic in which the production of goods and services is subordinated to a new global architecture of behavioral modification . . . 5. As significant a threat to human nature in the twenty-first century as industrial capitalism was to the natural world in the nineteenth and twentieth . . . 7. A movement that aims to impose a new collective order based on total certainty; 8. An expropriation of critical human rights that is best understood as a coup from above.

Here Zuboff is claiming that surveillance capitalism is transforming humans because the collection and manipulation of personal data are connected to behavior modification and to the very experience of being human. What is external to individuals changes them at the most intimate level for what is exteriorized as behavior becomes data that reshapes behavior on the reflective capacities of algorithmic and platform logics. This argument sets the stage for an understanding of social order reliant on the accumulation of data-as-commodity that constitutes new regimes of economic power that systematically undermine human rights and human nature. Extraction is but one goal. Prediction and sales target behavior control, and it is this claim that assumes interiorization. The goal is not to know what's next but to prompt the next action, the purchase, the vote, the choice, and to place users in a yellow brick road toward a promised land where users' hopes and desires meet the wishes of the market, the state, and the powerful, without friction.

These arguments echo those by Couldry and Mejias (2019), who describe the digital realm as a new *terra nullius*, a space of nondistinction, of chaos. The indexicalization regime that we call datafication is meant to make property, to make order, and to make profits. In step with ideas about wastefulness found in Aristotle and Locke, data has been assumed "to just be there, for the taking," and the contemporary forces of industry, epistemology, and technology are incorporating this "wasted" data into the regime of capital. Couldry and Mejias use Marxism to levy a critique of datafication based on the reasonable argument that the regime of data constitutes an evolving form of capitalism that uses human data for appropriation, for accumulation, and for further separating a class of people, the owners and controllers of the means of datafication, from the rest. Their assessment is partly historiographical:

> Just as industrial capitalism, according to Marx, changed society by transforming the universal human activity of work into a social form with an abstract dimension (via the commodification of labor), so capitalism today, in the expansionary phase we call data colonialism, is transforming human nature (that is, preexisting streams of human life in all its diversity) into a newly abstracted social form (data) that is also ripe for commodification. (Couldry and Mejias 2019, 32)

From industrialism and the regime of capital that inspired Marx, Couldry and Mejias identify a change, an expansion of capitalism, rooted in computation and the incredible capacity of today's computational technologies to insert themselves into almost every realm of life and make it data. In addition to Marxism, Couldry and Mejias use analytic tools from coloniality, a Latin American set of critical theories that attend to the ways colonialism survives in forms of sociality and ideology. With coloniality they can argue that what is different about this stage of capitalism is that what is "annexed" to the processes of wealth accumulation are not simply some raw materials (a term used by Zuboff) that are part of nature, land, gold, or silver. What is annexed, Couldry and Mejias claim, is human life itself, which becomes the new territory discovered and colonized by and with datafication.

Data colonialism and surveillance capitalism use contractarianism to build their arguments, but do so in particular ways. In Couldry and Mejias's work, contractarianism is framed by colonialism, and the authors repeatedly throughout the book compare user agreements to the *Requerimiento*, a 1513 Spanish document that the invaders would read to Indigenous communities before engaging in warfare and dispossession. The *Requerimiento* informed the people that all land, including Indigenous land, belonged to the leader of the Catholic Church, appointed by God to rule in his name. If they refuse, the *Requerimiento* spelled out the process of utter dispossession and subjection it would follow:

> But, if you do not do this, and maliciously make delay in it, I certify to you that, with the help of God, we shall powerfully enter into your country, and shall make war against you in all ways and manners that we can, and shall subject you to the yoke and obedience of the Church and of their Highnesses; we shall take you and your wives and your children, and shall make slaves of them, and as such shall sell and dispose of them as their Highnesses may command; and we shall take away your goods, and shall do you all the mis-chief and damage that we can. (*Requerimiento*, cited in Couldry and Mejias 2019, 92)

The document and the practice established a type of poisonous social contract, one meant to produce, legalize, and justify dispossession, slavery, and servitude. Couldry and Mejias find similarities in the way contracts anchoring the digital realm are constructed by corporations to be powerful, comprehensive, and impossible to understand (the *Requerimiento* was read in Spanish to non-Spanish speakers). These contracts, which are everywhere in our digital daily lives, establish legal ways by which users cede their property (user data) to the company without the capacity to reclaim it. Inspired by the cruel asymmetry at the heart of the colonial social contract, this asymmetry at the heart of digital contractarianism is nothing short of the legal architecture to produce new forms of human chattel.

Surveillance capitalism depends even more than data colonialism on contractarian arguments. Zuboff's argument, which periodizes history in terms of first modernity (early industrial capitalism and massification), a second modernity (liberalism, individuality, capitalism, and rise of neoliberalism), and a third modernity (capitalism with radical inequality in tension with liberalism and individualism), is argued in relationship to contract theory. The disjunctures between radical economic inequality and taken-for-granted liberalism are illustrated by reference to the massification of contracts dominated by corporations to the expense and abuse of individuals who are left with no recourse but to agree to terms, services, and goods in ways that take away their rights.

The massification of ever more complex boilerplate contracts, user agreements, and terms of service today define life in general, but even more dramatically in the digital realm, where almost every interaction is with or through private websites that impose contractual conditions that regularly take away the right to sue, the right to get damages, and the right to privacy. "Legal experts call these 'contracts of adhesion' because they impose take-it-or-leave-it conditions on users that stick to them whether they like it or not. Online 'contracts' such as terms-of-service or terms-of-use agreements are also referred to as 'click-wrap' because, as a great deal of research shows, most people get wrapped in these oppressive contract terms by simply clicking on the box that says 'I agree' without ever reading the agreement" (Zuboff 2019, 52–53). Designed to obfuscate, these boilerplate agreements bind the user to the corporation and, as legal scholar Margaret Radin (2013) argues, their massification erodes democratically earned rights: "This is the problem I will call 'democratic degradation.' Mass-market systems of form contracts that restructure the rights of users of products and services operate to undermine or cancel the rights of users granted by legislatures. In other words, these systems of contracts can delete rights that are granted through democratic processes, substituting for them the system that the firm wishes to impose" (16). Increasingly existing under a corporate legal regime independent from the state, the contractarianism at the heart of digitization is radically dissimilar from the political philosophy that Hobbes outlined and that many others have found crucial to the modern understanding of political subjects. Our desires for peace, order, and the ability to have an orderly future are no longer part of the contractarian equation, as corporations were never constituted to safeguard those wishes.

What Couldry, Mejias, Zuboff, and other scholars like Radin are describing is a contractarianism quite capable of generating order, as imagined by other contractarian thinkers, but in ways antithetical to the democratic and liberal hopes found in Locke, Rousseau, or Rawls. The massification of contracts today is "the hidden network," using Foucault's words, that determines new forms of intersubjectivity, ones set on a radical asymmetry between data corporations and users. Far from ushering in a social compact, as imagined by Hobbes and Madison, the massification of contracts means an order reliant on the systematic, unapologetic, and colossal transference of rights and property, not to the sovereign but to data companies. The authors also point to a new indexicalization regime, one in which the meaning of a promise, of personal consent, of a signature, is expanded to include a click, opening a web page, or scrolling a page down. All of these are forms of consent regularly used in the data universe, which means that, effectively, to simply "be" in the data realm is to consent to the asymmetries that befall us. As important, one of the most powerful forms of "extraction," using Zuboff and Couldry and Mejias's term, is the signing away of our personal data, our indexes, which are the basic building blocks of the new data economy. Imagine if the contractarianism theorized by Hobbes had been argued on the basis of generating huge wealth to corporations or the sovereign. Would any political philosopher have followed Hobbes's steps?

The strengths of these contractarian theories of the digital are many, and they include the recognition that datafication is rigged to benefit corporations and governments and that new forms of exploitation and extraction affect us all. For sure, contractarianism is in these important works a problem, but more has to be done. To continue the coloniality critique initiated by Couldry and Mejias, we need to examine the types of inequalities inherent in digital contractarianism. *A homophily of property and propriety is fundamentally flawed, and the subaltern perspective should account for difference.* And, fortunately, many scholars have argued that from predictive policing to data extraction, we all are set to lose, but the subaltern is set to lose more. Predictive policing and data extraction affect more dramatically the racial other and the Global South, as many have argued and shown.

From Life to Data

In Chapter 2 I argued that indexicalization is partly a cultural technique and used Bernhard Siegert's (2015) words to define it. He explains that cultural techniques "operationalize distinctions in the real," and he uses the example of a door to illustrate how opening and closing it constitutes (encodes) the distinction between inside and outside. "Concrete actions serve to distinguish them from earlier nondifferentiatedness. In more general terms, all cultural techniques are based on the transition from nondistinction to distinction and back" (14). As in Siegert's example, indexicality mediates between two worlds, two reals. A universe of nondistinct individuals is mediated through, and at the other side of the door appears a universe of individuals who are sorted, categorized, and addressed.

This sorting is crucial to temporality. It allows for the past to shape the future, as when someone's reputation, kept in memory through storytelling, shapes the way we treat this person today. A person, an index, a name, is classified as "good" or "trustworthy" for past deeds, and this person is treated with the benefit of those memories. A credit score tries to do the same at the social and economic level. We attend to our economic present and pay bills in time so that in the future, this credit score rises and thus we have access to the best loan percentage rates. The past shapes the future, and the number of such instances is significant. Our success in schooling looms over our decisions at the end of high school; our ability to drive safely determines our ability to have a driver's license; our vaccinations help determine health policies in the future. An ordered world is a world of prediction, one in which the past shapes the present to make the future.

Social order systems rely on prediction, but prediction means something different in different social orders. In-person interactions, for instance, are part of prediction processes reliant on tradition, habits, and the relative predictability of surroundings, our familiarity with them, and with the people that live within. Giddens (1991) explains this as follows:

> Trust, interpersonal relations and a conviction of the "reality" of things go hand in hand in the social settings of adult life. The responses of the other are necessary to the sustaining of an "observable/accountable" world, and yet there is no point at which they can be absolutely relied upon. Social reproduction unfolds with none of the causal determination characteristic of the physical world, but as an always contingent feature of the knowledgeable use of convention. (51–52)

In this description, trust depends on an observable and accountable world. We interact with others, even anonymous strangers, with the hope that what we see can be trusted, that our predictions will be correct, our inferences right. And, though our trust is sometimes betrayed, the types of interactions that yield the most predictable and beneficial outcomes quickly become convention.

However, human actions and interpersonal relations shaped by digitation have changed our relationship to prediction and trust. Datafication has added another layer of material and temporal complexity to life, one that is structured by its own set of rules, which are quite peculiar. This peculiarity is rooted in at least two reasons. First, datafication further fractures indexicalization processes in material and temporal ways. The digital realm is apart though interrelated from nondigital realms, those that we sometimes describe as brick and mortar, flesh and blood, analogue, or IRL (in real life) realms. It is as if instead of one door, indexicalization now is two different, self-referential doors, and most of us exist in this refractive multidimensionality. One door sorts, categorizes, and addresses individuals in their embodied selves, as they exist in relation to others, to physical space, to social norms pertinent to *anonymous copresence*, and to political obligations and privileges related to humans, citizens, and anonymous strangers. The other, constituted by a human/computer interaction, sorts, categorizes, and addresses individuals, their digital selves, as they exist in relation to other digital selves, digital spaces, and social norms pertinent to *anonymous absences*, a social space that Sherry Turkle (2011) at one point called "being alone together."

These are different but not independent dimensions of existence that shape most lives. They are connected by the properties of indexicalization, including anonymity, the capacity to further differentiate and process human reality. Each realm provides the raw material that will be indexicalized, processed, at the moment of transition, and thus becomes data on the other side. Just like human actions were captured by a computer interaction that ended in the LexisNexis giant data archive, the data archive that is LexisNexis becomes the new raw material that Palantir uses to constitute human-specific data that will stand for criminal investigation. If a person is found suspect and charged, they reenter the circuit of indexicalization and become datafied yet again, part of digital archives that will shape the person's future. Recurring, constant, the flow of real to data to real does not end. We are never just data. We are always process, nondifferentiated and differentiated, raw material and data, non-indexicalized and indexed, flesh and datafied bio-indexes (Deleuze 1992; Bergson 1975; Kreps and Muirhead 2019, 5). Referencing the work of Gloria Anzaldúa again, we exist in nepantla, a space in between the analogue and the digital where identity possibilities present themselves as open and sometimes painful (see Chapter 1, and Chapter 5 on anonymity and ontology).

As in nepantla, the pain in the digital realm comes from two directions. We suffer the consequences of our digital lives at the discretion of the corporations and institutions that collect our data, pool it, and sell it and produce a world of their control in which our digital actions and behaviors are simultaneously target (as when our shopping behavior changes because of data predictions) and currency (the new shopping behavior becomes data and reenters the circle of datafication). And we also suffer the consequences of our digital lives at the hands and whims of other users, who embrace norms of behavior unique to digital anonymity. The ontological security expectations found in Giddens that rely on trust and conventions do not apply. In social media, most of the time, you interact with anonymous strangers whom you cannot see and cannot quite predict. What would Simmel say about these anonymous strangers who lurk in the obscurity of the digital? What social contract do they follow? None that we can detect, for they are invisible to us.

The digital world is constituted not simply by humans acting rationally or in good faith and expressing their actual views and preferences about the world. The economy of anonymity has changed with profound consequences. The digital world is increasingly shaped by trolls and professional fakers, who often use anonymity to control public conversations, views, and preferences of users. This is partly a design feature of many digital spaces, which makes it extremely easy to foster anonymity, incentivizing behavior untroubled by consequences. Many studies have shown that trolls often exhibit psychological characteristics associated with psychopathy and sadism as well as overall lack of empathy (see, e.g., Buckels et al. 2019, 1–40; Sest and March 2017, 69–72). And other studies show that the availability of anonymity also invites trolling (Nitschinsk et al. 2022), which fits the common perception that trolls hide behind the veil of anonymity and, inversely, that the veil of anonymity invites the sadism that characterizes trolling. This anonymity is available through different means, including the simple and common practice of using nicknames and fake emails, all the way to creating personas or handles behind VPNs. The concern over the overall effect of trolling in public discourse is such that governments such as that of Australia have proposed anti-trolling policies, and others like that of the United Kingdom are trying to force social media platforms to perform stricter user verification tools and banning users who carry out abusive behavior online. But governments are also part of the problem, as many argue that Russia, in particular, has used trolling systematically to shape geopolitics (Jamieson 2020). But studies show state-sponsored trolling is much more common and Russia is far from being the only bad actor. One study alone by the Palo Alto organization Institute for the Future showed cases of state-sponsored trolling by the United States, Venezuela, Turkey, the Philippines, Ecuador, Bahrain, and Azerbaijan. Other studies add India, China, Iran, Pakistan, and Saudi Arabia, and the list keeps growing.

Further complicating the issue of trolling is the fact that it is also carried out by bots, artificial entities that use the presumption of anonymity and can have social media accounts and participate, shape, and troll the internet. These bots have a wide variety of capabilities. Some are simple and simply repost, for instance, while others are increasingly machine-learning entities capable of generating complex posts and opinions (Badawy et al. 2018; Kai-Cheng et al. 2019). These bots are typically designed to shape public opinion, spread misinformation, and reduce the ability and willingness of people to share their views. This widespread problem is such that Elon Musk's notorious offer to buy Twitter in 2022 fell through for what he claims is the widespread existence of fake accounts, often set and controlled by bots to shape perception and opinion. Kathleen Carley believes this percentage of bots to range from 5 to 35 percent, which means that at least one in twenty, and perhaps one in three, accounts and their activities are not human (Menn and Dwoskin 2022). Scholars credit these bots with shaping elections, constituting misinformation campaigns about COVID 19, and causing other informational maladies that define today's digital political ecosystem.

A second peculiarity of datafication relates to digital contractarianism. As in copresence, and in pre-datafied modernity, models of prediction are central to datafication, but these models exist outside the set of obligations represented in and by contractarianism. As Zuboff, Couldry, and Mejias argue, datafication depends on formal contracts, but these contracts no longer serve the user. They only tie the user to the rules set by the data companies, yet, as I mentioned previously, the contracts themselves are designed to be obtuse and incomprehensible to the average reader. Informal contractarianism, the type that regulates social interactions, is part of digital social life, and people who spend time in digital communities such as gaming, Facebook, Meta, or even 4Chan attend to the formal and informal rules of interaction that allow for belonging and that allow for crafting and managing their reputations. Yet, even in these environments, contractarianism plays a reduced role, for anonymity seems to empower some individuals to act in more antisocial ways than they would in other nondigital, social environments (Behm-Morawitz and Ta 2014; Brehm 2013; Hill 2022).

As surveillance capitalism and data colonialism propose, the peculiarities of datafication connect to the fact that digital indexes have become valuable commodities that have energized a thriving and growing data market. The LAPD will have options when it comes to contracting with private companies like LexisNexis, and LexisNexis will have to prove its relevance by expanding its data offerings, and it is always working on improving. The LexisNexis Risk Solutions division aggressively advertises to law enforcement agencies and promises to put criminal leads at their fingertips by placing at their disposal public records data (37 billion!) that can be processed by algorithmic tools that provide a virtual picture of an individual, definite identification, and visualization tools.[3]

The world of privatized big data is quite different from that of the past. While modernities have relied heavily on indexicalization and data, nation-states were often the greatest creators of data, and, as William Alonso and Paul Starr (1987) note, this meant that nation-states could control a great deal of the epistemic ground of statistic creation, even if the data itself was later processed in universities or private companies. In the hands of these institutions, data was a valuable public good. Injustices were performed and rationalized thanks to public data (e.g., the funding of public schools attached to property values that created huge inequalities in education), but these injustices were outcomes of bad politics that citizens could theoretically change by electing different public officials. Yet, already in 1987, when Alonso and Starr were publishing their book *The Politics of Numbers*, private data firms were growing in importance in the creation of data and processing of data. Increasingly, public agencies were relying on private firms for data, not the other way around, a fact that opened challenges of public trust (359). Public statistical processes could be open and made accountable to the public, but private data production is not. Alonso and Starr believe that statistics based on private data "offer the political process only confusion and mistrust," a state of affairs that has only been exacerbated today (360).

The datafied world is radically different from the one described by Alonso and Starr. Although the private sector of the economy has been for centuries collecting data in order to rationalize production, distribution, and sales, the privatization of data has dramatically grown in scale and importance thanks to new communication technologies (internet, world wide web), hardware (computer sensors, digital cameras, processing speeds), platforms, and infrastructure (optical cable networks, data storage, video surveillance). These are mostly controlled by private interests, from internet providers to platforms like Google, and, while the goals of governments were never truly or only beneficial to citizens, corporations have no obligations toward their users other than the ones laid out by their obtuse contracts and the ones set by governmental policies.

Prediction, the art and science that has the anonymous stranger at its core, is central to the flow that imperfectly sutures our fractured reality. Prediction is part of the social contractarianism that orders copresence, part of the relation between individuals, communities, and the state under governmentality (which includes the statistical turn and pastoralism as a sort of contractarianism), and part of datafication. But prediction can no longer be thought of in isolated ways. What we do in situations of copresence may end up datafied, and what we do in the digital realm ends up shaping copresence. Couldry and Mejias (2019) use the term "data relations" to outline the routinized way in which data appropriation happens and the way existing social relations become datafied (12). The cycle of life to data to life seems unending, and prediction is one of its core engines. We are always predicting (that is life), and predictive technologies are always touching and shaping our lives.

This is the clearest with personalization, which is ubiquitous. We simply cannot exist in the digital realm without being targeted by the predictive systems that personalize our taste, social circles, and news consumption. From unbound in a post-traditional order, from anonymous strangers, personalization tries to bind us back, make us legible, nameable, and predictable. We are always being theorized by computers, and this predictive work bleeds from the digital to the analogue world, giving form to our experiences of culture, community, and politics. Importantly, personalization equalizes us but also separates us. We are all subject to personalization, but the goal of personalization is not individuation. As Chun (2021) notes, personalization is a misnomer, for personalization works by the principle of homophily. The goal of algorithms is to constitute groups, not individuals, which is why Chun uses figures such as gated communities and segregated neighborhoods to talk about the way our digital lives are treated by the machines (24). The goal of computer algorithms is not to personalize our experiences but to place us in specific groups that can be targeted by similar messages, tastes, advertising, news, and friend possibilities. Dominique Cardon (2015) writes:

> In digital services, an algorithm truly "works" when it manages to bring closely together the elements of the environment in which it operates so that the behaviors of users are regulated by its verdicts and when the principles it implements nourish their representations. We can say it about Google's PageRank, Amazon's recommendation system, TripAdvisor's hotel ratings or the GPS embedded in cars. (85, translation by the author)

The algorithm's verdicts, its "suggestions," bring together different types of input that include personal data and are meant to suggest the best output *for* the person and for the group. We, users, encounter similar but not equal digital social worlds, and our experiences are shared with others whom we may not know nor care about.

The logic behind these algorithmic outcomes is, Chun argues, an overinvestment in homophily, which is the crucial principle shaping personalization and online communities. She shows that homophily fostered the creation of polarized "echo chambers," where clusters of like-minded individuals are bound together by shared hatred of an opposing "other." This phenomenon mirrors earlier critiques of mass media, where scholars debated whether media informed democratic publics or manipulated passive audiences. Her analysis traces homophily's roots to mid-twentieth-century studies of social groups, particularly attitudes toward integration in biracial public housing. The chapter also links theories of social influence, such as Katz and Lazarsfeld's "two-step flow" model, to modern network science. Their work, which identified "opinion leaders" as intermediaries in the diffusion of ideas, highlights the mechanisms by which polarized online neighborhoods arise and persist. This polarization, Chun argues, is like a magnetic force that organizes previously inert masses into clusters of opposing poles, repelling and attracting simultaneously. Ultimately, her discussion critiques how network science and data analytics, underpinned by homophily, reinforce social divisions. By framing bias and inequality as predictable or comforting, these systems perpetuate the discrimination they purport to analyze, which raises questions about how to navigate the tensions between polarization, ambivalence, and the potential for a more inclusive democratic society.

The result is a social space configured by the logic of segregation, which is why there are subtle and at times not so subtle differences between our experiences in IRL and in the digital realm. In analogue life, experiences are differentiated by the standpoint of the individual. In the digital realm, experiences are differentiated by the digital echo of our subjectivity and history, what John Cheney-Lippold (2017) and Bernard Harcourt (2015) call our digital selves and our algorithmic identities. Our digital selves may or may not resemble who we think we are. Cheney-Lippold analyzes how the National Security Agency (NSA) has, for instance, used digital traces to claim that someone has the digital signature of a terrorist. The NSA does not simply theorize anonymous strangers; it is part of the US security apparatus that carries out the so-called war on terror, a war designation that authorizes actual killings, even though a significant portion of the war is carried out in the digital realm. When an individual is placed by the algorithms in the "terrorist" gated community, this prediction can have dramatic consequences on the individual. Ultimately, our digital selves are more or less similar to our actual selves because they are constructions not of our making alone but of the technical operations at the center of computation, the material possibilities of our keyboard, the platforms that we use, the algorithms that we encounter, and the dizzying array of data calculations that any given platform or web page may use to determine our digital identity at any given time. Fluid, unsteady, more or less reliant on our embodied history, our digital selves have a spectral reality that nonetheless has digital and analogue effects.

I began this chapter by identifying the anonymous stranger in social theories of modernity and focused on contractarianism as a classic and lasting strand of such theories. In a modernity defined by the post-traditional, theorizing social order means building theories about individuals acting in the social without the safeguards of tradition, without the rules, conventions, strictures, and consequences of religion or kinship. In post-traditional societies, these safeguards have diminished, making prediction difficult. Contractarianism, formal and informal, as in Giddens and Goffman, injected a sense of predictability to human behavior and a sense that social order could be achieved in a modernity where subjects were imagined freer to pursue their wants and desires. Since Hobbes, contractarianism has offered a way of thinking about social order and has penetrated political cultures in the West, making contractarianism common and enduring. It is too part of social theories like those by Goffman and Giddens, theorists concerned with ideas of trust, predictability, and public behavior (performance) in modernity.

But a subaltern critique of contractarianism starts with the recognition that the project of contractarianism has never been fully realized. Scholars like Rose, Alexander, Mills, and Pateman have helped us understand that racial minorities and women have never fully belonged to the group benefiting the most from the social contract. Not only that, but as Mills helps us see, the social contract actively undermines the life chances of those who are not White, and, for this reason, the social contract must be understood as a racial contract that is meant to reproduce and reconstitute forms of racial difference and hierarchy. Liberalism is not, strictly speaking, a failed project. Liberalism works, but not in the way advertised by its advocates. Liberalism is the ground of inequality, and it is inherently illiberal. The social, as understood in a term like "a social contract," is a segregated space reserved for some, not all. The boundaries are not necessarily or only spatial, but they certainly are always classificatory.

As I show then, classical contractarianism seems to work by a version of homophily, but not by the version that Chun will later identify in reference to social and communication sciences at the base of datafication. Contractarianism is a political and moral project, and the behaviors that it is meant to produce and discipline are interactions regulated by law, overseen by the state or government, and ethics, shaped by habits and unequal customs. Contractarianism is predicated on a notion of sameness borne out of a shared vulnerability, what Hobbes originally identified as the life of danger and violence proper to life in nature, without law. Yet, as Mills (1997) helps us see, contractarianism is also predicated on an epistemology of ignorance, a commitment to "particular patterns of localized and global cognitive dysfunctions . . . producing the ironic outcome that" those in power "will in general be unable to understand the world they themselves have made" (18).

The subaltern critique adds different dimensions to contractarianism. The contractarianism of Mills and Pateman shows that the social contract is not the same for all and, thus, that the economy of anonymity is also based on inequality. The social contract is built around sexual and racial difference. Theirs is a critique of the assumption of sameness within racial and sexual difference, a sameness that may comfort the cisgender White male, but one that can subjugate sexual and racial others. If the subaltern critique is right, then contractarianism has always been based on a tension between sameness and difference that begins to look a lot like homophily. Homophily, which imagines a social fragmented and diverse, hypothesizes that segregation predicts political interest and behavior and, given the eugenic drive at its core, homophily also normalizes that in the competition between White patriarchy and subalterns, the racial patriarchy wins. Segregation is not only meant to mark the existence of different groups and the particular political drives and behaviors. Segregation also is meant to explain the lack of traction political projects borne at the margins have with hegemonic groups. Echoing the subaltern critique of contractarianism, homophily explains not only the political real but also its cruelty.

Datafication, however, is forcing us to reimagine social order and the type of subject this social order is engendering. Datafication has introduced new complexities to social order because datafication is transforming the economy of anonymity. The easiest way of thinking about these changes is by noting that classical and casual contractarianism is implicitly built on the idea of *anonymous copresence*, the interaction of an individual with anonymous strangers. What connects "civil indifference" to the individual in Hobbes's *Leviathan* is that these individuals interact with others in a nonviolent fashion. Perhaps for very different reasons, Giddens and Hobbes are imagining social order based on nonviolence as the standard by which ontological security can be fostered broadly in a post-traditional world. Prediction in anonymous copresence is at the core of these theories.

Datafication is, however, characterized by anonymous absences, social interactions between individuals with anonymous absent strangers who are inconceivable and thus untheorizable because individuals cannot see them or know when they will act and react to our actions, posts, comments, and words. And while this chapter has explored the ways data archives such as LexisNexis blur these forms of data-driven anonymity, at the level of absence, anonymity is widespread, but it is one that makes interactions unpredictable. The question of "How shall I live?" seems harder to predict. It is hard to exist in the digital realm without suffering some violent interaction from an anonymous other. It is hard to trust what others say, what others do. Violence, harassment, and hate are common, and so is misinformation. Ontological insecurity is expanding with the expansion of digital cultures and social media, and anonymity is partly the reason (Rainie and Anderson 2017).

But this is not the whole picture about the economy of anonymity in datafication. While horizontally anonymity is widespread and erodes ontological security, vertically, individuals lack anonymity and privacy. It is hard if not impossible to remain anonymous to the platforms, corporations, and the state in the social realm. When we act digitally, we become data and the interaction becomes grounds for theorizing us and shaping our lives in the future. Meanwhile, the anonymous watchers, whom Zuboff calls "Big Other," overlook, record, keep, trade, theorize, our actions. Our future partly depends on them.

The future has always been the center of theories of order. It is through order that the future becomes predictable, and we orient ourselves and our institutions toward order when this predictability is desirable or, perhaps more honestly, when the prediction is beneficial to us. Datafication is transforming the relationship we have with the future. We experience a present crafted by a past increasingly independent from the social coordinates we typically used to predict our future. Increasingly, hundreds of daily computer-mediated actions are outside the purview of our reflexivity and impact our present and future. You could have driven by the automatic license plate reader unaware that your license plate would be recorded and tied to a murder investigation; you could have "liked" a music posting by someone unaware that you have interacted with a person participating in a deadly gang war. What are risky behaviors today if we do not understand the parameters of prediction? What is ontological security today if we cannot even conceive what actions or choices today are building our future? The nature and life of our digital indexes, our data, escape our control. We do not know the world that this data will produce. We do not have a clue how data will shape our futures, for as long as data is stored somewhere, it can be reused and retheorized to generate new outcomes and conceptualizations of who we are, why we act, and how we are going to act. The anonymity of "Big Other" is not a metaphor. We actually do not know who owns our data, how many entities have it, who will use it and for what ends. And because of this, in a very real way, our future does not belong to us.

Five

Bordering, Anonymizing, and Inscription Technologies

Coloniality is a Latin American intellectual formulation that originated in the work of Peruvian sociologist Anibal Quijano in the early 1990s. Quijano (2024) used the term "coloniality" to refer to the ways in which colonial relations and ideas had survived independence movements in Latin America and could be found in epistemology, notions of ontology, and administrative practices. Latine philosopher Linda Martín Alcoff (2007) uses a coloniality and feminist framework to point out that Western philosophy is based on an economy of credibility associated with identity, gender, age, race, and citizenship. She argues that prior prejudices, biases embedded in hegemonic ideas about ethnicity, race, gender, and free or slave status, determine the evaluation of ideas (82). Like other coloniality and feminist theorists, including María Lugones, Enrique Dussel, and Walter Mignolo, Alcoff understands that the effects of coloniality are relational. They shape intellectual evaluations but also social, cultural, intellectual, and political relations and have hierarchical effects on subjects.

In attending to culture and ideology, Alcoff echoes most theories of race, ethnicity, and gender that understand racism, sexism, and/or xenophobia as ideological frameworks. From Karl Marx to Frantz Fanon and

Simone De Beauvoir, ideology, culture, and myths are used to explain racism, ethnocentrism, and sexism. But coloniality offers more than ideological explanations of discrimination and subject formation. Coloniality proposes that relations of discrimination often are embedded in, and are preceded by, administrative practices. Administrative practices, which often go unexamined as ideological, regularly perform the dirty work of ideology and constitute subjects *because* they shape the very biographical possibilities of individuals.

Elsewhere (Amaya 2013), I used coloniality to examine how administrative practices in the United States have worked alongside racist ways of knowing to construct the dehumanizing environment that undocumented individuals in the United States have to endure. In this chapter I want to expand further on my engagement with coloniality and administration by looking at technologies of indexical inscription and the way these technologies shape immigrant subjects by engendering forms of anonymity and, simultaneously, hypersurveillance. I focus on how two subsets of technologies of inscription shape the lives of immigrants and other transitional individuals to the United States: One set shapes immigrant subjects by forcing specific naming practices that produce particular forms of anonymity. In this case, inscription is erasure and then reinscription. To millions, including me, these technologies permanently mark the crossing of borders on someone's biography and are the first step to normalize historical and cultural erasures that impose majoritarian linguistic and ethnic identities. Bernhard Siegert (2015) notes that "by subjecting the unwritten life to the priority of legal writing, the *bios* becomes an element of the political body" (87). Life, narrativized with parameters established in migration law and policy, becomes politicized. It is partly in the rewriting of life during migration that the subject is ensconced in the new political body, with new legal biographical writing. This cannot happen without erasure, anonymizing, and, in this chapter, I treat name changes as examples of erasure and anonymizing. Whether imposed on the subject, or embraced as forms of agency and creativity, name changes are a way of silencing the past.

The migrant's new biography does not yield a subject equal to the rest of the citizenry. This is so partly because of migrants' biographical newness but also because a second set of technologies of inscription, biometrics, or what Iván Chaar López (2024) calls "the cybernetic border," places immigrants as subjects of radical surveillance, making it difficult for migrants to be anonymous to the eyes of the state. Migrant crossings thus are characterized by forms of social erasure from the perspective of the migrants and far-reaching forms of administrative surveillance from the perspective of the state. These crossings and the technologies of inscription they rely on are examples of subjugating asymmetries in the economy of anonymity. The migrant loses forms of identitarian power, part of their history, and control over their identifiers; the state becomes more powerful by subjecting the migrant to radical identification, indexical harvesting, and surveillance.

Technologies of indexical inscription are the means by which personal identifiers, indexes, become traces, etched in matter, history, and place. Jon Agar (2016) proposes that a technology of inscription is material (e.g., a piece of paper); it has substrata; inscription depends on writing technologies (e.g., a typewriter); inscription is formal (e.g., the spaces in the birth certificate that expect specific information); it is often shaped by informal or formal policies and regulations (e.g., the birth certificate is shaped by state's policies); inscription depends on knowledge systems to be interpreted (e.g., the bureaucratic knowledge that allows a state employee to know what the Local Registration District means in a birth certificate). Agar is interested in bureaucracies, and so is this chapter. Commenting on migration practices in sixteenth-century Spain, Siegert (2015) helps us see that today's US practices have long antecedents, and some are found already during the conquest and early colonization of New Spain. What is common across these centuries is that both bureaucratic systems participate in the constitution of "the modern subject as an autobiographical animal" (84).

This chapter adds to Siegert and Alcoff by engaging anonymity from the perspective of technologies of inscription, one inspired by Gloria Anzaldúa's work and life. These technologies include sites of inscription, which is another term for archives (D. Martínez 2022, 36). Like Siegert and Diana

Martínez (2022), I show that technologies of inscription are constituted to record some, not all, traces. Because of this, I add, the way these technologies are designed and implemented constitute forms of erasure and anonymity that reshape the life of immigrants and their self-understanding. And, because these technologies are applied massively, they give form to the economy of anonymity that surrounds and gives meaning to migrant lives and the body politics in general. In this chapter I focus on three aspects of inscription that shape the indexical lives of immigrants: materiality, writing technologies, and forms.

Immigration, Materialities, and Technologies of Inscription

In the United States, a nation that until March 1, 2025, existed without an official language, the logic of administrative practices has been brutally Anglo-centric even before President Trump. As a result, millions of migrants to the United States live under names that were adopted or imposed on them through the bureaucracies and technologies of inscription that they encountered when they first transitioned from their country of origin to the United States or through culture and economic pressure. Studies centered on migrations in the early twentieth century, when the majority of migrants were coming from Europe, show that between 33 percent and 75 percent of migrants adopted new names (Biavaschi et al. 2017; Carneiro et al. 2020). The variation depends on the methodology. Did immigrants change their full name? Did they change their given name but retain their family names (a more common practice)? These variations exist today, but I add even more. I consider that a migrant changes their name when they are forced or encouraged by social norms and technological structures to drop diacritics; when they need to drop portions of their names, as when author Marian Chia-Ming Liu dropped Chia-Ming; when they need to reorder their names as with migrants from China; or when migrants, especially from Asia, keep their legal names but adopt an Anglo first name in day-to-day interactions (Liu 2022).

The migration process is multigenerational, and millions of children with migrant parents, even if born in the United States, also live with the consequences of these bureaucracies, inscription regimes, and social pressures, and even though some of the effects are often lost in memory after a few generations, migrant biographies are marked by a truncation or bifurcation that never goes away. If who we are today is the result of our past, many migrant histories and genealogies show through their indexes the violent moment in which their ancestors left a nation and entered the United States. Just as a cut-down tree shows in its growth rings moments of bonanza and moments of struggle because of droughts or fires, our biographies and genealogies do the same through our indexes.[1] These are traces that tell us about change and that mark, in time and often in space, moments of deep transition. Importantly, these traces are material and are shaped by materiality, because materiality matters.

Popular depictions of Ellis Island migration processes, like the scene depicted in the 1974 film *The Godfather Part II*, portray a process where the new arrival, in this case the young Vito Andolini, enters a processing station and is unable to understand the questions of the migration officer. The official asks again, loudly, in English, for the child's name. The question is translated to Italian by a local translator, but Vito, overwhelmed, does not say a word. The translator looks at the card attached to the child's clothing and says to the officer "Vito Andolini, from Corleone," but in the noisy processing office, the official only hears "Vito Corleone," and that he writes down. In this case, the mistake at the root of the name change is due to the materiality of the inscription, its aurality. Registered in sound waves that compete with other sound waves in the busy place, the index traveled from mouth to ears, and in that short distance it changed. Vito Corleone is born. Vito Andolini is not gone but placed in a box of memories and documents that one may label "before."

Scholars interested in debunking the Ellis Island myth that name changes happened routinely at Ellis Island because of interactions like those depicted in *The Godfather Part II* have argued and shown that administrative processes made it practically impossible for that to happen. In reality, Rosemary Meszaros and Katherine Pennavaria (2018) argue, "immigration officials did not write names down—they checked them off on a list in front of them. In other words, the names were *already written down*.

The officials were not working with blank sheets of paper on which they created lists of newly arrived passengers, but with ship manifests, official lists of passengers who had disembarked." Just as materiality mattered for arguing the apocryphal story of changed names at Ellis Island, it is the materiality of inscription that debunks the myth. Name changes happened after migrations from Europe, but these changes were after arrival and often during naturalization processes.

Technologies of inscription are material recordings that allow for the dissemination of indexes, and some of these technologies make indexes relatively durable and stable, giving them a high degree of permanence and mobility, and, in so doing, these technologies shape an index's relation to social and power systems. Different materials offer different possibilities for dissemination and processing and, for this reason, for governance, management, administration, and control. The materiality of aurality, sound waves, is powerful but brief, and if the sound waves are not recorded or listened to carefully, aural indexes vanish and are subject to forgetting, misremembering, and misinterpretation. Listeners have little time to process what they hear and little time to react. *The Godfather Part II* depicted the evanescent conditions of aurality quite well. The immigration officer presumed to have heard what the translator stated and recorded the name according to his best interpretation of what he heard. When waiting for the name, the first name he heard was "Vito," and the last thing the officer heard, "Corleone," was inferred to be the last name. Materiality and hermeneutics combined to make the mistake credible.

Focusing on materiality changes the analysis of anonymity. Attention to materiality in technologies of inscription shifts the emphasis of research of anonymity away from issues of signification and recenters the technical, material, infrastructural, and technological. Jacques Derrida's concept of *différance* is a reminder that the referent that indexes aim to represent is always in a state of deferral. From the perspective of technologies of inscription, this process of deferral is not simply semantic. It is manifested in the material conditions of representation. The name written in the ship manifesto that was used by the immigration officer at Ellis Island was recorded first in other documents, including a birth certificate or church registry that one could find in Corleone, Italy. The materiality of the name Vito Corleone is always in a state of deferral, and its last instantiation is only as accurate as each process of recording that stands between the present and its origin. Even biological traces like DNA are always mediated and in a state of deferral. That is, the claim that a specific DNA represents an individual is based on technology that interprets a DNA sample; and the technology that interprets a DNA sample depends on other technologies such as a swab that can gather saliva, and so on. Emphasizing materiality, as Bernhard Siegert (2015) notes, is emphasizing the exteriority of the index and placing a "technical a priori" to the indexical archive (50).

Materiality places real constraints on indexicalization and in migration cases often constitutes forms of anonymity. Like Vito, at birth I was given a different name than the one I have today. I was born Héctor Germán Amaya González. As most in Mexico, I had two given names (Héctor Germán) and two family names (Amaya and González), for I was the product of two families, my father's family (Amaya) and my mother's family (González). My name's form was in itself material genealogical inscription that offered information about two generations, not one. That Mexico's naming tradition included two names materially gave space for indexing the two families that I came from. It was also patriarchal genealogical inscription. Amaya is my father's family name, and it was in the first position. My father's mother's family name was Flores, which was lost after one generation. González is my mother's father's family name, and it was in the second position and thus was marked to be lost one generation after. My maternal grandmother's name, Ramírez, was also lost by my generation.

Documented migrants have to fill out dozens, if not hundreds, of forms before they go from temporary residents (e.g., tourists, foreign students, foreign workers), to permanent alien residents (green card holders), to naturalized citizens. Like Form I-485 and California's birth certificates, forms in the United States have three spaces for names: first name (identified as given name), middle name (identified as a second given name), and family name. I have by now lived most of my life away from Mexico, in the United States (and Canada), and I am yet to find a single form from the government, corporations, or educational institutions that has a different material arrangement than first name, middle name, and family name. Three spaces mean to signify specific naming arrangements and meanings, and they universalize what is local. These three spaces are normalized even though the United States does not have an official language, and even though the United States is an immigrant society, full of people from all over the world with different naming traditions including my own, with two first names and two last names, but also traditions where the family name is first and the given name is last (China among others), or mononymic traditions as in Afghanistan or Mongolia. In states like California, where the majority have linguistic connections to either Latin America or China, birth certificates have the same three spaces inferring the same order and the same number. Most migrants, including myself, subject ourselves to these forms aware that however difficult it is to simply give up on our naming practices and our actual names, we must adapt. The materiality of the forms migrants encounter is nonnegotiable.

But forced adaptation is not adaptation. It is compulsion. It is under compulsion that the United States and states like California secure the name changes of millions of migrants. The material decisions carried out by the US and California governments, and the myriad agencies, businesses, and corporations that reproduce this state of affairs, are clear examples of Western-centrism, Anglo-centrism, and coloniality insofar as coloniality speaks to global asymmetries between Western nations and individuals or communities from the Global South.

I explore names and unnaming extensively in the next chapter, but here I need to state what should be obvious about the importance of these naming transformations that migrants have to endure. Names matter. They tell some of our history, our place of origin, the linguistic context in which we grew up, and they connect us to communities and nations that we love dearly, even if we are forced by violence or poverty to move away. When our names are changed or taken away without any type of dialogue, there is a rip in our biographies that is troubling for what it leaves behind and for what it promises ahead. Behind is the pride, history, and care that were represented when our names were chosen. Liu (2022) writes:

> Chinese names are incredibly purposeful. Many of them . . . are made up of three characters steeped with meaning. First up is the family name, known as the last name in many Western cultures and similarly taken from the father's side. This is followed by a name that is shared with your generation, often paternal cousins. Finally, there is the person's individual name. These names literally show not only our ties to family and history, but how we put them first. So, my full Chinese name is Liu Chia-Ming.

What is promised ahead is an assimilated identity, a sameness imposed not chosen, an identification that anonymizes us in two different ways.

A name change anonymizes our past from the perspective of the present. We are reborn at the border with new identities and histories; I remember the oddity of leaving Mexico where I was a Brown mestizo ethno-racially unremarkable and the crossing experience of learning that I was a Brown Latine male in the United States, a perpetual ethno-racial minority, a member of a category meant to signify social, economic, and cultural marginality. I was reborn as a subaltern, a Mexican, which I learned was a term used in the Southwest as an insult, a statement of derogation. From pride for belonging to a millennial civilization, I had to learn shame. All of this is not the result of the name change alone, but the name change is an element that marks the crossing and makes it permanent. I have by almost every measure defied the odds and live a life seldomly available to subalterns. But I remain marked by my name, which means not simply a story of success but also a story of forgetting.

It is tempting to disregard the social life of indexes when referring to materiality in favor of their juridical, political, and economic life. After all, a history of materials used to archive indexes (as in the forms mentioned previously) is also, partly, a history of materials used for ruling or governing complex social groups, from empires to nation-states. At the hands of scholars of the index, such as Foucault, Siegert, or Louise Amoore, these are material technologies central to governmentality.

But the material social life of indexes is more than what it means to states. It also involves the way indexes and their erasure are part of the everyday, part of the way we go through life and engage in social interactions modulated by our indexes. In those interactions, indexes are often inscribed in aural materials, in processes of mnemonics associated with conventions of sharing one's name with the expectation that our name will be remembered. Our minds are thus indexical material archives and processors, and particular technologies of remembering help us understand the world and organize it. We remember the names of those for whom we care. We have a hard time remembering names that belong to other linguistic and ethnic traditions. Our memory betrays our values and our histories. Like all substrata, our memory is not neutral; it responds to some incitements and disregards others. In its fundamental operation, it catalogues (what names do I get to forget?), systematizes (those names matter in these contexts), and records. Inscription speaks.

Migrants from non-Western linguistic traditions (from India or China, for instance), often change their names officially or at least unofficially in order to avoid being forgotten, confused, or misnamed. Historian Ellen D. Wu (1999) traces the process of naming among Chinese immigrants within a process of forced assimilation more common among second-generation migrants (24). As Laurence Barrett (1993) succinctly states, "The shortest route to WASPdom, which it was still the new arrival's destination of choice, was the swapping of an ethnic name for an 'American' one" (79). In the case of Chinese, the name swapping is even more dramatic than for migrants from Latin America, for at least Latin American immigrants use a phonetic alphabet. Chinese immigrants begin the process of changing names with the process of transliteration, the writing of all elements of names into phonetic translations that can be represented in the English alphabet. The first element to go is visual inscription (from Chinese characters to the alphabet), and typically pronunciations, which almost never can be represented alphabetically. A second element of name assimilation is changing the order of one's name to fit the Anglo tradition of using the family name last instead of first as it is common in China. It is not uncommon that first-generation migrants also adopt a social name to be used in the United States, even though they retain the transliterated version of their Chinese names in official US documents. Most of my students from

China, who are Chinese citizens, do this, and it is very likely that their American student names will be used for as long as they are in the United States. Many of the name changes that Chinese immigrants and their kids undergo relate to the materiality of sound and memory. As Wu (1999) helps us see, individuals often changed names simply to be understood by non-Chinese speakers and to be remembered (32). The threat of being forgotten, misidentified, or simply remembered as a nameless face looms over every migrant from East Asia and other non-English-speaking countries.

Although it is common to think that our hearing and our memory are "interior" mechanisms because they happen in our bodies and in our minds, they are not. They have been shaped and polished by custom and tradition to such a degree that we must understand them as social and political technologies of inscription. When we claim that we cannot understand someone's name or that we cannot remember it because the name is strange to us, what we are actually saying is that our senses are tuned to reality specifically, not generally. That is, sounds are heard and memorized based on the cataloguing mechanism that is our senses and our memory. One may reshape the catalogue, retrain our ears and our memory, and one may get better at understanding and remembering a name pronounced in a different language, but the cataloguing is always limited. Never do our senses become attuned fully to reality. Never does inscription present the real. Inscription, as Derrida would put it, is writing.

Timothy Lenoir (1998) connects Derrida's concerns about signs and inscription to debates in science as a way of reframing the question of realism versus idealism. Lenoir notes that Derrida's research project was concerned with arguing that writing and inscription preceded presence and orality. Against philosophical traditions that considered writing secondary representation and orality primary, Derrida challenges the priority of orality, and of presence, and argues that the thing, reality, the referent, cannot be distinguished from the sign, the index, writing. "Writing, embedded within an entire economy of signs, is thus constitutive of meaning rather than a passive medium for restoring the presence of language to thought" (Lenoir 1998, 5). Even in presence, our memory, our senses, are not fully ours. Writing, inscription, constitute them. Lenoir adds: "Derrida concludes that once it becomes plain that the signified is indistinguishable from the trace, that, as he phrases it, 'the trace affects the totality of the sign in both its faces,' once, that is, it is realized that the signified is originally and essentially trace, that it is always already in the position of the signifier, the metaphysics of presence must recognize writing as its source" (5).

If we think of our listening and our memory as cultural techniques crucial to indexicalization in copresence, we must then recognize that the main affordances of these mechanisms, the sensorial and the mnemonic, are to sort the world into familiar and unfamiliar, kin and foreign. The category of foreign, even at this material level, at the register of the sensorial and the mnemonic, starts with material unfitness, material inscrutability, material evanescence. The foreign is, at this level, anonymous for it cannot be named; it cannot be registered or written. The foreign thus enters our lives without a history, inscrutable, subject to misperception and forgetfulness. The material reality of the foreign does not fit or match our perceptual sensors or mnemonic techniques. This may explain why in the presence of the foreign we often feel provincial, little, ignorant, and unkind. Because we are.

I remember when I was a young immigrant to Canada, I was working bagging groceries at a supermarket in Calgary. The bagger for the next checker was an older Chinese man, with a kind handsome face, skinny, and tall. He was old enough that his back curved a little into a hunch. His English, like mine, was rudimentary. One day he shared a bit of his story while eating lunch. He had come relatively recently to Canada, and though he had a PhD in nuclear chemistry, the only job he could find was bagging groceries. I felt shame. At that time, I had one degree from Mexico and was working on my MA at the University of Calgary, and for that reason I had felt superior to those around me, and I had felt mistreated by a system that had me working for a lowly wage even though I had more education than most people. I felt shame when I heard his story because I had imagined him as less educated than me. I felt shame because I was faced with my prejudices. I still feel shame because I don't remember his name, and this forgetting is not simply due to time (this happened after all decades ago), but due to my listening and mnemonic limitations.

The material social life of indexes is often in conditions of copresence, and thus the need to reflect on inscription by our senses and memory. But the material social life of indexes is also shaped by history and politics. To make sense of the unnaming and renaming that migrants often undergo, one must understand these processes as embedded in particular histories. It matters that Mexican immigrants, subjects of the cultural and economic empire that is the United States, are forced to renounce their names in order to be accepted. It matters that Chinese migrants were first forced labor to the United States. It matters than when Japan was an enemy of the United States in World War II, Japanese Americans suffered pressure to change their names. It matters that migrants from Vietnam or Korea after painful wars adopted measures including naming that would make their past partly invisible.

Sounds are also indexical archives that record historical and political patterns. In Spanish, names associated with femininity tend to have fewer "o" sounds and more "a" sounds. In English, names with "ie" sounds, such as Maggie, Trixie, Barbie, are associated with younger women. We sometimes take joy mispronouncing some names and use this mispronunciation as a power game. For roughly a decade I lived in Austin, Texas, and one of the most important streets in the city is called Guadalupe, a name that is sacred to Mexicans and Mexican Americans, for it is the name of the most important figure in Mexican Catholicism, "la Virgen de Guadalupe." Austinites seem to take particular joy in butchering this name, and I always found it interesting that the same people who would secretly laugh at those mispronouncing the word *croissant* would have no problem mispronouncing *Guadalupe*. Power games.

In day-to-day interactions, our bodies function as substrata for categorical indexes. We are racialized because of our color, judged attractive because of our weight or height, deemed sexed because of our body features, and judged elegant because of our gait. Our bodies are thus indexical archives too, and they are key to establishing what we mean to others and to ourselves. The hermeneutics of embodied indexes are longer than history, as Darwinian doxa would have us believe. The myth and/or science of the "survival of the fittest" is nothing but the expression of the eugenicist impulse at the heart of humanity, an impulse made action by way of the interpretation of body signs, first, in the relative and cruel candor of the signs of health (who is the strongest or the fastest or the smartest?) and, second, in the perturbing discourse of social potential (who can live the easiest in this society?). Our bodies are texts advertising health or prospects, and most decisions associated with body lore, from the fetish of muscle strength (even in a society of machines) to the fetish of skin color in multiracial societies, are a testament to the importance of body inscription and its accompanying hermeneutics. Inscribed in our art (from pre-Columbian sculptures of women in childbirth to Michelangelo's *David*), and perhaps even in our genes, we see a human history that has depended on the cultural interpretation of embodied indexes to determine identity and value.

In all these instances, the materiality of inscription, which depends on particular infrastructures, allows for the recording, reproduction, and processing of indexes (Bowker and Star 1999, 33). A trace cannot exist without substrata; the clay that captures the footprint is as essential as the foot that pressed the clay. Indexes and inscription are entwined. This entwinement follows material logics. However, processes of deferral are also processes of reinscription and thus rematerialization. A clay footprint may be photographed and printed on paper; the photograph may be digital and recorded as a digital index; and so on.

While not everything can be digitized, current technology allows for the digitalization of almost every index, and this means that the materiality of digital indexes has gained enormous importance. Yet, digital indexes represent further analytic complications because these indexes are imprinted alongside metadata, and thus, they never sit alone. Imagine a footprint recorded in a clay patch that automatically stores the identity of the person whose foot was imprinted, the type of shoe the person used, the time that the footprint was recorded, and that gives us the clues as to how to find more traces like this and link them together. The materiality of digital indexes is not simply entwined with the index: It is entwined with a host of other capacities, including the capacities to become memory, calculation, and theorization. In addition, digital indexes can be endlessly reproduced, stored, and inserted in different interpretation schemas, as when personal data of one digital purchase is used to infer future shopping preferences of the user. For these reasons, digital indexes, again, pose different questions about materiality, including questions pertaining to the boundary between the material and technological, the archival and theoretical, and embodiment and indexes.

The materiality of indexical inscription is grounds for common forms of anonymity, indexical dissociation, but the process of crossing borders is also one that renders bodies into data, into digital indexes of many sorts. Today's migrants in the United States face a border logic of securitization and militarization that has escalated since 9/11. Elsewhere I have shown (Amaya 2013) that these terrorist events became grounds for this escalation:

> With political maneuverings that marked the betrayal of the 9/11 victims, nativist politicians used the attacks on the Twin Towers and the Pentagon to engage in a political and legal war against undocumented immigrants in general and Latin American immigrants in particular. Citing border-security concerns, these politicians pushed for the further militarization of the border with Mexico. The four-thousand-mile Canadian border, huge and porous and patrolled by less than 7 percent of the Border Patrol personnel, never became the issue. It was always the border with Mexico, already militarized thanks to the successive presidencies of Reagan, Bush, and Clinton, which would receive the bulk of the new discursive and economic resources to stop all crossings. The Bush administration militarized the very institutions in charge of immigration, refranchising the Immigration and Naturalization Service (INS) into the Immigration, Customs, and Enforcement (ICE) under the securitizing umbrella of the Department of Homeland Security (DHS). (71–72)

Nativist discourse after 9/11, which has escalated during Donald Trump's ascendency in politics, normalizes the perception that immigrants from Latin America pose a risk to the security of the nation, and this risk discourse routinely dehumanizes.

Part of this dehumanization is to make all immigrants subject to risk assessment for they/we represent risk, not life, and, because of this, the migrant must be anonymized, deprived of the complexities of life, identity, and embodiment. Louise Amoore (2006) writes about the same escalation and risk logic as follows: "The authority of risk profiling in the war on terror precisely relies upon the representation of a world that would be safer if only ambiguity, ambivalence and uncertainty could be controlled" (338). The immigrant becomes understood through the logic of risk, and the job of state agencies is to determine a risk profile that makes the immigrants unambiguous, subject to calculation and state actions. She continues: "In effect, the place of science and technology in fighting the war on terror is ever more secured if we overstate the coherence of the grip it has on life itself" (338). In her work, and in the work of others interested in the militarization and securitization of the border between Mexico and the United States, risk will be managed through the development and deployment of unprecedented technologies of inscription and surveillance. These include electronic fingerprints, facial and gait recognition, and iris scans (342).

Another layer of securitization, explored at length in Iván Chaar López's (2024) work, is less about biometrics than about bodies, and these include intrusion detector sensors and drones that are tasked with automatically detecting and identifying whether bodies in the vast expanse of the border between Mexico and the United States are those of animals or humans and, if humans, of intruders (8). These technologies, which sometimes rely on heat sensors, are the ultimate anonymizing technology. Humans become red flashes on a dark screen, but in the context of the border, the red flashes become anonymous invaders that need stopping.

The war on terror has been partly fought with biometrics (Amoore's argument), and the ongoing colonization of process that normalizes jurisdictional logics over bodies and surveillance systems (López's argument) has rendered migrants into datafied bodies conceptualized by theories of intrusion. In this process of indexicalization, the migrant becomes subject to risk assessment and profiling, and the migrant's indexes become subject to theorizations and analyses to make migrants predictable and accountable. The desired outcome of these theorizations is to be able to sort migrants into categories like legitimate (business, tourist, leisure, and so on) and illegitimate traveler (terrorist, trafficker, immigrant, and so on) that can thus activate specific security protocols for specific individuals. Lives lose individuality; life becomes anonymized by erasing anything that cannot be sorted, categorized, and made accountable to specific relational protocols. These protocols will dictate who is welcome and who will be placed in highly constraining situations, including temporary detention and imprisonment. All categorizing anonymizes because categories, by definition, are meant to treat us as sets, groups, not as individuals. But risk categories are some of the most reductive; so much life cannot fit into risk logics. One social media link, one streaming of a documentary, one text to someone who texted someone considered a terrorist, and an individual becomes riskier to the eyes of the state. The rest of life is thrown away.

But the rest of life cannot be thrown away; even if surveilling institutions tend to be reductive, life is irreducible to any one aspect, and the surveilled are aware of that. People, and migrants are no exception, belong simultaneously to several categories; they lead a complex life with multiple social roles that blur the line between who is welcome and who is not, between rights and obligation. Such complexity is captured by Asad L. Asad in his book *Engage and Evade* (2023), who demonstrates the "prudence" of undocumented immigrants with US citizen children in navigating institutional surveillance (15). He shows the double-edginess of surveillance "dangling the threat of societal exclusion alongside the promise of inclusion" (13), a double-edginess that undocumented immigrant parents, themselves doubly categorized as undocumented noncitizens and as citizens' parents, manage by simultaneously evading it for fear of deportation and engaging with it in hope of future inclusion in society. Knowing that "their attitudes, behaviors, and transactions are on full display," while also recognizing that "authorities lack the resources to evaluate them as whole people in any one interaction," they exploit what Asad describes as a mutuality of surveillance in which the surveilled immigrants exhibit agency, though restricted, by themselves surveilling the "laws, regulations, and policies that these authorities enforce" (18). Through this mutual surveillance, they enact their own risk assessment to inscribe their own records. They engage in "selective engagement" (20) with the surveilling institutions "depending on where they are being watched, who is watching them, and what is at stake" (18) to generate their records, a material inscription. Aiming to avoid exclusion and hoping for future inclusion, they create a paper trail that would maximize benefits while minimizing risks, records that show that their law-abiding qualities outweigh their immigration status. This perpetual maneuver is indispensable for someone embodying and aligning with the expectations of multiple, sometimes conflicting, social roles, someone navigating a precarious legal status that necessitates institutional evasion and the duties of parenthood that necessitate institutional engagement. This multiplicity of life, this irreducibility, and their awareness of it, grant those undocumented immigrants a fractured agency to tread the blurry lines of their differential categorical indexes.

However, this complexity, as shown previously, is lost on some of the technologies employed by the surveillance apparatus. From the perspective of corporations like Accenture, which sells biometric systems to the US government in general and US Customs and Border Protection (CBP) in order to construct what Amoore calls the biometric border, and Anduril Industries, which sells the drone and sensor system Lattice to the US Department of Homeland Security (DHS), the challenge is to identify sensorial technologies that can capture unique elements of human bodies that can then become concrete indexes to be added to databases crucial to advanced analytics and predictive models. The goal is not simply to identify but to understand the individual. For this reason, what Accenture has been selling to DHS and CBP is a biometric *and* biographic identity management system that helps border agents and customs officers determine who can enter, who can remain, or who needs to be detained or denied access (Lynch 2012). What begins at the level of the materiality of our faces (crucial for visual recognition), our fingers (for fingerprints), or our eyes (iris recognition), and the sensors that translate these materials into traces (cameras, scanners), ends up in databases that connect to other databases with the goal of painting a biographical picture of who we truly are. Travelers in general, and migrants in particular, are subject to systematic identification, and one cannot go through the process of migrating without accepting the inscription regimes that CBP and DHS have made normal.

Writing Technologies and the Anonymized Immigrant

The Anglo-centrism of US administrative practices is manifested in the writing technologies that function as the primary means to inscribe immigrants into official records. These writing technologies include alphabets, typewriters, keyboards, and also policies or practices that normalize some ways of writing over others. Together, these writing technologies constitute and reproduce Anglo-centric practices within the agencies, institutions, and bureaucracies, and here I focus on two particular writing technologies that shape naming practices: Anglo-centric keyboards, which are used in practically every instance when a migrant encounters state institutions; and institutional policies and practices that marginalize or proscribe the use of diacritics, which is a way of marginalizing the languages used by the great majority of migrants to the United States (e.g., Spanish, Chinese, Korean, Tagalog, Arab). These Anglo-centric writing technologies are forms of political power that participate in the constitution of the immigrant subject as a subaltern, which is why they matter. Importantly, this power is exercised over names, by dissociating, decentering, or erasing non-Anglo forms of personal identification.

Writing technologies have always shaped writing, and, for this reason, writing technologies have shaped storytelling, history, culture, and administration, the very logic of governance. Sometimes, the power of writing technologies is in the very materiality of writing, and alphabetical writing is a great example of this connection. For centuries now, alphabetic writing has been inscribed on paper, the substratum that allows for indexical archives to exist. Writing was done only by hand in the European context until the fifteenth century. Before, writing as a social tool was carried out by scribes who were highly regarded professionals capable of clearly and often beautifully replicating text. With the advent of the printing press, the writing technology added technical and material layers, including the skill and craft of the printer, the quality of the types and press, and the quality of the paper used. The relative centralization of printing meant the increasing standardization of spelling, syntax, and inflection and made it natural to regard some sounds and some letters as belonging to the nation. As Friedrich Kittler (1999) states, “It is no accident that the invention of the printing press coincides with the inception of the modern period” (199). In this understated way, he replicated what Francis Bacon had argued about revolutionary technologies, which included gunpowder, the nautical compass, and the printing press. As I noted before, Eisenstein (2012) shows with a great deal of detail what Bacon and Kittler imagined or inferred. The emergence of the printing press constituted print cultures that would revolutionize knowledge distribution and production. What we have come to recognize as early modernity, the rise of a new intellectual, political, and religious order in Europe in the sixteenth century, can be attributed to printing, which facilitated the rise of national languages, diminished the power of Latin and thus the Catholic Church, and helped the dissemination of revolutionary knowledges, including the writings of Martin Luther, who published his *Ninety-Five Theses* on October 31, 1517. Only seventeen days later this broadsheet was published in London. And, as the saying goes, the rest is history.

Kittler (1999) has argued that the typewriter transformed writing partly because it constituted a space in between hand and paper, a space occupied by a machine that makes writing a technological artifice and desensualizes writing. A series of inventions for roughly a century, the typewriter enters the social unconscious after Remington, typically in the industry of war, releases in 1881 what would become a bestseller. The world changed. In 1870, in the United States, there were 154 typists, and almost 95 percent were men, who had followed the gendered tradition of clerking with typing. But the Remington changed things. As Martin Lyons (2021) notes, the universe of typist grew exponentially, and by 1930, there were more than eight hundred thousand typists and more than 95 percent of them were women. The typewriter transformed writing and inserted a gendered machine in the middle and a new cog in the industrialization and bureaucratization of the world.

As James Beniger (1986) shows, the typewriter joined telegraphy, rotary power printing, the transatlantic cable, the telephone, motion pictures, and the radio as the technological basis of the information society that within the span of a century transformed the world (7). Besides writing itself, the typewriter transformed bureaucracies. It is perhaps unsurprising that the rise of the information society, the century of statistics, and modern governmentality happened roughly at the same time, aided by the massification of technologies like the typewriter, which made possible the creation and reproduction of ever more records. What in Foucault's work is the centering of knowledge of the population as the defining characteristic of modern governmentality, in Beniger and Kittler's work is partly the implementation and massification of record-keeping technologies like the typewriter and, later, the keyboard. And the records that these technologies kept were often population records and individual records: indexes, in the abstract form of statistics; indexes, in categorical form like labor, health, and class; and indexes in the concrete form of debtors, managers, and worker roles.

Writing technologies like the typewriter and, later, the keyboard, have specific linguistic logics that typically match a nation's linguistic identity and corporate preferences. When Remington created the typewriter, the instrument was designed to mechanize writing in English and the keys translated that logic. Over the course of decades, Remington and other makers of typewriters created machines for specific languages. For Latin America and Spain, machines routinely included the letter "ñ," and many others introduced the innovation of dead keys, which marked but did not advance the paper and thus allowed for diacritics like accents, the circumflex, the grave, the tilde, or the overdots to add linguistic possibilities to typewriters without adding too many more keys.

This means that the typewriter and later the keyboard have had the potential to be multilinguistic writing inscription systems (even if bound by the Latin alphabet) but rarely have been used like that in US administration.[2] The reasons are partly the machines but also widespread practices and policies. For instance, diacritic marks are not supported in some federal documents, including passports. This means that at minimum, most migrants from Latin America, and many from Europe and the Middle

East, will lose part of their names that lend aural specificity and national specificity.

In the state of California, diacritics have been banned from official documents since 1986, when Proposition 63 was passed. This proposition made English the official language of the state and passed with one of the biggest margins of victory (73.25 percent versus 26.75 percent). As in other parts of the nation at the time, Proposition 63 was part of the mainstreaming of nativism, which used Anglo-centrism as one of its most successful platforms (Tatalovich 1995). Since then, diacritics have been excised from official documents, including birth certificates, driver's licenses, and others. At the moment of this writing, the California State Legislature is contemplating a new state bill (AB77) that would again allow for the use of diacritics in official documents like birth certificates, death certificates, and others. AB77 was introduced by representative Blanca Pacheco of California's 64th district as a way of franchising migrants like her parents who, from Mexico, never got to see their names spelled correctly. AB77 would also franchise immigrants from Vietnam, France, Germany, Turkey, and the Middle East (De La Fe 2023).

The failure to honor language specificity of individuals residing in places like California has anonymizing effects because it erases heritage and identity. Nancy Chaires Espinoza and Pablo Espinoza, who are Nicolás's parents and the inspiration behind Pacheco's AB77, have declared that their son Nicolás needs the diacritics, the accent, as a way of indicating the correct pronunciation of his name but also to mark his deep connection to Mexico and Ecuador, the places where Nancy and Pablo were born. The diacritic is thus part of the story that Nicolás's name tells others about who he is, and without it, his parents imply, Nicolás's story would be incomplete.

The erasure of diacritics, and the anonymizing it produces, is carried out also by other important institutions that manage knowledge systems. One of the most important of these institutions is the American Library Association, which does not recognize diacritics and has, for this reason, failed since its origins to properly name, catalogue, and thus serve the intellectual work of authors, creators, and historical figures from other linguistic traditions. Laura Langberg (2020) shows how this English-centrism is inscribed in libraries across the nation, creating barriers to finding work by many authors:

> Several months ago, in a meeting, a coworker brought up an issue she had noticed when searching for Spanish-language materials in our catalog—words with diacritics appeared incorrectly, though inconsistently so. For example, the author of the book *Aristotle and Dante Discover the Secrets of the Universe* appears in the catalog as Saaenz, Benjamin Alire; Saenz, Benjamin Alire; and Sáenz, Benjamin Alire. These results are not interchangeable; typing "Saenz" into the catalog will yield results for Saenz and Sáenz but will exclude anything found under Saaenz. This is troubling for several reasons. First and foremost, it renders many items unfindable. Who will think to keyword search for Saaenz, or espaanol (which yields 465 results in the catalog), or Maarquez (71 results)? If items cannot be found through the catalog, they are only findable by physically browsing the stacks. This decreases circulation and leads to prematurely weeding these items from the library. Additionally, by allowing words to be misspelled and therefore unfindable in our catalog, we are sending the message that words and names that are not English are not important. (19)

As an author, I can assure you that there is no greater damage to my career prospects than to be invisible and thus discardable, the two outcomes that Langberg mentions are inevitable when diacritics are proscribed. Authors are made invisible, erased from the record, uncitable, and, thus, forgettable, which makes the intellectual history of the nation and the world as represented in our library catalogues misshapen by Anglo-centrism.

Langberg reminds us that this failure of the library system has been perpetuated in the computer era, even though barriers are increasingly minimal given the astronomical growth of computing and database capacity. Encoding standards, in other words, continue being used to reconstitute these Anglo-centric practices. The standard coding system used by library systems is the old code ASCII (American Standard Code for Information Interchange), which has 256 characters. These include letters of the English alphabet and some codes to improve transliteration, but other languages than English were largely ignored (Langberg 2020, 21). In the last few years, Unicode, which seems compatible with ASCII and supports more characters, has added characters including emojis and bidirectional formatting. But library systems still cannot recognize the "ñ." "By not fully adopting an encoding standard which recognizes the languages our patrons speak and request materials in, we are sending the message that their needs and the materials they request are less important than those of English speakers" (21). The problem also affects academic careers in the United States and abroad. The unwillingness to inscribe diacritics in libraries reproduces an intellectual history that privileges the contributions of Anglo writers, securing citational practices that marginalize non-Anglo academics in the United States by unfairly ballooning the citations of Anglo authors and securing they have greater impact and reputation.

Writing systems are part of the administrative decisions and structures that force migrants into changing their names, and if the issue is clear with diacritics, it is even clearer when transliteration from languages like Chinese is a first step into being "marked" as legible in US bureaucracies. In all of these cases, writing systems operate not only as inscription technologies but also as border techniques meant to translate an individual into a subaltern subject, marginalized often by race and ethnicity, but one that is willing to comply to radical personal changes in order to reduce the risk projection to others. These writing systems are a material part of the borderlands, that space in-between that Gloria Anzaldúa describes as situated in between two realities that compelled identity transformations (see Chapter 1). The ones I describe here are, however, outside the purview of control of individuals involved in the bordering process. Neither the migrant nor border officers or border workers can change anything about the way writing systems operate. Indexical dissociation is baked in, decided as normal and desirable, embedded in the material technologies and writing systems, and outside the reach of the migrant and other users. The outcome of indexical dissociation, and the particular type of anonymizing this dissociation produces, is predetermined. The bordering system is many things, including a system that speaks and does it clearly in English: If you wish to keep your name, or have your name written and pronounced in the right way, or have your name represented in systems of knowledge like the library system, don't come. We don't want you. On the other hand, if you are willing to give up name, race, history, and nationality, if you are willing to plead fealty to the nation, to English, every time you use your anglicized name, we want you.

Anonymizing Forms

Name changes happen for many reasons, but a significant subset of changes are reactions to or forced by technologies of inscription that the immigrants encounter throughout all the bureaucratic processes of bordering. These reasons include the nature of the forms an individual has to fill out to produce a file that the US government will need to keep track of the migrant. Jon Agar (2016) researches "the file," which is one of the most important and ubiquitous technologies of inscription in modernity. To him, the file is an informational technology that is material, stores and organizes information, and is designed in such a way as to be part of a system or registry. The file has a form, and this form structures the encounter between the file creator and file user. What is standard in a file is often part of a rule system, and the rules are often derived from what is standard in a file.

This does not mean that forms do the power work they do without the individuals that use them. Forms shape, but their lasting impact is in the coming together of the form with the bureaucrat or individual filling out the form. The bureaucrat may make mistakes due to ignorance, laziness, lack of training, or prejudice. I introduced Anzaldúa in previous chapters to clarify the liminal and subjective work of indexicalization and of anonymity. Her work has inspired many to research and theorize migration processes. Moreover, her own biography offers a lived account of them. Diana Martínez (2022), in researching through Anzaldúa's papers, found the following:

> Anzaldúa's original birth certificate is rife with errors. It gives a different spelling of Anzaldúa's name. Whether this was the name her mother chose or a clerical error is unclear. Instead of Gloria Evangelina Anzaldúa, her name reads as "Eve Angeline Anzaldua." There is no street or number listed in the section designated for the mother's residence; it notes only that her mother resided in Hargill, Hidalgo County, Texas. The response to the question "Legitimate?" is "YES." Her parents' genders are reversed on the document, and their names are misspelled. Instead of Urbano, the certificate reads "URBANA." Likewise, her mother's full maiden name reads "AMALIO ANZALDUA." Not only is her mother's name misspelled—it should be correctly spelled "Amalia"—her maiden name was not Anzaldúa. At Gloria's birth, her father was twenty-three and her mother was sixteen. Anzaldúa was born in Raymondville, Texas, and the Department of Health Bureau of Vital Statistics received the document on November 4, 1942. (37)

Martínez details a huge number of errors in this relatively simple form meant to set the institutional stage for Anzaldúa's biography. These errors were absurd and include mistakes in the very name Anzaldúa (which include the lack of diacritics), mistaking the name and gender of the parents, and failing to write down the address where she grew up.

While I noted earlier that sometimes state bureaucrats (border agents, border workers, city workers) have little control over inscription systems, this example shows that these workers are themselves cogs in the machinery of inscription. The person who wrote down the data necessary for Anzaldúa's birth certificate in Texas was uninterested or unprepared to do the job, and the errors that Martínez notes are closer to the types of errors people complained about at Ellis Island. Here, however, we have evidence that naming changes were sometimes at the hands of state bureaucrats. I begin this section with this example to show that forms play a significant role in properly identifying individuals. I use the term "properly" to highlight the fact that forms reconstitute hegemonic ways of classifying humans. That is, individuals are identified not based on reality but based on how reality has been "formatted" by inscription systems.

The adoption or imposition of new names on immigrants does not happen typically at the border or at points of entry. Most name changes happen after arrival, and, when formalized, they become so in processes of naturalization. But they continue happening even after. Let's not forget that Anzaldúa was born in Texas. Let's not forget that laws about diacritics are experienced by immigrant communities as onomastic coercion. Étienne Balibar (2002) has noted the following: "The borders of new politico-economic entities . . . are no longer at all situated at the outer limit of territories: they are dispersed a little everywhere, wherever the movement of information, people, and things is happening and is controlled" (71). I would add to this spatial logic a temporal one. Bordering does not end at crossing. It can continue over generations, as Anzaldúa's case illustrates. Amoore (2006) writes the same: "Read in this way the border becomes a condition of being that is always in the act of becoming, it is never entirely crossed, but appears instead as a constant demand for proof of status and legitimacy" (348).

Migrants' naming practices are shaped not only when migrating but also if they have children and have to adopt naming practices that fit the cultural, regulatory, and epistemological expectations of birth certificates, as in Anzaldúa's case. As a file, birth certificates are issued by states. In mine, in California, a state where 28 percent of residents are foreign born, and where 40 percent of Californians are Latine and 15 percent are Asian American and Pacific Islander, birth certificate forms do some of the work of normalizing Anglo naming practices and making these official (Johnson et al. 2025). The California birth certificate, like Form I-485, is a specific type of file designed to become part of a registry in the State of California. A birth certificate has fields for state file number, local registration district and certificate number; for naming, it has the same Anglo standard fields, first name, middle name, and last or family name; sex (boy or girl); date of birth; hour of birth; place of birth; name of father and mother and the birth dates of both mother and father; address of parents; and so on. This form—this certificate—is in possession of the state and of the parents. Parents are obligated to use this form for all sorts of purposes, and at each instance the field's information becomes active and transfers, moves from this file to another, the name of the child and parents, the date of birth, their sex, and other genealogical information.

The birth certificate form alludes to a bureaucracy (i.e., local registration district, organized numerically) as a set of offices and districts that could connect to the birth certificate, where the original of the form would be archived and would give the form its official character. The form can then become part of a registry where that certificate would join millions to show a population as an aggregate of concrete individuals. The form is also part of reproducing heteronormative ideas of childbearing and family. It asks for the child's sex and thus expected an official medicalized interpretation of physiognomy (that is, a penis; that is, a vagina), and that official pronouncement of male or female becomes attached to the body of the child, like an appendix, marking but not fully certifying gender and sexuality. Dimorphic heteronormativity is reified by the two gendered fields designed to record the name of the mother and the father. These two fields act as implicit arguments in favor of heteronormativity as they make it impossible to declare any other type of gender or sexual combination.

As lasting as forms can be, they are also sites of struggle, and people try to correct them in order to be properly indexed. The legislation that Representative Pacheco is trying to pass, AB77, which would make diacritics legal in California again, began with parents who wanted to name their newborn child Nicolás Agustín but discovered that the state would not allow the diacritics. Their fight is about fixing the rules by which birth certificates are completed, which would also give the opportunity to others to "fix" their birth certificates and officially embrace their real names. In Anzaldúa's case, her name was misspelled until she was thirty. Her grandmother, Martínez tells us, corrected the name from Eve Angeline to Gloria Angelina, but she did a second correction. She "also altered the race category from 'Mexican' to 'white'" (37). Perhaps out of care, trying to protect her from racism, Anzaldúa's grandmother also erased her Mexican and Indigenous heritage. Forms speak, but they do not speak only reality. They speak the ideology of the state and at times also the ideological struggles of those who use them.

In this way, autobiography is a contested space even for the subject.

Diana Martínez (2022) writes: "Anzaldúa kept all versions of the birth certificate, creating her own personal archive. Together they create a new text that performs outside the role of official documentation, serving to bring together aspects of her identity across time and space. . . . However, as I examined the documents, I felt that Anzaldúa's voice was 'missing.' She did not go in and fix the errors; her grandmother made the changes" (38). Martínez continues by pointing out that Anzaldúa did, however, write a short story that uses the autobiographical to illustrate the difficulties she experienced with her name.

In this short story, Prieta is in her first day of school, surrounded by English, a language she does not speak:

> She notices cues and determines that the teacher is calling roll because, when the students around her catch their name, they respond. Prieta gets in trouble for not hearing—or rather, not knowing—her name. Her family's reliance on her nickname, "Prieta" or "Prietita," makes it impossible for her to know her official name, "Gloria." She is unable to explain that she goes by "Prieta," and as a result, the teacher punishes Prieta for misbehaving. The story continues with a lapse in time: an older Prieta explains the confusion with her name and the changes made to her birth certificate. The tone of the story shifts; she clarifies that her name is the basis of her awareness and power. (39–40)

As Martínez shows, Anzaldúa uses this story to theorize her own relationship to her name, and the awareness, reflexivity, and agency of the child at the center of the story represent that agency and reflexivity that Anzaldúa in general locates in migrants. In this case, forms present an acknowledged problem that fuels the mistakes by a teacher who has a name in her roster, another form, that has no referent in the real. Martínez also notes how the very materiality of these interactions between subjects and indexes constitutes the space of struggle that Anzaldúa tries to understand. The form, and its solidity, is made worse by a teacher who cannot speak Spanish and cannot pronounce the name in front of her. Even when Prieta understands the error and learns to say "present!" when her official name is called, she still has difficulties with her teacher's accent and often cannot hear her name and continues being punished. Forms, materiality, and writing technologies, all together, are technologies of inscription that determine a person's relationship to the state but also a person's relationship to bureaucracies, to their peers, and to themselves.

What characterizes Form I-485 and California's birth certificates is common among most technologies of inscription and corroborates what Agar, among others, proposes. A technology of inscription is material; it depends on writing technologies, forms, shaped by informal and formal policies, and knowledge systems. I have shown that each of the constitutive elements of a technology of inscription (a technology's materiality, formality, and registry system) has the potential to transform the names of individuals migrating or has the ability to push individuals to change their names on their own volition.

Inscription, in other words, constitutes indexical dissociation and produces types of anonymity among migrants that have lasting effects. We, migrants, are partly disconnected from our past, our history, our linguistic traditions and forced into forms of reinvention that may carry benefits but also mark many of us as perpetual subalterns. But the goal of this chapter was also to explore what I mean by the economy of anonymity, and the case of migrants offers a revealing example of how this economy of anonymity functions and how it is transforming. Technologies of inscription tell us some of this story.

Migrating involves at least two processes of indexicalization and multiple technologies of inscription. One of these processes, exemplified here by naming changes and other types of cataloguing that try to make immigrants from the Global South "legible" to the hegemon, normalizes indexical dissociation. In this exchange, to use economic terms, the new arrival agrees or is compelled by inscription technologies (which include aural and mnemonic perceptual mechanisms) to change some aspects of their names (diacritics) or acquire new ones. When people pronounce my name "Hector" in English, as opposed to "Héctor" in Spanish (and, yes, the "h" is 100 percent silent), I do not correct them. When my colleague born in

East Asia adopts a nickname common in the Anglo name catalogue to present themselves to others in daily interactions, without giving up their legal name, they have, as I have, acquiesced to the change in the spirit of making daily life easier. This does not mean that we are okay in general with giving up or changing our names but understand this as a trade-off, and migration is all about trade-offs.

This process of indexicalization, which involves anonymizing, is inscribed in aural form, has mnemonic outcomes, and is long lasting. The bordering process does not end with naturalization; it happens in every social interaction where the judgment of kin or foreign is at stake. And, in my experience, this happens numerous times daily. The bordering process is not only characterized by interactions with state agents, though these matter a lot; the bordering process is part of every social interaction in which epistemic credibility, using Alcoff's (2007) term, is at stake. Anzaldúa's short story is a clear example in which the bordering process is carried out in schools and a case in which the epistemic credibility of the child, Prieta/Gloria, was shaped by the teacher's ideas about race and ethnicity.

The second type of indexicalization involved in migrating and bordering is clearly a top-down process that exacts radical forms of surveillance over the bodies of migrants. CBP and DHS have made sure that migrants have as little access as possible to anonymity by attaching border logics to our bodies. What Amoore (2006) calls the biometric border signals the turn to digital technologies and inscription regimes, but also a particular "exercise of biopower such that the body itself is inscribed with, and demarcates, a continual crossing of multiple encoded borders" (337). Our bodies are inscribed with border logics; they become part of the circuitry of surveillance that complements the sensorial systems, the cameras and scanners, that will trigger specific state actions based on the logic of risk prediction. While migrants have some agency in the previous model of indexicalization, in this one, we have none. We are not subjects; we are objects to be surveilled, understood, theorized, and, always, contained.

Mitchell Dean (2010), a scholar of governmentality, may call "assemblages" what I here call the "economy of anonymity." We would both agree that these economies or assemblages are more complex than having or not having anonymity. The two types of indexicalization I have presented here, with an emphasis on technologies of inscription, are part of the same economy of anonymity or assemblage. They show that economies of anonymity are not simply distribution systems but constitutive systems. They exist always in the dialectic of identification and anonymity, the two forces that constitute identity at any given time. Yet, against Dean (2010), I also show the benefits of attending to "the divisions between state and civil society and between public and private spheres" (37) and have tracked down identificatory complexities that exist in private spheres, at the level of the self and subject, while connecting these to what Dean calls "the routines of bureaucracy; the technologies of notation, recording, compiling, presenting and transporting of information, the theories, programmes, knowledge and expertise that compose a field to be governed and invest it with purposes and objectives; the ways of seeing and representing embedded in practices of government; and the different agencies with various capacities that the practices of government require, elicit, form and reform" (37).

In current socio-technical regimes, an economy of anonymity and migration is characterized by a radical asymmetry (and for this, the term "economy" is more useful than "assemblage"). A person's agency is harnessed to the project of hegemonic construction at the same time that biometric and cybernetic borders make sure the migrant is always already treated within the grammar of risk. Amoore (2006) writes it beautifully: "I have argued that the biometric border signals a dual move in the contemporary politics of the war on terror: a significant turn to scientific and managerial techniques in governing the mobility of bodies; and an extension of biopower such that the body, in effect, becomes the carrier of the border as it is inscribed with multiple encoded boundaries of access" (347–48). The technologies of inscription used in these surveillance processes inscribe bodies into legible risk narratives that determine who crosses, who is detained, who is stopped, and who can continue. Much like I argue about how our senses and mnemonics constitute a grammar that cannot attend to the real, these processes cannot see the real migrants nor understand them.

Six

Unnaming, Renaming, and the Economy of Anonymity

Names matter. Sojourner Truth helps us see how much they matter with a few words describing why she adopted her name and what her birth name meant to her:

> I had my freedom, my freedom had me. I know freedom made me change, but I needs a new name now. Isabella don't fit me no more, so I asked God to name me. The Lord gave me "Sojourner," because I was to travel up an' down the land, showin' the people their sins an' bein' a sign unto them. Afterwards, I told the Lord I wanted another name 'cause everybody else had two names, and the Lord gave me "Truth," because I was to declare the truth to people. (Truth qtd. in Stowe, 1863)

Indexical dissociation also matters. Yet, names have a complex relationship to anonymity. In many cases related to women from the nineteenth century, anonymity was the technique that allowed authors to publish. In these cases, names given at birth needed to be hidden for these women to be able to share their art and ideas. Truth, however, reminds us that names given at birth do not necessarily or simply represent us. Names given at birth can have anonymizing effects. In her case, the name Isabella Bomfree was her slave name, and this name made invisible her inner freedom. It made her discountable, an object, chattel, and only through an act of self-creation that included removing a birth name could a new name represent her as a free individual (Emmelhainz 2012; Piepmeier 2004, 127). Names, like other natural language indexes including sex, gender, race, and ethnicity, have the capacity to point but also to give meaning to the person or to the body. For that reason, names (and other natural language indexes) shape identity and can be central to existing in nepantla, in the in-between that Gloria Anzaldúa theorizes as a birthing space (see Chapter 1). Truth illustrates this birthing process, the importance names have in it, and the fact that reinvention is often connected to pain and forms of subjugation organized around ascriptive characteristics like race, ethnicity, gender, sex, and nationality (see also Bering 1992).

The previous chapter showed how technologies of inscription shape asymmetries in the economy of anonymity. This chapter shows how a single but rich and complex type of concrete index, the personal name, gives form to specific features of the economy of anonymity, to the way anonymity is distributed, used, and placed in hierarchical, oppressive, agentic, and traditional social arrangements. The chapter also models research on the economy of anonymity by showing a methodological approach anchored on the following axiom: *An economy of anonymity depends on economies of identification, on the way identifiers are used to shape the social and individuals.* This is so because both anonymity and identification are particular manifestations of indexicalization, the cultural technique and nepantla *dispositif* that produces or manifests possible variations rooted in the indexical, two of which are anonymity and identification (see Chapter 1). That anonymity depends on identification is clearer with natural language indexes like names, races, ethnicities, genders, and so on. With this category of indexes, indexical dissociation is much more than misidentification. As Truth reminds us, indexes like names give us meaning. Analyzing an economy of anonymity from the perspective of an index like names should reveal more than a network of indexes. It should reveal a world textured by the semiotic and cultural richness of those indexes.

When I argue that an economy of anonymity depends on economies of identification, I am arguing that anonymity uses the same sociotechnical locations that give life to an economy of identification. Because books require identifiable authors, they can be used by anonymous authors. Because bodies "should" present gender, they can be used to generate dissociation from gender categories. Not all forms of identification (e.g., DNA) give space for dissociations, which means that the density of an economy of identification is greater than the density of an economy of anonymity. But they both overlap. When anonymity is manifested, it is manifested on a location that makes identification, and disidentification, possible. This is why a first step toward understanding an economy of anonymity shaped by names is understanding naming practices. In particular, the chapter argues that the crucial element of naming that one must understand in order to make sense of anonymity is power or, better, the connection of naming to different articulations of power, subjugation, and identity.

Power in names is complex. Names acquire power within the context of signifying systems shaped by tradition and law, and at this level, the power of naming is of a word or words that give cultural and legal meaning to a person, to a body, and to the actions of that person and that body. As Truth clearly understands, *unnaming and renaming are also about the power of words to give meaning to a person and to a body in front of others and in front of the law.*

Names are complex also because they are one of the oldest indexes, the oldest markers that connect an individual to a sign or symbol. We probably had some version of names as soon as we, as a species, developed language. Naming has grown with humanity, and, unsurprisingly, naming practices are the richest indexes in terms of variability across time and across places. This richness is partly due to cultural variations between groups, particularly variations in language, political structure, kinship, family life, and tradition. But the richness of naming practices is also due to the fact that names are words and words have a huge array of possibilities for variation in meaning (Davies 2000, 16; Matthews and Hornblower 2000). One word can be joined with a second and create a new one, as in the portmanteau. The same occurs with names, as when *Child-* (fight, in Prankish) is joined with *Bert*- (bright) to create Childebert, an early Prankish royal name (Wilson 1998, 71). Names also invite different significations by way of connotation, metaphor, similes, and other literary tropes. Some names function as indexes and as metaphors or similes, as when a warrior is named Bear or a king Childebert; names also function as indexes that connote class, kinship, region, or ethnicity, and their signification is hardly exhausted by their connotative power. So, the richness of names is partly the richness of language, and the diversity of naming practices is partly the diversity of culture.

The power of names is not simply semantic. Names are given, acquired, or selected, and the processes that attach a name to a body are manifestations of power and identity, or power *in* identity. It matters whether a name is given as part of the birthing process, or in a traditional ceremony (e.g., the crowning of a queen or a king), or through marriage, or acquired as a part of a professional performance (e.g., stage names). Naming and renaming matter because each naming process means power. The power of naming, unnaming, and renaming is a social, political, and often legal power to vest others with meaning and to determine how those who are given names will be seen, interpreted, categorized, treated, and governed.

In the spirit of understanding the economy of identification that serves as ground to the economy of anonymity, the next section provides historical context for naming practices that can illuminate contemporary power relations in diverse nations like the United States. To me, this means addressing four things: naming in Europe (as many of our traditions are, due to colonialism, inherited), in the Americas, in US slave society, and in colonial settings, in particular the Spanish colonization of Mexico and the British colonization of the United States and Canada. This also means an expansion on how names operate as indexical materials shaped by particular technologies of inscription that produce contingent relational outcomes. The section will show that names do power work even when the individual is absent. Some of this power work is not rooted in the capacity of names to single out an individual but in the capacity of names to connect individuals to categories like gender, race, and ethnicity.

The last section examines five types of unnaming and renaming present in US society that have given form to the economy of anonymity: agentic dissociation, as in cases of anonymous women authors; forced dissociation, which I exemplify with naming practices common in slavery and those imposed on Indigenous communities in the United States and Canada; disciplinary indexical dissociation, which I illustrate with colonial practices in Mexico over Indigenous populations; traditional indexical dissociation, which I show in the context of First Nation practices in the Canadian West and marriage naming practices in coverture; and indexical dissociation as self-creation, which I show in relationship to contemporaries like Sojourner Truth but also sexual and gender minorities that seek new names that better describe who they are.

Naming Practices and the Index

As a general rule, naming systems and practices gain complexity as societies become more intricate. James Scott (1998) notes how little premodern states knew about the people they ruled over, and this lack of knowledge was proportional to the amount of information about the population states gathered, collected, and used (102). Clay tablets, like those used in Sumer, were expensive, needed a great deal of human and physical infrastructure to make them and keep them, and could hold relatively little information. This meant that fewer of these records could be kept, and since these records operated as knowledge about the economy and Sumerian subjects, relatively little was known. Scott also notes how much by comparison modern states know about their populations. By our modern standards, state power in the premodern was highly inefficient. But the evolution of the state has not been a teleological movement toward efficiency. Different states throughout history had different degrees of administrative sophistication, and, for this reason, it is wise to start a historical understanding of naming practices in Europe, even if the Sumerian example can powerfully set the tone. Ancient Rome, a centuries-long political formation, allows us to analyze the full arc of Western naming practices from traditional to administrative back to traditional.[1] Rome is also a useful reminder that Western naming practices today may change tomorrow, and, for all I know, tomorrow's naming practices may revert back to traditional ones.

The arc of naming practices is partly related to complexity. As ancient Rome gained in size, age, and political ambition from the Roman Kingdom (753–509 BC) toward the Roman Republic (509–27 BC), Romans, who had originally one name like most groups around them, adopted a second and later a third name.[2] The Roman Republic and later the Roman Empire (27 BC–AD 476) are associated with the famous *tria nomina*, the set of three names that included a given name (e.g., Gaius), a kinship name (Julius), and a nickname or epithet (Caesar). This practice became common at the height of the republic, the moment when the Roman state had grown in complexity, ambition, and population (Gavrielatos 2017, 155; Wilson 1998, 4). The *tria nomima* eased political tasks such as arranging elections, economic tasks such as taxation, and the military task of conscription. It also allowed for easier recognition in the city of Rome itself, which grew to one million inhabitants by the first century AD. In all of these cases, naming is central to the knowledge techniques required and used to operate, make feasible, and even make possible the Roman state. How could the state tax such a huge population without a way of distinguishing individuals on the tax rolls? During the Roman Republic, how could the state have a semblance of democracy without a way of identifying and recognizing individuals and their political rights? Who was a citizen? Who was not? How to keep track of the huge wealth extracted through wars of empire, and how to regulate an individual's obligations and hereditary rights without formal legal hereditary rules anchored on an identifier? Names are thus not simply a footnote in the history of state power. Names have always been a central technology of knowledge for state making and statecraft.

Rome offers other lessons about naming and power work. In Rome, names did more than allow the state to organize, administer, and control large populations. Names were also constitutive of social units of different scale and function and always essential to the marking of family kinship and family boundaries. Neither kin nor family can be historicized or theorized without attention to names. Second names in Rome, *gentilicium* or *gens*, constituted kinship structures, joining families for hereditary, religious, and political practices. One had the ethical obligation of helping one's kin marked by *gens*; one gained prestige or lost it thanks to their *gens*; one survived if the *gens* survived. Even in the late Roman Empire, the *tria nomina* was often abandoned for a single name, a patronymic transformation that reflected the weakening of old social organizations and that marked the rise of new power among new native groups in different regions of the empire.

Names also constitute the smallest social unit, one-on-one relationships. Roman citizens used their name to produce specific interactions with other citizens, as when patricians, long considered more powerful than the plebeians, used their *cognomen* (their third name, often a nickname) to mark status and impose respect (Gavrielatos 2017, 185). The *cognomen* was traditionally only a marker of the patriciate, and in formal occasions, during Cicero's time, aristocrats were addressed by *praenomen* plus *cognomen*, and by *cognomen* alone in informal occasions.

Names produced specific interactions in other ways too as in the way naming is partly constitutive of patriarchy. At the societal and state levels, patriarchy is manifested the clearest in patrilinear, agnatic relations, that is, on the ability given to males to reproduce their names and property relations through their offspring and the inability of women to do the same. Matrilinearity, or the privileging of cognatic ties, have been part of European history, even in Rome, in the later Republican period. Naming practices during the Middle Ages reflect also a complex intermixing of agnatic and cognatic practices, as in Prankish practices during the fifth century that used cognatic naming elements alongside or instead of agnatic elements (Story 2005, 197; Wiszewski 2010, 367). But these cases are the minority. Patrilinearity in property and naming have been the norm, and naming forms and practices convert the spirit of patriarchy into the intimate power work that produces gender property disenfranchisement and the invisibility of women in the public realm.

As the continuity of patriarchal naming practices suggests, the history of naming is not teleological. That a society has a naming system apt for complex administration does not mean this system will last. The Roman Empire fell in 476 to mainly Germanic tribes who used only one name, a practice that became quickly common among the newly conquered.

Within a century, Germanic names accounted for half of names in Gaul, which was once part of the Latinized Roman Empire, and by the ninth century it was Latin names that had become rare, particularly in the north and east of Gaul (Burns 2003, 362; Wilson 1998, 65–69). Germanic naming traditions were quite different from those of the Romans. German names were created and were rarely repeated (Pohl 2021, 36). Most names were dithematic in that they were composed of two names together and, in so doing, the Germanic practice enormously expanded naming possibilities. Gender was indicated in the second element, and men and women could use each other's names (Wilson 1998, 75). Although typically patrilinear, descent was broadly bilateral, and women could inherit land (77). Although Germanic names were rarely repeated, and they were all given, they constituted kinship that was marked by shared elements, as when King Theuderic I names his son Theudebert, who in turn names his son Theudebald. Although names were rarely repeated, over generations one may trace a lineage by reference to the repetition of some ancestral dithematic names like Childebert or Chrodobertus, or some elements like *Theude-* or *Child-*.

Though not teleological, naming systems do tend to gain complexity proportional to the complexity of the state, and the complexity of the state grows as population and territory grow. While most of Europe used single names during the Middle Ages, second names were slowly added to eventually become the norm, and this happened from the tenth to the fourteenth century, in which population doubled (Hey 2000, 3). In France, the use of second names began to increase in the eleventh century and by the thirteenth century constituted the majority (Evergates 2007, 133). In England, a similar transition happened between the eleventh and the thirteenth centuries, but the second names were often simply the office a man held and were not commonly used in social situations. In Venice, second names can be found as early as the eighth century, and by the end of the thirteenth century almost all records in places like Perugia, Cremona, Florence, and Tuscany included two names (Wilson 1998, 117).

These second names were not necessarily family names yet. It took time for second names to become that. Originally, they had a huge range of significations. They were marks of character, as when nicknames were adopted; of profession, office, and even physical traits, as when a heavy and big person is given the last name Quarey, after *carré* (four-square), or when a dark-skinned person is called Le noir. Second names were also references to moral behavior as in Constanz (constancy) or Probus (honest). Animal names were used to mark metaphoric connections to moral characteristics, as when dogs are used to refer to faithfulness in names like Caignet or Le Quien, and roosters were used to denote vanity as with Coquart or Coquel. The variation of practices is too great to mention here, but suffice to say that second names, which eventually became family names in Europe, illustrate the huge literary and signifying range of words, which makes naming traditions so rich and complex (Hey 2000, 40; McKinley 1990; Wilson 1998, 118–23).

The stabilization of second names as family names (in China, the order is inverse) has taken time, and it is still not universal. Iceland does not use that naming system, nor does Ethiopia, Somalia, or Myanmar. However, today the majority of nation-states use standard naming systems that include a given name and a family name. In England, this practice happened by the fifteenth century, but even in Europe this practice sometimes took centuries to become normal. The Lisbon earthquake of 1755 allowed Portuguese authorities to understand the benefits of surname standardization, and it is thus after 1755 that the Portuguese made standard family names mandatory, as well as their registry.

Standardizing family names permitted a huge range of practical administrative, political, and military tasks, and, as James Scott (1998) hyperbolically argues, one cannot conceive of modern statecraft without this stabilization. To those nation-states that have used family names, these allowed for stable and often rigorous tax rolls, property rolls, conscription lists, and property deeds as well as for rationalizing laws of property, heredity, and political membership (65). Unsurprisingly, states are the main forces behind the adoption and stabilization of family names. Scott illustrates the extent to which states will go toward this goal with the example of the Philippines, where, under Spanish rule in 1849, people were by decree forced to take surnames for taxation and census purposes.

Governor Narciso Clavería y Zaldua, a utilitarian and technocratic state builder, ordered the making of a catalogue of nouns and adjectives of nature, geography, and the arts to be used by Filipino officials to assign permanent surnames. The *Catálogo alfabético de apellidos*, a robust 141-page book with more than sixty-one thousand surnames, included names in Spanish but also names in Tagalog, Ilocano, Boholano, and other adaptations of, for instance, Chinese names (Ocampo 2013). The names were not randomized or fully imposed. Scott notes that "in practice, each town was given a number of pages from the alphabetized catalogo, producing whole towns with surnames beginning with the same letter" (1998, 69). For a long time, one could tour the Philippines alphabetically. In addition, the father or the eldest person in a family was given the opportunity to choose a surname from the section of the *Catálogo* allocated to that parish or town (Martínez-San Miguel 2014). Clavería was aware of the huge social imposition of mandating last names, and to secure adherence to the practice, schoolteachers were ordered to force their students to use only the new surnames, and priests, military, and civil officials were ordered to accept only official petitions, deeds, and applications from those who use their official two names.

Calling these massive anonymizing processes "standardization," which is the term adopted by the literature, is a huge oversimplification and one that attends only to the state and its goals. To individuals and families who underwent these important social phenomena, every standardization meant anonymizing, forgetting, and erasure. Imagine being a Filipino at the time in which Governor Clavería y Zaldua forced you, your family, your kids, your parents, to renounce your names and adopt new ones, mostly in Spanish. How can we imagine such demoralizing, denigrating, and massive colonizing imposition? Changes to the economy of anonymity create winners and losers, wealth and trauma, invisibility and visibility.

As these vignettes into the history of naming illustrate, names perform functions essential to the state, the family, the kindred, society, and politics. Names are indexes of individuality and connect specific bodies to specific histories. *They are the connecting tissue between the bio and politics in the term "biopolitics."* Aristotle famously said, "Man is by nature a social animal," yet, society depends on indexes to graft identity and difference, and humans have used names as the ontic operators trusted to connect a body to a biography and to a political and social identity. This indexical capacity of proper names depends on the thesis that names are referential, and we recognize this thesis as dependent on social conventions. François Récanati (1993) states this indexical property of names as follows: "For each proper name there exists in principle a social convention linking that name to a definite individual called its bearer. This individual is the referent of the name" (139). Even though we accept that one name may have multiple bearers, the social conventions surrounding names also tend to include the notion that one will be able to solve this problem of ambiguity with context and that in context we will be able to fully determine indexicality. For philosophers and linguists, the ambiguity problem is often a problem of name to body referentiality, as in Récanati's case. It is a problem rooted in the fact that names promise concrete indexicality but rarely deliver it.

Yet, the problem of ambiguity can be posed differently. *Proper names are not only indexical because they connect a name to a specific body. Proper names also connect a specific name to specific systems of power, and they are involved in power games and power work that may or may not require the presence of the individual.* In some cases, as when a name exists to be part of a tax roll, the connection between name and body is utilitarian, and what is usable about a name is precisely its concrete indexical property, that a name can point toward a specific bearer. But names are more than the promise of concrete indexicality. Names are used and interpreted to convey extra-indexical information about the bearer, what in the previous chapter I call categorical indexicality. We receive an email signed by "Jane Smith," and we assume the bearer is a woman. This is so because we embrace the thesis that Jane is woman's name, and it is very likely that until proven otherwise, we'll continue holding on to the assumption. I have a Latine name and happen to be Brown. My son has a Latine name, and he happens to look White. He may one day prove wrong someone who presumes that his name points toward a Brown Latine. Clearly, the categorical information conveyed by a name is an assumption, a calculation that the likeliness that Jane is indeed a woman is quite high. But calculations fail, and Javier, my kid, looks White.

The fact that assumptions connect names to systems of power such as gender, ethnicity, and race does not make their power work less insidious. Many studies have shown that in hiring processes, the categorical information of names can determine who gets a "callback." Marianne Bertrand and Sendhil Mullainathan (2004) showed this in the context of race in the United States. They sent roughly five thousand résumés with similar characteristics to respond to different job ads. Stereotypical White names like Emily Walsh and Greg Baker were assigned to half of those résumés. Stereotypical Black names like Lakisha Washington and Jamal Jones were assigned to the other half. White names got 50 percent more callbacks. Later, the researcher upped the credentials of another set of résumés and used the same logic of White and Black names. White names with higher credentials got an extra 30 percent bump in callbacks while Black names got none. This means that even with higher credentials, Black names yielded a power deficit, a distressing notion.

Similar studies have proved the power of gendered names. Corinne Moss-Racussin and colleagues (2018) conducted a study in which faculty in STEM fields were asked to evaluate a curriculum vitae (CV). Different faculties were given the same CV with the only difference that the CV marked the academic record of either a person named John or Jennifer. Even though STEM academic units in the United States face consistent pressure to achieve gender parity, Jennifer was less likely to be selected as mentee, as a lab researcher and, when given a position, was offered a smaller salary, roughly 13 percent less than fictional John. What I am suggesting here is that names do power work beyond their capacity for concrete and categorical indexicality. In the Moss-Racussin et al. study, as in Bertrand and Mullainathan's, names invite inferences about competence, capacity, kinship, appeal, and performance, suggesting that names have a categorical range of power effects way beyond concreteness. While these power effects are possibilities, the likelihood that over a lifetime an individual won't be impacted by the categorical power effects of their name is quite small. In fact, researchers such as Gregory Clark et al. (2014), who use surnames in order to track down and understand social mobility in history, in different contexts, must account for the fact that names that connote less status will have a negative effect on social mobility. Elite surnames, the authors posit, may take ten or fifteen generations to become "average in status" (107). Names do power work, even if we sometimes may need large data sets to see it. Most of us carry our names always or at least for decades, and many times these names, not us, are subject to evaluation, from job applications, school applications, all the way to credit and mortgage applications. Not only that, but our names do power work when we are not present and at different times. While my body can be involved in, at best, a limited number of interactions at any given time, our names can be simultaneously involved in different power games across geography and time, multiplying the chances of being affected by our name's categorical power effects.

At the categorical level, ambiguity is the capacity of names to signify membership in different groups with specific histories and signifying power. I have a Latine male name, and, until proven otherwise, I am presumed to be the bearer of the population traits of Latines, their histories, and of men and their privileges. This type of ambiguity is unique to naming, as the categorical is the property of names because names are words, and words can and often have poetic, discursive, and symbolic meanings. In this ambiguity, names are different from other indexes like DNA or a passport number. They are, however, similar to some biological indexes such as phenotypes, which are also subject to aesthetic, symbolic, and discursive judgment.

The signifying capacity of names simultaneously connects individuals to a diverse array of power systems, from our taxes to our gender, and they are typically socially productive in complex ways for this very reason. Names have power effects that are hard to predict and often hard to understand. But we, the name bearers, tend to feel this power either as the power of accountability, promised by concrete indexicality, or the power of prejudice, due to categorical indexicality.

The Power of Unnaming and Renaming

Anonymizing is sometimes about impunity, but not only. Different forms of renaming offer different social possibilities. Some are symbolic and traditional, as when Charles Philip Arthur George Windsor was renamed King Charles III in September 2022 after his crowning as the king of the United Kingdom. Unnaming and renaming are also part of social pressures on individuals, as when an immigrant changes a name to acculturate, which I dealt with extensively in the previous chapter. Other forms of unnaming and renaming are forced on individuals and are part of systems of subjugation. Indeed, the sheer number of instances in which indexical dissociation, unnaming and renaming, are used coercively is remarkable. From patriarchy, to slavery, to colonialism, the history of humanity is full of instances in which the subjugation of a people is done by and made evident in the imposition of names and in the symbolic use of names to mark boundaries of membership and, more recently, citizenship.

Given this, an analysis of an economy of anonymity based on names is incomplete without exploring voluntary and involuntary forms of indexical dissociation, or the uses of unnaming and renaming as techniques for coercive, disciplinary, traditional power, as well as for the purposes of self-creation. Here I want to analyze further the five most common types of anonymizing: (1) agentic indexical dissociation, the type of anonymizing most referenced in the literature; (2) forced indexical dissociation, as in master-slave naming practices, which are practices exclusively concerned with subjugation; (3) disciplinary indexical dissociation, which refers to naming and unnaming processes that are the result of cultural, social, and technological pressures that push individuals to accept onomastic dissociation; (4) traditional indexical dissociation, which involves naming practices ensconced in tradition, and for that reason, they give little or no room for rejection and offer some social rewards in exchange; and (5) indexical dissociation as self-creation, or the ways in which individuals change their indexes in the process of creation and adaptation. The sections on agentic indexical dissociation and self-creation are relatively brief because I have explored them extensively elsewhere. Chapter 2 explores some possibilities and challenges of self-creation. Chapter 3 is based on a complex case of agentic anonymity. I also explore disciplinary indexical dissociation in Chapter 5 but add some cases to illustrate its historicity here.

As the cases discussed will show, these five types of dissociation are not always clear-cut, and a single type of practice may show characteristics proper to the other types of dissociation. Sometimes, forced dissociation prepared the ground for disciplinary dissociation practices, which gave way to new traditional types of indexical dissociation. Aware of this complexity, I use this typology to illustrate sometimes subtle differences that need particular types of attention.

Agentic Indexical Dissociation

The traditional history of anonymity shows that hiding our names or changing our names can be experienced as freeing. Nepantla is sometimes that. Yet, that anonymity is understood by many as a practice of freedom and, in some instances, as essential to freedom of expression is not simply due to the characteristics of anonymity as an ontic operator. This understanding is at least partly historical; it is constituted through time and in time. It has coalesced in discourse that places anonymity at the center of the publicity and political tactics of the marginalized. This is perhaps nowhere clearer than in the use of anonymous tactics by women in literature, a practice common today (J. K. Rowling and P. D. James use initials that dissociate their author names from gender) but one that has a long history.

In the English world, anonymous publishing was not only the purview of women. During the last half of the eighteenth century, over 80 percent of all novels were published anonymously. Although the percentage decreased during the nineteenth century, the practice remained common. *The Dictionary of the Anonymous and Pseudonymous Literature of Great Britain*, published by Halkett and Laing in 1850, lists work by almost every well-known author (Mullan 2007). The reasons for their anonymity were varied. Aristocrats, for instance, hid their identity with anonymity, as in the case of Walter Scott, who feared that publishing fiction was unbecoming for a clerk of sessions and might ruin his aspiration to become a judge. Often men used pseudonyms, a common technique of dissociation in literature, as a form of artistic expression, as in the cases of Jozef Korzeniowski (Joseph Conrad) and Eric Arthur Blair (George Orwell). In general, women authors had other reasons, among them those noted by Cheryl Turner (1992): "the detrimental impact that their sex might have upon the earning power of their writing, particularly early in the century; the fact that it could undermine a proper evaluation of literary merit, either through premature rejection and ridicule, or through over-indulgence and condescension; and because the stigma of 'unfeminine' behaviour remained attached to authorship throughout the period" (95).

Though the anonymous publishing decreased during the nineteenth century, the practice remained common. At issue were not simply the increasing reach of copyright and the commercialization of the novel. Some authors used their names but signed away their copyright. Others like Jane Austen did not use her name but kept the copyright. Austen tended to pay for the publishing herself and gave a percentage of the sales returns to booksellers. But she was anonymous, and it was her brother who communicated with her publishers. Mary Anne Evans, writing as George Eliot, would ask George Henry Lewes to handle publishers too. So, at issue with women authors was not only gendered norms of public discourse (as illustrated by the Brontë example in the introduction) but also the legal prohibition to keep the money they earned and to inherit property, a prohibition that came to an end only with the Married Women's Property Act of 1870 (Griffin 2003, 4). Women used anonymity and pseudonymity to push back against gendered norms of public discourse and, to a degree, against coverture.

Anonymous publishing is one type of agentic indexical dissociation, but others like anonymous political actions, whistleblowing, trolling, adopting pseudonyms in digital environments, using a VPN, or using a mask in a protest, follow similar sociopolitical patterns. Individuals need or want impunity in particular social locations and use anonymizing tactics to make it possible. Typically, those using this type of anonymity carry on most of their lives with their original names, and the anonymizing is only tactical, for some situations and environments.

Forced Indexical Dissociation

Traditionally, master-slave hierarchies have been established partly through naming practices, and they are the clearest example of forced indexical dissociation. Slaves have been forcefully separated from their birth names or the naming traditions of their ancestors as a way of disconnecting them from their history and kinship traditions (Spillers 2003). Forced unnaming and forced naming have been used as ways of establishing ownership over slave subjects. These anonymizing practices have been diverse throughout history but had the common characteristic of giving the slave owner the right to impose a new name on each slave, if he wished to do so. In Classical Rome, slaves were sometimes owned by individuals and sometimes by cities and other organs of the states. In general, slaves had a single name given by the master followed by a reference to the owner. For instance, "Martialis C. Olii Primi or Martialis the slave of C. Olius Primus" (Wilson 1998, 25). Yet, a good portion of Roman slaves were unnamed and simply referred to sometimes, for example, as "Marcus's boy," or something to that effect. Similarly, most slaves in the British colonies, and later in the United States, were given a simple English name and at times a second name designating the owner or the plantation to which they belonged. As Omi Leissner (1997) notes, "[Slaves] were denied fixed names for they were legally defined as chattel. Hence, abolitionism regarded the slave's right to name themselves as of primary importance" (109). Haig Bosmajian (1974) observes that "the power that comes from names and naming is related directly to the power to define others—individuals, races, sexes, ethnic groups" (5). Or, as Valerie Alia (2007) argues, "Any substantial regime change or change of dominance and power is inevitably accompanied by changes to personal and place names. Taking control of naming is an important component of the process of assuming political power and is a fundamental part of social and political change. This kind of renaming can indicate either subjugation or liberation" (10). In slavery, indexical dissociation must be seen as an act of coercive symbolic power set to define a human being as chattel. The power work is done both by the imposition and the dissociation that is used to disconnect individuals from their preslavery selves. Anonymity is a double move: (1) indexical disassociation, then (2) indexical reassociation so that the individual is dislocated and disoriented and then relocated and reoriented.

In order to understand the impact of forced dissociation in slavery, it is wise to begin by recognizing the particular importance naming had in Sub-Saharan Africa, the place of origin of the majority of individuals subjected to slavery in the Americas. While the region is enormous, there are a few continuities worth mentioning. Among Northern Sotho-, Southern Sotho-, and Botswana-speaking people, names held significant spiritual power, and they were hidden from strangers and shared only with trusted people. They believed that one could cause you harm if they reverse the meaning of your name. Among the Botswana-speaking people of South Africa, the word for name is *Leena*, which translates as "staying behind," as "immortality," and names bear an immortal energy (Fitzpatrick 2012, 26). Among the Yoruba of Nigeria, naming happens seven days after birth, and during that time, parents and other family members consider their affairs in order to choose a name. There are two kinds of Yoruba names. One is a given name that is meaningful for kinship; the other is a "Oruku Amutorunwa," or a destiny name, which is given by the heavens. The emphasis of naming and spirituality is also part of African Muslim traditions, which were common in Sub-Saharan Africa during the centuries of the slave trade. Either in Arabic or in local languages like, for instance, Swahili, names were chosen to indicate the relation to the Creator (Zawawi 1998, xiii).

The emphasis on spirituality was not monolithic. For instance, Ghanaian naming practices often followed the days of the week (Agyekum 2006, 215). However, it is unquestionable that for the majority of those who were subject to slavery, their names were significantly more than an identifier (Abarry 1991, 157). Names connect them to their spiritual world, to their cosmology, and to the spiritual visions their parents and relatives had for them. Names were part of the symbolic and social practices that defined their self-description and deep subjectivity, and removing these names simply aggravated the utter pain and inhumanity of slavery.

The removal began during the Middle Passage, often by using branding that marked the captives as property of colonial authority and/or of the slave merchants. The baptism of slaves also led to further branding, with the cross superimposed on the royal arms. Captain Thomas Phillips observed and described the baptism carried by Portuguese and Spaniards as follows:

> In the early seventeenth century, it became customary for slaves in Africa to be baptized before their departure from Africa. This requirement was first laid down by King Philip III of Spain (II of Portugal) in 1607 and confirmed in 1619. The slaves had, as a rule, received no instruction whatever before this ceremony, and many, perhaps most, of them had no previous indication that there was such a thing as a Christian God. So the christening was perfunctory. In Luanda, the captives would be taken to one of the six churches, or assembled in the main square. An official catechist, a slave, say, who spoke Kimbundu, the language of Luanda, would address the slaves on the nature of their Christian transformation. Then a priest would pass among the bewildered ranks, giving to each one a Christian name, which had earlier been written on a piece of paper. He would also sprinkle salt on the tongues of the slaves, and follow that with holy water. Finally, he might say, through an interpreter: Consider that you are now children of Christ. You are going to set off for Portuguese territory, where you will learn matters of the Faith. Never think any more of your place of origin. Do not eat dogs, nor rats, nor horses. (Phillips qtd. in Thomas 1997, 396)

This horrifying account concisely presents unnaming and renaming as part of the culture and subjective strategies used to transform into, or at least mark, these Luandans as property. Baptismal names were not necessarily the only ones imposed on slaves. In the ships, they would often be named with numbers or after things such as mainstay, cat's head, bulls eye (all of these are parts of ships), or simply with derogatory nicknames. When they arrived at the slave markets, they would often be renamed again with European-styled names such John or Mary. Richard Burton (1999) argues that "the 'unnaming' and 'renaming' of new arrivants from Africa was, for the slave masters, an integral part of the act of taking possession" (38). This was true at every instance of unnaming and renaming.

As in Rome, most slaves in the American British colonies had only a first name. Commonly, this was given by the slave owner, in particular if the slave was going to work in the owner's house. Most owners chose names that were easy to pronounce and remember, and most were common English names. Some African names or Anglicized versions of African names remained in circulation both in British North America and in places like Jamaica. Other names like Becky and Sukey were common among slaves because, though English, they had sound similarities to African names (Leissner 1997, 125). The variety of names and naming practices attests to the fact that there was not a single rule or policy followed by slave owners. Yet, naming was, as a rule, used to subjugate or, as Burton argues, to mark possession (see also Leissner 1997, 123).

Naming mattered to slaves, and they clearly understood the power of slave society's naming practices and fought back. Slaves would almost never use the diminutive on each other, and it was not uncommon that slaves were also given "secret real names" (Burnard 2001; Leissner 1997). In public, they may use the English name, but in private they would use the African name. It was also common to use the English name as a sort of temporary nickname, and the African name was understood as the real name. When the Emancipation Proclamation (1863) passed in the United States, some four million ex-slaves adopted surnames, which had been denied by slave practices, and adopted names that clearly meant to shed any residue of the slave system. Names like Freedman, Freedland, Justice, Lincoln, and Grant were common. Ordinary English names such as Jones, Smith, and Harris reflected a desire to be seen as regular, Anglo, free people. In these cases, slaves and emancipated slaves used renaming as practices of freedom in order to push back against the dehumanizing character of forced anonymity (Leissner 1997, 128).

Yet, not every aspect of slave society's naming practices could be undone. Hortense Spillers (2003), referencing the work of Claude Meillassoux, argues for the need to understand these naming practices as participating in the constitution of a kinless subject, one trapped in the "vestibular" space of in-betweenness between slave society and the slaved. In terms of this book, this vestibular space is a particular manifestation of nepantla, which is a more capacious location or birthing space, one that yields different outcomes, including the vestibular. Names can hold us in the painful vestibule of genealogical identity. Spillers continues: "In effect, under conditions of captivity, the offspring of the female does not 'belong' to the mother, nor is s/he 'related' to the 'owner,' though the owner 'possesses' it, and in the African-American instance, often fathered it, and, as often, without whatever benefit of patrimony" (2003). Naming here is indexical of this vestibular state that Spillers later clarifies as follows:

> If North American slavery in its laws outraged the classic status of motherhood in the African case, then it asymmetrically complicated notions of fatherhood. In effect, the African person was twice-fathered, but could not be claimed by the one and could not be claimed by the other. The person, following the "condition" of the mother, very often bore only a first name—Niger I, Niger II, Phoeby, Cassius, Jane, Sui, and so forth. While the suppression of the patronymic engenders a radically different social and political economy for African-Americans, it involves us, relatedly, in nested semiotic readings: the African name is not only "lost" to cultural memory, but on that single ground the captive African is symbolically broken in two—ruptured along the faculty of a "double consciousness" in which one's cultural membership in the American one remains inchoate. A social subject in abeyance, in an absolute deferral that becomes itself a new synthesis, is born—the African-American, whose last name, for all intents and purposes, becomes historically X, the mark of his/her borrowed culture's profound illiteracy. (232)

Outside the rules of kinship made evident in naming practices elsewhere, Spillers clarifies the conditions of a multigenerational trauma at the core and origin of the Black experience. What is mothering when the offspring belongs to the master? What is fatherhood in this context but a biological process outside the rules of nature and the rules of politics?

Slavery is sometimes explained from the perspective of biopolitics, as a sort of domination over flesh. In Michel Foucault's work ([1978] 1990), biopolitics is all about the bios, the social and political side of the body, the fact that bodies are disciplined into lives that can be managed, understood, and reproduced to reconstitute populations. Georgio Agamben's (1998) work criticizes and complements Foucault by arguing that some bodies are treated not as political constructs and the rights this politics inheres but as bare life, animals, flesh that has no rights within the polis. Spillers helps us see that even biopolitics cannot fully explain the slave subject, for this subject is equally expelled from relations of obligation inherent in the natural world and the relations of obligation at the core of the political. Neither bios, nor *zoē*, the term Agamben uses, the result is a third space that can be transversed but not settled.

Naming practices in slave economies illustrate some of the ways in which names are forcefully transformed, and future generations cannot fully recover traditional ways of naming. Yet, in the constitution of private and community naming practices connecting to traditional preslavery life and languages, slave societies also illustrate modalities of resistance that can be found among other subjugated populations in the Americas.

Similar tactics of resistance were used by Native Americans in the United States, whose naming practices have changed dramatically throughout the centuries of settler colonialism. Forced naming dissociation was central to the nineteenth-century efforts by the US government, and this is nowhere clearer than during the late nineteenth-century efforts to use the education of Native children and youth to minimize Indian resistance and address the Indian problem. The most notorious and influential of these educational institutions was the Carlisle Indian Industrial School in Pennsylvania, which was founded in 1879 and (re)educated more than ten thousand Native students from almost very Native nation in the United States, including Puerto Rico.

This institution's goal was to continue the nation-building project and, as Jacqueline Fear-Segal and Susan Rose (2016) note, to "transform Native children from 'savagery' to 'civilization'" (2). Children were sometimes forcefully recruited; some were sent by their parents, who were convinced that Carlisle would provide a proper education; some were prisoners of war. The goal was assimilation, and the tool was rupturing the link the children had with Native cultures and Native knowledge. Kids were forced to speak English and were never roomed with members of their own Native nation.

The project, funded by Secretary of the Interior Carl Schurz, promised a cheaper way of eliminating the ongoing rebellions. Schurz famously justified the school by arguing that it would cost a million dollars to kill an Indian in war, but only $1,200 to school an Indian child for eight years (Fear-Segal and Rose 2016, 7).

As with slaves, the first step into this process of stripping these children of their traditional identity was the removal of their Indian name and the imposition of an Anglo name. Barbara Landis (2016) describes the experiences of the first sixty-six students arriving at Carlisle as follows: "Just as Adam named his subjects in the Garden of Eden in order to exercise dominion over them, so did the Carlisle administrators rename those first children from the Sioux agencies" (91). In *My People, the Sioux*, the autobiography of Luther Standing Bear (1928), one of Carlisle's most famous graduates, vividly describes the experience:

> One day when we came to school there was a lot of writing on one of the blackboards. We did not know what it meant, but our interpreter came into the room and said, "Do you see all these marks on the blackboard? Well, each word is a white man's name. They are going to give each one of you one of these names by which you will hereafter be known." None of the names were read or explained to us, so of course we did not know the sound or meaning of any of them.
>
> The teacher had a long pointed stick in her hand, and the interpreter told the boy in the front seat to come up. The teacher handed the stick to him, and the interpreter then told him to pick out any name he wanted. The boy had gone up with his blanket on. When the long stick was handed to him, he turned to us as much as to say, "Shall I—or will you help me—to take one of these names? If it right for me to take a white man's name?" He did not know what to do for a time, not uttering a single word—but he acted a lot and was doing a lot of thinking.
>
> Finally he pointed out one of the names written on the blackboard. Then the teacher took a piece of white tape and wrote the name on it. Then she cut off a length of the tape and sewed it on the back of the boy's shirt. (136–37)

As Standing Bear describes, for most children their "Christian" names were the first thing they were forced to learn in English and the first word they learn to write. In these cases, the imposition of names coincides with new methods of inscription, writing, and new ways of self-narration that transformed generations of Native Americans. That we have Standing Bear's autobiography today, and that I can read it and cite it, also speaks to the introduction of new authorial practices that allowed for new archival methodologies and knowledge formations.

Efforts to erase Native American culture never succeeded, and this is partly because of writings like Standing Bear's, which preserve history, rituals, and challenges, and partly because many Native Americans were and are committed to acts of physical and cultural rebellion and survival. Institutions like Carlisle may have succeeded at normalizing Anglo names among Natives, but like African Americans in different contexts, Native Americans have used competing traditional naming practices that connect today's naming culture to the past. Lakota Sioux children were the first students forced to assimilate at Carlisle, but today, the Lakota carry on the naming practices of the past alongside those imposed by settler colonialism. A Lakota, for instance, may have an Anglo name, a Lakota name by birth, another name as an honorific after a significant deed has been accomplished, and a secret or spirit name only known to the individual and the medicine man. In the multiplicity of names one finds the struggle, the negotiation with the present and the past, and the efforts to preserve power structures that can compete against settler hegemony.

Disciplinary Indexical Dissociation

When indexical dissociation is used for subjugation, dissociation marks a break between past naming traditions and future ones. The transition between past and future naming practices is sometimes violent and rather clear, as in slavery and the Middle Passage, but sometimes changes to naming are part of the general cultural and symbolic erosion and transformation that a community suffers after colonialism or after experiencing the long-term effects of cultural imperialism. In places like central Mexico, which were ruled by the powerful Aztec Empire before the Spaniards arrived, the imposition of naming practices was secondary to the savage conquest that preceded it.

The Aztecs spoke Nahua, and the term "Nahua" refers to a linguistic grouping of many ethnic communities. The Nahuas in central Mexico before the Spanish conquest in the early sixteenth century used naming systems sometimes reliant on the calendar or a characteristic of the child or in memory of a special event that had happened that day. Names were unique. Single names were common among the lower classes; composite names were common among the aristocratic class. Whether children were named after the day on which they were born depended on advice regarding the type of day and, if the day was deemed unlucky, would be named after a different day (Krickeberg 1961, 71). Boys would receive names of animals, and girls of flowers or names that would give them the favor of deities. Among the Mixtecs, children were given a second name when they were seven, and they would end up with names such as a Mixtec princess named "13 lizard—turquoise butterfly": 13 lizard is the date; butterfly and turquoise are attributes. Although this princess's second name is beautiful and poetic, as a rule female names were not this colorful and were often simply indications of birth rank and date. The most common female names indicated birth order: Tiacapan (Eldest), Tlaco (Middle), Teiuc (Younger), Xoco (Youngest), or Mocel (Only) (Horn 1999, 107). In general, names given to males were more diverse and colorful, and second names were not family names except in the case of some royal dynasties (107–8).

Naming practices after the conquest must be understood within the context of religious and political practices of assimilation and exploitation. They are part of a disciplinary framework that resulted in the eventual formation of new practices and new traditions. The Spaniards legitimized their colonial greed and violence in religious terms, and the Catholic Church served as the institution mediating between the dark colonial impulses of the political and military occupation, the wars of dispossession and conquest, and the establishment of the *encomienda*, a Spanish labor system that had evolved from forms of communal slavery in the Iberian Peninsula. In the Americas, as it was prior in the peninsula and against the Muslim communities, the *encomienda* granted a Spaniard absolute rights over the labor of Indigenous communities in specific locales. Abolished officially in 1721, the *encomienda* and, later, the *hacienda* systems, which more resembled the system of indentured servitude, shaped colonial society, creating a racial system of subjection and legal frameworks of exploitation based on race and ethnicity.

Early examples of renaming in classic narrations of the conquest such as Bernal Díaz del Castillo's *Historia verdadera de la conquista de la Nueva España* ([1576] 2010) describe the military conquest as essentially religious. Yet, even such description represented the renaming of Indians as the result of coercion, albeit as always justified by the ritual of the Catholic baptism. In the seven mentions of these renaming rituals, the majority describe baptisms of individuals who did not speak Spanish and who could not understand what was happening to them. In some of these cases, the individuals are prisoners of war who are given the name Melchor and Julían; in another instance, Díaz del Castillo describes how after a battle the Spaniards perform the baptism of eight young women who will be given by their fathers to Cortés and his soldiers. The harshness of these descriptions is not apparent to Díaz del Castillo, who justifies every military and coercive action in the name of God, the church, and the salvation of the Indians.

The harshness of the conquest gave way to the harshness of political, social, and legal subjugation. Yet, over the centuries of colonialism, the role of the Catholic Church in New Spain regarding naming practices became more nuanced than the church's coercive role early in the conquest or during the Atlantic slave trade, mentioned earlier. This is why I use these postconquest examples of disciplinary indexical dissociation. Even though some coercion persisted, priests pushed but not always imposed Spanish names among the Indians. More commonly, priests would advocate for the adoption of given names that connected a child to the saint associated with her or his birth. Rebecca Horn (1999) proposes that Nahuas may have been open to this practice as it resembled their own preconquest use of the calendar to name children. Baptism rolls show that by the early seventeenth century, most Nahuas were named after the saints assigned to their birthday. Even though some Nahua names persisted as second names during the sixteenth century, they became extremely rare by the early seventeenth century. A practice of adopting a Spanish given name, particularly the name of a saint, also as a second name became common. So, a person may be called Juan Diego, with Diego acting as a surname.

The disciplinary power of religion and culture facilitated the transition to colonial naming traditions. For instance, the reasons for the adoption of such second names, Horn (1999) shows, were not simply religious, as many of these names were also meant to link a person to a place or a parish; places named after saints were very common. In addition, Nahuas also commonly adopted Spanish surnames, particularly those of prominent people, which explains why Cortés, the surname of the conqueror, became the most common Nahua surname drawn from the Spanish by the mid-sixteenth century. Spanish surnames of commoners were also used by Nahuas, but while surnames of aristocrats and prominent people often became family names, commoner surnames did not (104–22).

Over the centuries, Spanish surnames all but erased Nahua names. The sometimes subtle, sometimes direct coercion by the church and the forces of racism compelled most Indigenous people in New Spain and then Mexico to adopt Christian and Spanish names. This adoption was never total, and, as Mauricio Melendez Obando (2001) notes, Indigenous names were more likely to survive in places with large Indigenous populations to begin with, like Mexico, Guatemala, and Peru, than in the rest of Spanish Latin America. The survival of these names meant not simply the survival of a word. They typically represent the survival of a cosmology and rituals that sutured individuals to their collective past and that illustrated methods of survival during colonialism. The evidence of these practices cannot be found in baptism rolls, which index a community from the church and state's perspective. The evidence tends to be anthropological, as these practices are often hidden and private or semiprivate, and they are often under threat of disappearing, as they exist alongside social, political, and legal pressures by majoritarian forces and state institutions to erase the Indigenous past.

Anthropologists Ana Sagi-Vela González and Ursula Thiemer-Sachse (2005) illustrate the survival and fragility of these naming practices among the Ayuuk or Mixe, an Indigenous community of northern Oaxaca in what is today known as Sierra Mixe. The relative isolation of this community allowed for a continuity of traditional practices well into the twentieth century. The influence of the Catholic Church constituted the basis of hybrid naming systems but did not translate into the abandonment of preconquest practices. At least one of the names of the Ayuuk remained traditional, assigned through the ritual usage of a *xemabie*, a lawyer or priest, a person knowledgeable of the Mixe calendar. This lawyer reveals the Ayuuk name to the parents of the newborn on the third day of their birth. The child is thus assigned *xi*, sacred names, which include calendrical indexical names. In the same ritual the child is given *tona*, companion spirits, which are typically animals or forces of nature (e.g., thunder), which protect the child. While the *xi* was calendrical, the *tona* was assigned based on a ceremony involving the dispersal of ashes outside the birthplace followed by the lawyer interpreting these ashes. These names connected a child to a culture, but also to a date in the calendar, to forces of nature, and to a spiritual road map.

The cultural and cosmological edifice that gave an identity to the Ayuuk has been eroding, or perhaps changing shape or adapting to the pressures of the nation-state and the national imaginary. If at one point naming in Ayuuk meant the use of animals and things in nature, after colonialism naming was done in Spanish and often after church saints. But naming is again evolving. Sagi-Vela González and Thiemer-Sachse identify three forces pushing these changes: first, the growing influence of evangelical religions, which move people to comb the Bible to find and use names like Aarón or Absalón; and second, the growing process of acculturation and migration back and forth to the United States, which have normalized names like Erika or Wilson. Last, there is a resurgence of Ayuuk names that follow the cultural and political revindication of Indigenous life and culture, a sort of contemporary *indigenismo* that has popularized traditional names, particularly those attached to the mythical and historical world of the Ayuuk, such as Konk, a hero from the wars between the Mixes and Zapotecs. The traces of the traditional naming system are found not only in the resurgence of Ayuuk first names but also on the tenuous hold family names have in the communities and the ongoing practice of choosing one's last names. As in Spanish, the Ayuuk have now two last names, but these follow random patterns or no pattern, reflecting choices where state bureaucracies would give none. Most Mexicans use the Spanish tradition of two last names, with the first being the first last name of the father. That means that naming is patrilinear. But Spanish also uses the mother's first last name in the second position and thus is a tradition that attends to the mother's ancestry, even if this is within a patrilinear system. The Ayuuk may use any order for the two last names, and these may not represent family names.

While in slavery and colonialism naming practices reflect a desire by the slaveholder or colonial power to use names as indexes and forms of subjection, often with the goal of easing administrative tasks, imposing new naming systems is a temporal disciplinary tactic. It disconnects individuals and communities from past histories, past power structures and systems, and past ways of self-narration. Anthropologists sometimes refer to the connection between past history, self-narration, and power structures as kinship chronotopes, temporal structures of power that mark an individual's changing place in a community (Ball 2015). With the destruction of kinship chronotopes, slaveholders could impose a new naming system and force individuals to connect to new forms of government, bureaucracies, and ways of being known, governed, disciplined, and administered. Past and future orientations are disrupted when old names are forgotten and new names are adopted or imposed. Over time and generations, individuals and communities become natural members of the new order, marked by colonialism and new systems of race and ethnic hierarchies.

The imposition of naming systems does not only congeal over generations. Naming, unnaming, and renaming destroy and reconstruct an individual's sense of self and juridico/political location in a single lifetime. This is particularly traumatic when these impositions disrupt tradition and an individual's sense of history, as in slavery. But less traumatic transformations to an individual's historicity due to disciplinary dissociations have profound social implications, and these are clear in cases of mobility and migration.

Dissociational naming practices are used by new populations as social tactics signaling, for instance, their willingness to assimilate or to reinvent themselves in a new sociopolitical context. In some cases, as when massive migration from Europe to the United States used Ellis Island as a key point of entry, migrants would change names as ways of anticipating ethnonationalism or racism, or as a way of responding to the challenges of acculturation (see Chapter 5). Many immigrants start the process of self-creation that often is needed to function in a new society by changing given names. And, as an added benefit, the immigrant increases their chances of survival by adopting names that connect to positive categorical indexes. Perhaps this is the reason that at the beginning of the twentieth century, "Schmidts" became "Smiths" in the United States, and right now, someone like popular singer Peter Hernandez decided to change his name to "Bruno Mars" or film actor Oscar Hernández changed it to "Oscar Isaac."

Whether it helps immigrants reinvent themselves or not, naming practices can be seen as ways of exerting control over new populations, force new populations to Anglicize their names, and force them also to write these names in Latin alphabetic script, even if the names were originally inscribed in, for instance, logosyllabic script such as Chinese or abjad script such as Arabic. In many of these instances, nonstate institutions participate in processes of disciplinary dissociation that push for immigrants to acculturate.

The effects of disciplinary indexical dissociation in a society can be massive. In the United States alone, there are millions of people whose birth names are no longer theirs because of similar technological disciplining with systems that cannot understand that sometimes the first name is the family name (Korea), that sometimes one has four, five, or six names (Latin America, among others), that sometimes a given name is followed by a patronymic and then by a surname (Russia), that sometimes one has only one name (Afghanistan), or that sometimes one has three given names and no family names (Somalia).

The effects of disciplinarity can also be subtle, as these effects tend to offer social rewards to individuals for transforming their names, and, because they are presented as choices, name dissociation can easily be interpreted as adaptation, as normalcy, and as sacrificing something small, a name, for something bigger, belonging. And a name change indeed can reward a person with an easier path toward belonging and at the same time do that other thing that critical scholars like me fear: reproduce the idea that Latines do not belong or reproduce the notion that the Indigenous past is unimportant and inessential.

Traditional Indexical Dissociation

Most immigrants like me embark on dramatic personal changes that often include letting go of our names out of necessity and perhaps as a tactical solution to the complex problems of belonging. But there are many others who adopt new names as part of tradition, as part of rites of passage that mark a new stage in life. The different names that a person accumulates are typically part of their kinship chronotope, a marker of an individual's changing role in their communities. These traditions have disciplinary effects, but these effects are ritualized and they are not the product of a person's choice. I did not grow up knowing that I would decide to change my name, but members of communities in which tradition dictates that a member's name can change, such as among the Lakota, grow up with that knowledge. Names, therefore, can mean something quite different as these traditions negate the idea of the fixity of a person's name.

A powerful example of this difference can be found among the Tsimshian. Anchored by the Skeena River, which flows west from the Cariboo Region of British Columbia, Canada, to the Pacific, the Tsimshian are a Native American tribe with communities along the Skeena River and the coast. Their naming practices are traditional, ancient, and current.[3] Names are at the center of tribal organization and help constitute the basic weave of humans that we call Tsimshian society.

What differentiates Tsimshian naming practices from others is the ontic value of names and their standing as the actual members of Tsimshian life. As a Tsimshian once put it, "People are nothing. They're not important at all. It's the names that are really real" (qtd. in Roth 2008, 30). Strictly speaking, Tsimshian traditional names are not given to individuals, but individuals are given to the names. Names are the social spaces from which power and property rights and property relations emanate. Marcel Mauss, writing in 1938 about these naming practices, puts it as follows: "On the one hand, the clan is conceived of as being made up of a certain number of persons, in reality of 'characters' (personnages). On the other hand, the role of all of them is really to act out, each insofar as it concerns him, the prefigured totality of the life of the clan" (Mauss qtd. in Roth 2008, 31). Names are thus the reality of the tribe, and an individual who is conferred a Tsimshian name in the traditional potlatch ceremonies becomes the latest embodiment of that character and inherits their history as well as their property and honorifics. While embodied social relations undoubtedly exist, "the names themselves constitute a web of social relations that are manifested through and known by the practice of bestowing and using personal names" (33). These relations are prefigured by the names, and they outlast the name bearer. Strictly speaking, Roth notes, "names incarnate in individuals so as to make them their own ancestors" (3).

Although matrilineal, Tsimshian society's naming practices have similarities to those of some aristocratic royal houses in Europe. For instance, the recognition that one becomes the name is similar to an individual becoming, let's say, the crown, and thus the monarch. What is different is that in European aristocratic societies, individuals occupying specific names, such as the Earl of Arundel (an earldom that originated in 1176), represent that name but they are no longer considered as representing the latest instantiation of a social persona that began nine hundred years ago. At best, Edward Fiszalan-Howard, the current Earl of Arundel, represents a past social location that is alive today mostly in memory.

In Tsimshian society today, as one hundred years ago, a name bestows an individual a social persona, a specific history, distinctions, and wealth, which is for the most part nonalienable. The name is always central to the history of the Tsimshian, their migrations, the relationships to others, to land, and to nature. One thus inherits those histories, relationships, power, and obligations, and one becomes part and a character in the origin stories of the tribe. Today's Tsimshian naming system is the same as one hundred years ago and is the same accumulated history and social relationships of the tribe. Even if some stories of how some names came to be are being lost in time, with the names and thanks to their ontological status, the Tsimshian maintain the social relations these names inherited.

The Tsimshian have faced all the challenges that a colonized people would after almost two hundred years of occupation. Like many, they had to adapt to the impositions of the English and later the Canadians, and they have adopted English names. These are registered in birth certificates and used by and for activities related to broader Canadian society and the Canadian state. Yet, the English names die with the individual, while the hereditary Tsimshian names are immortal, or at least as immortal as human legends can be. The duality, nonetheless, points to the fact that the Tsimshian have no choice but to participate in colonial ways of subjectivity and self-construction. Contemporary traditional naming practices may be consistent with past naming practices, but what they produce is not only the contemporary Tsimshian world. They also have the capacity to construct a competing modality of personhood that can withstand the ongoing challenge of settler colonialism.

Tsimshian naming practices illustrate a way of withstanding the cultural and political impositions of settler colonialism using parallel naming systems: one that marks the continuation of tradition; the other that marks Tsimshian both as colonized people and as Canadian citizens. The Tsimshian traditions, by design, insert an individual into a new history and a system of obligations and rights that increases the individual's power and worth. But traditional indexical dissociations can be embraced with the opposite goal in mind.

In the Tsimshian tradition, an individual's kinship chronotope marks a new legal standing in the community, granting the individual new public and juridical powers. In contrast, changing names after marriage is part of the power work of patriarchy, and it is meant to reduce a woman's legal standing and control women's power. The Western patriarchal tradition is part of the influential English system of coverture, which was inscribed in English law for centuries and has influenced much of the world thanks to colonization. Coverture was a rigid system of subjugation that not only forced patrilinear relations but nullified the political and economic rights of women.[4] Women adopted their husbands' names, and it was through their husbands' legal rights and reputations that women were citizens of the state and members of the public. These names constructed formal and informal hierarchical relations between individuals, helping form specific self-descriptions through the standardization of forms of interaction and intersubjectivity.

Coverture became hegemonic in Europe only relatively recently and became the norm in England after 1400. Before coverture, naming designations were varied and complex, most of the times following agnatic patterns, but not always, as is particularly clear in the Germanic traditions. Women's second names, in particular, included nicknames, names of places, kinship, and sometimes a feminized husband's name. Although after 1400 and even earlier in France, women of high standing sometimes kept their family names, patrilineal descent was the norm, and naming practices in England became more standardized, with most women taking their husband's second name and offspring taking the father's second name (Wilson 1998, 172–74). Matronymics, which had been a minoritarian but persistent tradition in Europe, became extremely rare as the early modern set in.

As second names became standardized forms of family names throughout the fifteenth and sixteenth centuries in England, the second name became a symbol of the family and its survival through agnatic descent became inscribed in law. By the eighteenth century, William Blackstone (1753) writes about these relations in his famous legal treaty as follows: "By marriage, the husband and wife are one person in law; that is, the very being or legal existence of the woman is suspended during the marriage, or at least is incorporated and consolidated into that of her husband: under whose wing, protection, and cover, she performs everything" (Book I, chap. 15, 279). What would be called "coverture" was specified here in the belittling of the legal and personal standing of women and her dependency on and subjection to her husband. As in the Tsimshian cases, this tradition had powerful ontological effects. By the mid-nineteenth century, the practice of referring to married women by their husband's names had expanded from the upper classes to most of British society and to the United

States, and it is for this reason that Elizabeth Cady Stanton rejected the practice and created the simile between married women and slaves to make her point:

> I have very serious objections . . . to being called Henry. There is a great deal in a name. It often signifies much, and may involve a great principle. Ask our colored brethren if there is nothing in a name. Why are the slaves nameless unless they take that of their master? Simply because they have no independent existence. They are mere chattels, with no civil or social rights. Our colored friends in this country who have education and family ties take to themselves names, even so with women. The custom of calling women Mrs. John This and Mrs. Tom That, and colored men Sambo and Zip Coon, is founded on the principle that white men are lords of all. I cannot acknowledge this principle as just; therefore, I cannot bear the name of another. (Stanton qtd. in Leissner 1997, 114)

Notice how Cady Stanton's rejection, as powerful as it was in the context of her times, did not extend to a rejection of her husband's last name but was simply the refusal to be called Mrs. Henry Stanton. It should be noted that Cady was her maiden name, and she accepted her husband's last name as it was customary, and that Henry, as it was customary, did not take Cady as his other last name. Cady, her family name, moved to the middle name position. Today, Elizabeth Cady Stanton is written about regularly and is typically referred to as Stanton, not Cady Stanton. My library at the University of Southern California lists her work under the letter "S." Even though her name is part of feminist history, it is treated in a way that reproduces the agnatic, patrilinear, and patriarchal tradition at the base of coverture.

Indexical Dissociation as Self-Creation

I began this chapter with a quotation showing how Sojourner Truth, born a slave, described her renaming. Her given name was Isabella Bomfree, a name she left behind when she escaped in 1827 and ran away to a nearby farm owned by abolitionists, the Van Wageners, who bought her freedom for $20 (Painter 1996). In 1843, already a notable speaker, she changed her name to Sojourner Truth. As declared in the quotation, she needed a new name because Isabella no longer pointed to the right person. I see this act of unnaming and renaming different from those described earlier that I call disciplinary indexical dissociation, which includes migrants changing their names. While there are elements of self-creation in these disciplinary practices, the act of renaming is a response to external pressures. In Truth's case, and in the cases I examine later, renaming is an expression of an internal desire to be identified in the right way. The given name, in this case Isabella Bomfree, no longer shows the self; indeed, in these cases, names given at birth hide the self (Bomfree is a Dutch name that marks its bearer as White and European), and birth names produce feelings of invisibility and anonymity. Names can produce these feelings because names are not only indexical. Names connote information about the bearer that sometimes betrays the bearer's identity. Given names can have anonymizing effects.

Previously I mentioned other examples that fall into this category, including the way in which slave naming practices in the United States were resisted by slaves, who would often have two names, one forced upon them by their owner but another, the true name, that they would use among their community. Other instances of indexical dissociation as self-creation include the millions who, once declared free by the Emancipation Proclamation of 1863, chose different names to mark their new identities, their rebirthing.

Today, examples of indexical dissociation as self-creation are common, particularly in relationship to sexual and gender identities. Trans, intersex, gender fluid, and nonbinary persons often seek new names and new pronouns that better describe or connote who they are. In these, as in other cases involving other subjugation systems like slavery and settler colonialism, names given at birth betray the self that the names mean to help define. While most people experience some harmony between name and self, trans, intersex, and gender-fluid individuals can experience their names as alienating, false, and inauthentic, and only renaming can restore some harmony to the subject.

Although all instances of unnaming and renaming point us to the importance of natural language indexes to self-identity, instances of self-creation show that naming and anonymity are more essential to the subject than we give them credit. When Anzaldúa uses the term "birthing" to describe nepantla; when Truth uses the notion that "freedom made me change" and thus she needed a new name; when Spillers describes the vestibular as the perpetual state of slaves, mothering, and the patronymic, they are all arguing that names have ontological capacities. I expand on this insight in Chapter 2.

This brief historical review of naming gives a glimpse into the cultural, political, social, and identitarian richness of naming and unnaming practices. Names, the most consequential of all indexes, have helped structure the social world by mediating between individuals and individuals and institutions. They are an essential part of how people treat each other and are as important when they represent individuals in their absence. Bound to specific names, we experience the positive and negative consequences of what our names mean to others, and, as data, inscribed in tablets, lists, forms, and series, they have shaped state and social practices from slavery to taxation. Importantly, the reflective way in which we use names and think about them has made naming and unnaming part of complex power practices meant to disarticulate established structures, including some crucial to our understandings of self-construction. Sometimes the uses of anonymity are meant to temporarily change power relations and are used tactically, as when Austen decides to publish anonymously but otherwise keeps her name and the rest of the power relations associated with it. Other times, unnaming and renaming are part of strategic practices that signal a form of rebirthing, as when a member of Tsimshian society is given an ancestral name. Not every rebirth is meant to benefit the individual, and slave name changes are a harsh example that one may lose a name and be given another one in the painful process of moving from human to chattel.

These practices have radically different outcomes, some benign, some empowering, some cruel and nasty. Yet, all the practices rest on a similar theory about naming, one shared by slave merchants and Tsimshian leaders. Names are the connecting tissue between individuals and power structures, and if we wish to separate someone from their past, invent a new future, one can use unnaming and renaming as ontic operators that produce that first new reality, the moment of change, the fracture, the disjuncture in self-construction. The theory often works. In colonial settings, in places like Mexico, where 93 percent of the population is mestiza, our names are Spanish. Our Native American DNA, my own, important as it is, has no history or specificity and has little chance of inspiring specific solidarities and social projects.

Conclusion

Thirteen Properties of the Economy of Anonymity

Changes to the economy of anonymity are happening faster than changes to our political imaginaries. The effects are sometimes tragic, as in Lucy's case (Chapter 3), and sometimes comic. On September 21, 2022, Disney+ began streaming *Andor* (created by Tony Gilroy), a story about Cassian Andor (played by Diego Luna), a spy, thief, and rebel whose character is central to the film *Rogue One* (d. Gareth Edwards, 2016). In *Rogue One*, Andor is one of two heroes who deliver the plans of the Death Star, the weapon central to the first *Star Wars*, and, for this reason, Andor is a crucial character in the multi-billion-dollar franchise. In episode 7 of the series, Andor is yet to become a spy working for the rebellion, but he is wanted by the Empire for a huge robbery, and, in the twisted action/detective plotline, Andor tries to hide from the Empire by using the fake name Keef Girgo. Replicating the tactic used by the Brontë sisters, by Thomas Paine, by Anonymous, and many others, Andor uses indexical dissociation to fight against the powerful. Yet, when I saw that in this sci-fi narrative anonymity meant simply taking a pseudonym, I laughed. The very thought that in a future aided by computers an Empire may rule without DNA-based identification systems seemed preposterous to me. If in the

1770s Jeremy Bentham wished for an identification system where our names would be tattooed on our bodies, what chances are there that in our near and far future, DNA and other biological markers, inescapable, won't be the bases of democratic and nondemocratic ruling? Chances are zero. DNA and other biological markers are already central to social order and to ruling, and there is nothing in our present that suggests that the use of these biological indexes will not expand and reach all facets of life.

Yet, the show *Andor* needed hope, and the writers knew that anonymity would justify it. If Andor could hide from the Empire, hope and the resistance would survive. I use this example to illustrate what perhaps by now is obvious. If even a fictional rebellion in the Star Wars universe cannot exist without anonymity, without the ability to dissociate ourselves from our indexes, the question becomes whether our futures are all fundamentally shaped by the growing asymmetries between anonymity and surveillance in a socio-technological present ruled with/by computers and in a political context in which absolutism, authoritarianism, and fascism are increasingly common. If even our fantasies of freedom depend on anonymity to be plausible, can freedom exist in a socio-technical and political future that harnesses the power of biological traces to know or predict what individuals do or plan to do? This is a future where our indexes are inescapable, attached to our bodies *because* they are our bodies. If our bodies are our shackles, can anybody be free?

We have come to associate agentic anonymity with rebellion, and this association has primed us to think that anonymity is eminently, or at least importantly, a social good and it should be protected. This important perspective is not particularly new or original, as it is shared by thinkers as different and as old as Benjamin Franklin and as new as Helen Nissenbaum. Anonymity, these thinkers believe, is essential to our capacity to exist in a social order that requires occasional redirections, revolutions, if you wish, and in a social order where speaking to power is often dangerous. The tragedy of our socio-technical history is that increasingly, technology has made it harder to be, to act, and to feel anonymous. Lucy could, in an almost foolish way, assure herself that her identity was kept safe, even though digital environments made it extremely hard to be truly anonymous. Her miscalculation was tragic. How many are at this very moment similarly miscalculating vulnerabilities when engaging with communication technologies? If Franklin and Nissenbaum are right, if all we have left are self-deceiving myths as in *Andor*, we are indeed in trouble. It is unclear how the direction of our socio-technical decisions could generate anything other than benign or malevolent totalitarianism. The Empire, indeed, looms ahead.

This concluding chapter brings together insights peppered throughout the book and organizes them in three particular areas of emphasis. The first attends to some of anonymity's connections to the social by elaborating on the notion of an economy of anonymity. The second emphasis synthesizes insights that shape identity theory and ideas on the subject. In addition, I show how a subaltern perspective gives analytic meaning and focus to the economy of anonymity and to this book's theories on the subject. Last, I show how subaltern analytics can help us understand the social multiplicity represented by the digital and the analogue.

The Social Properties of the Economy of Anonymity

When directed upward, toward those in power, agentic anonymity is indeed essential to the very possibility of political progress and change. But there is more to anonymity than whether anonymity can help us oppose power, which is why this book has also presented a different perspective on anonymity from the more conventional agentic perspective that Franklin (2016) and Nissenbaum (1999) provide. I have introduced the term "economy of anonymity" to help us understand the importance of embracing a systemic perspective on anonymity. This system is not as tightly woven as the system of indexicalization in which anonymity operates, but it is sufficiently dense to recognize it as an economy, as a structure that helps determine power at the macro and micro levels. An economy of anonymity has different properties that shape the meaning and social outcomes of anonymity at any given time and in each instance. In what follows I list the most evident of these properties and their effects on subjects and the social. Each of these properties has been shown and analyzed in the chapters preceding this Conclusion, but here is the first time that I bring these insights together.

(1) *An economy of anonymity is given form by distribution systems that dictate who can have anonymity, on what conditions, and what individuals, communities, or institutions can use it and for what ends.* Some of these distribution systems are socio-technical, as in the inscription technologies that, I showed, shaped the unnaming and renaming of immigrants (see Chapter 5). Others are socio-scientific, as when health practitioners establish anonymous organ donation or when medical institutions claim scientific knowledge to assign sexes (Chapter 2). And yet other distribution systems are political, as when journalists embrace the notion of anonymous sources in order to protect those who speak to power or when publishing practices normalize gendered authorial practices (Introduction, Chapter 1). Each of these distribution systems behaves as a normative framework that shapes how individuals connect to each other, to institutions, and to power.

(2) *In an economy of anonymity, distribution systems have directionality.* Anonymity, I have argued, is indexical, which means that anonymity is vectorial. It has a point of origin, a direction, and target(s). The point of origin can be a person, a social agent, but it can also be an institution. The direction can be upward, as when Andor tries to fool the Empire; downward, as when a slave master forces a new name upon a slave; and horizontal, as when a social media user takes a pseudonym to comment on other users' views. The directionality of anonymity partly explains anonymity's effects on power, and vice versa.

(3) *Whoever controls anonymity controls the relationship with the target and, often, controls the target.* As with other distribution systems, it matters greatly who or what imposes or generates anonymity on individuals and the direction or target of anonymity. Almost instinctively, we know that when agents choose anonymity, they do it to control some social and power relation. This is why we think Andor may succeed at pushing back against the Empire or that Mary Shelley did right by choosing to publish *Frankenstein* anonymously. When an agent chooses anonymity, the agent

controls that relationship. But this is not because anonymity naturally favors individual agency but rather because in these instances, agents control the origin and direction of anonymity.

In this book I have shown also the importance of recognizing, identifying, and researching instances in which anonymity is initiated by institutions or communities. Particular cases like naming and renaming of individuals under coverture, slavery, colonialism, and assimilationist forces in immigration revealed this important strand of anonymity (Introduction, and Chapters 2, 3, 5, 6). In these cases, individuals have to relinquish names, and thus self-identity, to become proper subjects of power. Women were and are forced by convention to take their husband's name. Slaves, colonized subjects, and immigrants have been pushed or forced to relinquish their names to become chattel or to become assimilated, de-subjectified into a different people. The old indexes go. The new ones mark you, mark me, as a controlled subject or an object, empty of will and of freedom. The ontic technique of indexical dissociation has social ontological outcomes (Chapter 2). New beings are created, and this process of creation often requires a first step, the normative, traditional (Chapter 6), or coercive imposition of new indexes and the social and legal traditions that support them. Anonymity has a vectorial property, and this vector is the vector of power. It matters who or what initiates the anonymizing.

(4) *When anonymity is directed horizontally, anonymity reshapes the social and communities.* Horizontal relationships are between individuals or communities of relatively equal power. For instance, two social media users have roughly equal power, and either or both often have the ability to use pseudonymity to hide their identity. Alcoholics Anonymous explains their uses of anonymity as follows: "In stressing the equality of all A.A. members—and unity in the common bond of their recovery from alcoholism—anonymity serves as the spiritual foundation of A.A." While AA also uses anonymity to hide the identity of members from the public and the press, anonymity helps establish the principle of horizontal relationships at the heart of their mission. Each member is equal to each other in relationship to the disease, and each needs the others' support for

their recovery to succeed. I expand on the subjective and ethical effects of horizontal forms of anonymizing later, but, first I briefly analyze other directionalities.

(5) *When anonymity is directed upward, anonymity gives the capacity to individuals and groups to undermine or oppose the more powerful.* This anonymity is vertical, and it originates in a lower social stratum. This is the anonymity that often inspires and gives hope to the less powerful. It is the anonymity at the center of the example in *Andor* and the type of anonymity Lucy mythified. It was the anonymity that allowed anonymous writers like Jane Austen, Mary Shelley, and Thomas Paine to exist in the public sphere and the anonymity that lionized the hacker activist organizations like Anonymous. The conscious manipulation of indexes has been a tool of the subaltern, a crucial element in the hidden transcripts that anthropologist James C. Scott (1990) repeatedly encountered in different contexts at different times. The first paragraph of this celebrated book establishes the importance of anonymity directed upward by arguing that the subordinate routinely avoided direct confrontations with the powerful and instead "adopted the safer course of anonymous attacks on property, poaching, character assassination, and shunning" as political tactics (17). Anonymity was not the only socio-technical tool at their disposal. Arguing for the intrinsic power and need for privacy, Scott reminds us that "slaves in the relative safety of their quarters can speak the words of anger, revenge, self-assertion that they must normally choke back when in the presence of the masters and mistresses" (18). That is, subalterns using these tactics understand how indexes work, the way in which technologies of inscription work, and the relational technologies indexes activate. They are able to calculate consequences and act accordingly.

(6) *When anonymity is directed downward, the outcomes of anonymity benefit the goals of the powerful.* I have already noted instances in which anonymity starts from above (e.g., coverture, slavery, and immigration), and the outcomes are terrible. But downward anonymity is not automatically bad. When an institution asks for anonymity, anonymity may have positive effects on individuals as in the case of the anonymous vote, which protects voters from potentially vindictive elected officials. Sperm donations

or organ donations are typically anonymous to protect the donor from legal or ethical repercussions. When laws protect the right of protesters to use masks (as is the case in thirty-three states in the United States), these laws are trying to encourage public debate and political dynamism. In all of these cases, the targets of anonymity have less power than the institutions regulating anonymity, but the anonymizing benefits the anonymized. That said, the reason these forms of anonymity are institutionalized is not to primarily benefit the anonymized; it is to pursue the goals of the institutions. Democracies need legitimacy, and the anonymous vote is one instrument to achieve this. Corporations or institutions that depend on sperm or organ donors need the participation of people, and they use anonymity to encourage it.

(7) *The powerful often control all distribution systems, shaping also horizontally and upwardly directed anonymity.* In the United States, where the powerful in politics systematically court the powerful in the technology sector, as was happening with President Trump and Elon Musk, the expansive datafication regime is increasingly emptying out the hidden scripts' repertory. Conflicts over digital identity are rarely resolved through standard juridical processes, even if these indeed exist. In 2005, the US Supreme Court upheld the right of anonymous blogger "Proud Citizen" to remain anonymous, stating unequivocally that "bloggers have a strong First Amendment right to speak anonymously." Yet, this is also the same legal and security regime that showed, thanks to Edward Snowden, that the US government is routinely spying on citizens and governments all over the world, with the cooperation of telecommunication giants and the tech industry. The First Amendment right of digital anonymity is almost irrelevant in a technological and juridical realm that has normalized data gathering, and this normalization, controlled by the technology corporate sector, shapes all anonymity. Those who forced the disappearance of Lucy and her partner in Mexico never sought legal means to find their identity. They simply used superior technological means to identify Lucy and her partner.

(8) *Anonymity is valued more by the subaltern, just as identification and surveillance are valued more by the powerful.* To the powerful, anonymity

has some value, but it is often small. Anonymity is only a part of a structure of domination. The slaveowner used renaming, indexical dissociation, as a brutal cultural symbol to erase the slave's past and redefine them as chattel. But the importance of renaming vis-à-vis kidnapping and taking coercive and legal possession of an individual is relatively minimal. The effects of racist laws, for instance, were and are greater. In other words, the slave system did not depend on renaming but used it to signify it and reconstitute it. It did, however, depend on racist law.

By contrast, anonymity, disguise, and privacy play a crucial role in the struggles the weak engage with against the powerful. And, while this book has shown that anonymity is in more places than we typically consider, in the final instance, from a social and political perspective, indexical dissociation is more important to the subaltern than it is to the powerful. This means that from the macro, societal perspective, the digital realm is constituting a social order that will unquestionably benefit the powerful. All the questions about the present and future of datafication point toward potential socio-technical answers that will make surveillance ever more powerful, algorithmic injustice ever more present, and capital extraction, of the types analyzed by Couldry and Mejias (2019) and Zuboff (2019), ever more systemic. Nothing but fantasies point our futures in the direction of *Andor*.

Yet, a subaltern critique cannot end with the recognition that anonymity is valuable to the subaltern, which is where a lot of scholarship ends. In this book, a subaltern critique has more dimensions than value. It is a critique with a positionality that recognizes that power is structural and systemic. For this reason, I have used the economy of anonymity as a strategic perspective that allows us, and even compels us, to engage questions about indexes from systemic vantage points. Understood as a cultural technique, and as a border *dispositif*, I have argued that anonymity is crucial to the organizing of human groups and crucial also to self-recognition and identity. Because of this, anonymity helps us see patterns and prospects associated with the introduction of new socio-technical systems grounded in indexing, from facial recognition and fingerprinting to other forms of surveillance. Those who study the data sets that train machines' "senses" to identify specific individuals or behaviors alert us to the uses of the relatively anonymized sets of faces and actions that end up sharpening the AI skills. In places like the United States, these data sets are often collected without the consent of individuals and continue being used even if they needed to be and were not erased. Our indexes may participate in forms of power that we may oppose, that target us unjustly, or that undermine our sense of privacy and our ability to be anonymous in digital public spaces. Importantly, the analytics of anonymity can help us understand what outcomes are likely when specific indexical technologies and practices are introduced and to recognize that there is a range of possibilities that may need to be explored to understand outcomes. These possibilities will connect order and identity, epistemology and phenomenology, subject and being. Engaging anonymity requires us to understand the socio-technical ingredients at the heart of indexical play that include, at the very least, indexical materials, technologies of inscription, and relational technologies.

But this book does more than argue that anonymity is the other of surveillance and datafication and that anonymity should be treated, like privacy, as essential to the social and political well-being of individuals. This book has shown that anonymity also shapes subjectivity, which means that the economy of anonymity is more than a socio-technological structure that controls some of the levers of power.

Subjective Properties of the Economy of Anonymity

(9) *The economy of anonymity textures the subjective realm, the space of possibilities, desires, identities, and experiences that give meaning and shape to being in time, in context.* This book expands understandings of anonymity and the subject first by noting the limitations in the literature. Most research on anonymity has a version of the individual, but one that rarely interrogates subjectivity. Most studies of anonymity, after all, are interested in what in this book I call agentic anonymity, and, in these studies, anonymity allows for some forms of agency to exist. Women writers can publish; trolls can criticize and taunt; journalistic sources can talk; and voters can vote. At this level, anonymity is a social tool or cultural technique that

helps agents acquire impunity, and individuals using anonymity are a sort of rational, reflexive actors choosing pathways to accomplish their goals. They have a macro understanding of the consequences of their actions, which also means that they act within the constraints of normative understandings of good and legal behavior.

Yet, once we define anonymity as indexical dissociation and recognize institutional and contextual anonymity, this approach to anonymity seems rather limited. As a scholar, once I identified anonymity in slavery, coverture, and colonialism, I recognized that a perspective anchored in agency was quite limited. Agentic anonymity mattered, but anonymity was more than that. Scholars like Gloria Anzaldúa, José Esteban Muñoz, and Mariana Ortega and novelists like Ralph Ellison, Margaret Atwood, and Percival Everett helped me glimpse the missing parts.

Nothing that I had read on anonymity from the agentic and rationalist perspective could help me explain what indexical dissociation was to and in subjects. Let me explain my bafflement by exercising the humanist privilege of treating art as evidence and repeating the quote that opened this book:

> My name isn't Offred, I have another name, which nobody uses now because it is forbidden. I tell myself it doesn't matter, your name is like your telephone number, useful only to others; but what I tell myself is wrong, it does matter. I keep knowledge of this name like something hidden, some treasure I'll come back to dig up, one day. I think of this name as buried. This name has an aura around it, like an amulet, some charm that's survived from an unimaginably distant past. I lie in my single bed at night, with my eyes closed, and the name floats there behind my eyes, not quite within reach, shining in the dark. (Atwood 1986, 84)

This insight into a psyche shaped by anonymizing may be Atwood's, but different versions of the same painful experiences are in Alex Haley's *Roots*, Percival Everett's *Erasure*, and Ralph Ellison's *Invisible Man*. I saw echoes of the power that anonymity has in the subject while reading Anzaldúa's work on the borderlands, in the words of Sojourner Truth, and in Lucy, the central character in Chapter 3. And then I turned this insight inward and began to realize my own history, shaped by migration, unnaming and renaming, the hypervisibility and invisibility of being a Brown male body in racist contexts, the oddity of being me, with this body, with these concrete and categorical indexes, in this profession, and recognized more and more common features of the power of indexical dissociation in my soul. I not only understood Offred: I identified with her.

To the scholar of identity, to someone trained like me, all of this was relatively new. Identity scholarship is built on the notion that identity matters and that who we are and how we positively identify ourselves are roughly the same thing. We highlight the fact that identities are relational, in a system, and thus that negation is part of the identity process, but in practice, positive identity wins over. The negation of relational identity is partly quasi-Saussurean and cognitive: I am Latine because I am not Black, or White, or Indigenous, or Asian American, or Pacific Islander. But in practice, identity theory constitutes and reconstitutes a positive, affirmative notion of identity that allows an individual to claim: "I am Latine because I am x, y, and z." Other ethno-racial identities may help us understand boundary conditions (e.g., Afro-Latines are both Black and Latine), but these boundary conditions simply redefine the category. Complexities are resolved by redefinitions, and we are quick to accept that Latinidad is multiracial, for instance. To start from the perspective of identity means to reconstitute it.

Identity theory in ethnic studies is partly attentive to scholars like Anzaldúa, but the condition of being in the borderlands seems specific enough to categorize it as a particular, not general, human condition. And, while Latine scholarship may embrace the notion that many Latines are more like Anzaldúa than they are not, and that these Latines live and experience life from two national perspectives, both perspectives are defined mostly as affirmations. Anzaldúa *was* US American *and* Mexican; I *am* US American *and* Mexican; Jennifer Lopez *is* US American *and* Puerto Rican, and so on. The positive relationships, the affirming relationships, take precedence over anything else. Our hybridity is the coming together of two substances, two affirmations, and two ontologies.

Thankfully, Latine studies is not static, and, in general, the discipline is moving away from embracing only positive identity and ontologies of affirmation. Scholars like Muñoz, with his book *Disidentification: Queers of Color and the Performance of Politics* (1999), and Ortega, with *In-Between: Latina Feminist Phenomenology, Multiplicity, and the Self* (2016), have turned away from the axiom of identity and opened new avenues of interrogation.

Anchored in identity questions important to Anzaldúa and other Latine scholars, Muñoz's argument is set against Louis Althusser's notion of interpellation, the identificatory technique that Althusser uses to illustrate ideology. In Althusser, we are interpellated by ideology, and our response locates us in the social structures as subjects. In Muñoz's work, people who are erased by ideology, like queer people of color, can respond to hegemonic ideological interpellations only at great cost, and, for this reason, disidentification is possible and even needed for survival.

Muñoz does not use the term "anonymity" once in his book but uses ideas of invisibility and erasure, which depend on indexical dissociation and often imply anonymizing processes. In my terms, Muñoz is concerned with forms of invisibility and erasure that are the result of an economy of anonymity that is given structural form by the anonymizing that happens to subaltern subjects absent from culture, misrepresented, or dismissed. From Frantz Fanon's (1952) dismissal of Black queerness, to the absence of Brown queerness from the queer cultural canon of the time, Muñoz pushes back against the anonymizing erasures that shape the lives of queers of color. In his work, queer Brown performances, which are characterized by the play of indexes, are essential to the self-creation these subjects routinely do. Muñoz theorizes these performances in ways that echo my analyses of indexical changes (e.g., Sojourner Truth and the Tsimshian in the previous chapter, Nex Benedict and Herculine in Chapter 2, immigrants in Chapter 5) to explain and trouble the relationship of indexical dissociation to the subject. Fusing our analytic vocabularies, queer Brown performance is a type of agentic anonymizing crucial to self-creation. Muñoz and I are in agreement on most things, including the following: Indexical play is fueled by the dialectic of anonymity and identification, and disidentification is one of its possibilities.

In my read of Muñoz's work, the economy of anonymity textures the subjective realm, an insight found also in Ortega's analysis of Latina phenomenology. Ortega, whose work is essential to this book, also uses the work of Anzaldúa to theorize a phenomenology of multiplicity that can better account for the lived realities of Latines in the United States, but one that also explains the lived realities of many others. Like Muñoz, she uses ideas of subject fragmentation for her phenomenology, but her conceptual toolkit includes ways of conceiving power outside the top-down structure at the heart of Althusser's work and, by extension, Muñoz's. One senses in Ortega a notion of power that is also fragmented, refracted, and multiplicitous, which produces the need to conceive of a subject whose mastery of the environment requires multiple hermeneutic codes and performance possibilities.

Different as they are, Muñoz and Ortega push ethnic (and subaltern) studies away from identity resolutions based on affirmation. Subaltern subjects are not constituted by ideology in the model proposed by Althusser. Subaltern Latine identity does not simply represent the imaginary relationship of Latine subjects to their real conditions of existence. Muñoz reminds us that the real conditions of existence, which are sometimes painful and even deadly, also interpellate us and force our attention away from ideology to craft performances of subjectivity that counter the oppressiveness of the dominant. The subaltern subject (Muñoz's work allows for some generalization) incorporates negation, not simply or only affirmation, and disidentification, two powerful ontic operators. And, negation and disidentification cannot exist without indexical dissociation. To the interpellation of ideology, the subaltern answers, "I am not who you claim I am." Or, as Atwood helped us vividly experience in the nightmarish world she created for us: "My name isn't Offred."

In Anzaldúa's work, subjects like Offred are common. She belongs to *los atravesados*, the category of humans who are fragmented and multiple by necessity or choice. With a mixture of biological, ethical, racial, and sexual indexes, she describes subalterns in the process of becoming ("who cross over, pass over"), of movement. Becoming is crucial to Anzaldúa's theories of the subject, and Ortega reminds us that so is multiplicity. Multiple and always in the process of becoming, the subaltern subject is as much "I am" as "I am not," the result of a dialectic of identity and anonymity without resolution or synthesis. The subalterns' hybridity is the coming together of two or more substances and affirmations; but also, and more primordially, it is the coming together of two or more absences and negations. Indexical dissociation is always already in identity, and not simply because identity is relational, but because identity is fragmented, unstable, dynamic, and *irresolute*.

The subaltern here is a model of being inspired by actual historical subjects. The model is not Offred but Anzaldúa. And, as a model of being, the subaltern makes it easy to understand how an ontology of becoming is needed and thus, how anonymity and indexical dissociation are part of subaltern ontology. But it would be an error to claim that only subalterns, as historical subjects, exist in the throes of becoming and, thus, to believe that indexical dissociation shapes the lives of only those who are subalterns.

One changes when one needs to adapt, and one needs to adapt when one's being does not match the standard or norm or when circumstances transform context (Deleuze and Guattari [1987] 2005, 291). We may define the standard or mode of being as that of the White cisgender male and thus assume that White cisgender males are not in the midst of becoming. This thesis would allow us to cleanly rearticulate a separation between subalterns and White cisgender males, and that may keep things clean, but reality is messy. Every human may experience nepantla, the in-between, at one point or another, even White cisgender males. In some milieus, it is some form of subaltern archetype that may constitute the standard, and this matters to those who exist in those milieus, and this matters to those who, like White cisgender males, do not fit the standard (see Amaya 2024). And, last, when circumstances transform context, as is happening today with the generalized effects of environmental challenges, many, regardless of ascription, will become like *los atravesados*, migrants, the ones who cross over, pass over, and the half-dead. Becoming is coming.

We can generalize cautiously in the following way:

(10) *Like identity, anonymity is part of human ontology, but not every*

human is equally shaped by it. As I showed in this book, subaltern historical subjects, including women, sexual minorities, immigrants, and ethnoracial minorities, tend to be forced into processes of becoming that include indexical transformations. In the previous chapter, I used the terms "forced indexical dissociation" and "disciplinary indexical dissociation" to attend to these power moves and the way these impositions or coercions mark the subaltern as subaltern. But the chapter also identified two other types of anonymizing, "traditional indexical dissociation" and "indexical dissociation as self-creation," that show anonymizing in processes of becoming at the center of the social, as in tradition, and at the core of agency, as self-creation. The former includes naming and human categorizing processes common in Indigenous cultures but can also include religious traditions based on conversion and other "normal" categories of being that we embrace in the process of becoming modern, like those related to education and political conviction. One is expected to become "college educated" or "blue collar" and believe in "liberalism" or "conservatism." Traditional forms of being are process oriented.

(11) *An economy of anonymity includes, and depends on, intersubjectivity and the micro-asymmetries anonymity constitutes.* Indexical dissociation as self-creation refers to instances of indexical play that allow individuals to experience multiple social domains as if they were multiple beings. There are two sides to this process. The subject side is aware of the multiplicity, and these experiences require reflexivity and a working theory of how identity and indexes function in different domains. When an immigrant faces a border officer, the immigrant has a working theory of how to present themselves and what descriptors to use. The border officer is, however, privy only to the performance of the immigrant in that moment. People at the border have these experiences routinely, but the insight of multiplicity applies to many others, including, for instance, social media users who rely on nicknames and pseudonyms to embrace identities different from the ones they may have in real life (IRL). Ortega and Anzaldúa may have been inspired by the borderlands, but their ideas of nepantla and multiplicity explain well the multiplicity of social and material domains that the digital and the analogue have made normal. This means that today more

than ever in history, subjects are defined by agentic indexical dissociation and indexical play and by the micro-asymmetries these bring to life.

I am not suggesting that nepantla is everywhere or some sort of facile generalization that may romanticize the conditions of the subaltern. Nor am I suggesting that the subaltern is the future of all, in the same playful way in which sometimes we say that "woman is the future of man." What I show with this book is that subaltern theory has paved the way for an understanding of the multiplicity of social domains that can be used to theorize other multiplicities, including the multiplicity created by the digital and the analogue, which envelops most.

Ethics of the Economy of Anonymity

(12) *Because anonymity and impunity give form, meaning, and value to the micro-asymmetries of the economy of anonymity at the interpersonal level, anonymity shapes ethics and social trust.* The conditions of multiplicity characterize most of our lives, and they are reshaping what it means to be human, to be moral, and to be honest, as much as they are redefining the role trust and truth play in our lives. More than ever in history, we have access to impunity, thanks to casual and tactical horizontal anonymity, and we can be immoral and unethical without affecting our reputations and daily lives.

This outcome would not be surprising to Immanuel Kant (1991) who, in *Perpetual Peace*, argues that "all actions affecting the rights of other human beings are wrong if their maxim is not compatible with their being made public" (126). Kant is forwarding here a notion of ethics and governance that depends on publicity and openness, one that is also limited by its overreliance on the notion of a "rational actor." If what we do needs to be hidden, it is probably immoral. Contrariwise, if what we do to others can be shared openly and can be debated, it is probably moral and right. While Kant's notion of ethics is not without detractors (including me), it remains a common understanding of public virtue, and Kant's "publicity condition" continues influencing today's understanding of publicness, particularly arguments about the politics of visibility. Yet, the publicity condition seems incompatible with agentic anonymity, and the different effects of the practices of dissociation illustrate what I call the "anonymity condition," which may help us also refocus our attention on anonymity's role in ethics and governmentality.

Agentic anonymity is not in tension only with Kant's notion of ethics. Agentic anonymity is also in tension with any post-Levinasian understanding of ethics, or any ethics of recognition or identity as imagined by Axel Honneth (Honneth 1995; Levinas 1969). After all, agentic anonymity depends on misrecognition or at least the deflection of identity, and it is questionable whether one can use these important strands of ethics to help us understand an ethics of anonymity. The issue is twofold: In the digital realm, anonymous social interactions seem to invite a great degree of unethical behavior. For instance, the Pew Research Center recently released a report pointing out that 41 percent of US residents have personally experienced some form of online harassment and nearly a fifth of them have experienced severe forms of online harassment, including physical threats, harassment over a sustained period, sexual harassment, or stalking from anonymous sources (Vogels 2021). Yet, the issue is not only that agentic anonymity seems to invite unethical behavior but that anonymity is also used in ethical and even emancipatory ways. How do we think about an ethics of agentic anonymity? Or, even better, what is an ethics *with* agentic anonymity?

Ethics and identity have always connected, and they do so more evidently in what some philosophers call "prudential rationality," or the type of self-judgment that attends to the likeliness of harming our future self if what we do is deemed unethical and punishable. Kant's publicity condition is one example of prudential rationality. In cases of prudential rationality, accountability matters. If today a person does something immoral or illegal and others find out in the future, that person will be accountable and will suffer the consequences. But if the ground of accountability depends on identification, then prudential rationality becomes less important to a person and to a society. That is, prudence matters because a person's future self can be punished or criticized for unethical behavior today only if present self is positively connected with future self. But if the person uses anonymity today, future self is off the hook.

Common notions of ethics that fit into prudential rationality cannot easily adapt or explain ethics and the multibody problem. Agentic anonymity cannot be used in every action in the analogue realm, though it is readily available in the digital realm. Regardless, only some actions can be anonymous, not all. So, while prudence may shape some ethical behavior, it is secondary or unimportant to the subset of actions that are anonymous. From the perspective of an individual who has two or more realms in which to act (e.g., digital and analogue, at least), and the ethical relationship that such individual has with themselves, multiplicity is a problematic, a conundrum. How should I behave? How should any of us behave given the increasing role of impunity?

Can prudence matter and not matter at the same time? Strictly speaking, no. If a person is prudent only when all actions can be connected back to them but not when actions are anonymous, we don't call that person prudent. They may be tactical, as when someone slows down their driving when they enter their own neighborhood but speeds in other neighborhoods. They may be experimental, as when someone adopts another sex identity in an avatar to experiment with subjectivity and intersubjectivity. But we could also call them hypocritical, in particular when the outcomes of actions are unethical or illegal. While prudence has been a virtue particularly defined by its future and public orientation, we call a hypocrite any person who practices a virtue (kindness, loyalty, fairness) only when they can be identified, but disregard these virtues when anonymous or in privacy.

(13) *The economy of anonymity connects the interpersonal to the social, thus helping us understand current and future power structures.* Agentic anonymity is about public actions, words, and performances. When these actions are directed up, toward the powerful, they are one of the scripts that subalterns use to oppose the powerful. But when actions are directed horizontally, as when a troll insults a social media user, that person is shaping the public realm and making it not simply agonistic, which is a feature common of publicity, but harmful. When a person participates in the public sphere but hides behind anonymity, that interaction opens up new ethical possibilities and judgments. Multiplicity and anonymity shape an

individual's sense of what is prudent and what is right, and they shape also the digital social environment by making it harder to predict. Anonymous strangers are everywhere in real life. But their presence is more dramatic and consequential in digital environments. Plenty of research on trolling, cyberbullying, and other forms of digital harm place anonymity as a factor that engenders these antisocial behaviors (Barlett et al. 2016; Li et al. 2022; Nitschinsk et al. 2022, 2023; Ludemann 2023; Macaulay et al. 2022). The magnitude of these many instances of incivility gives meaning to the digital social environment, forcing recalculations on overall social trust, making it harder to exist and to speak without the fear of harm and harassment. Our circles of trust in digital realms are shrinking thanks in part to anonymous trolling but also because of the way platforms reify homophily, the idea that our digital neighborhoods should include only those who behave or think like us (see Chapter 4).

All of this is happening at the same time that surveillance makes it harder than ever to be anonymous to those in power. While digital corporations seem to be nurturing horizontal anonymity, they knowingly or unknowingly sow distrust among the population and thus help create and fortify divisions, a sort of "divide and conquer"; the powerful are also committed to radical identificatory techniques to increase surveillance and control. Without question, this identificatory asymmetry will be essential to the reproduction of surveillance capitalism and data colonialism but also to the increasing weakening of democratic values and to the rise of authoritarianism. The powerful succeed when the weak are fragmented, mistrustful, and unable to believe in solidarity and the possibility of allyship.

Yet, this book has done more than explore the economy of anonymity and how it shapes power. Chapter by chapter, page by page, this book has argued and shown a novel way of thinking about anonymity and a new way of using anonymity to make sense of society and subjectivity. I call this way of thinking about anonymity subaltern because of the examples I use, the voices I elevate, and the questions that I privilege. Subaltern analytics, given focus by border scholars, is helping us glimpse the problem of material multiplicity, of existing in different social realms, a problem magnified by new technologies of anonymity. Material multiplicity engenders the related problems of ethical multiplicity, phenomenological multiplicity, and ontological multiplicity. I began sketching these problems in this book and Conclusion, but much needs to be done. Questions abound because these problems cannot be perceived by single perspectives but only by circling around the multiplicitous subject, as proposed by Ortega, and by accepting, in humility, that any one perspective is highly limited and cannot help us see or understand multiplicity. If we cannot see it, we cannot think it, and we cannot solve it. Standing in front of this monumental shape-shifting subject, given three-dimensional complexity by the negations of anonymity, I wonder: Where should we go? And, how should we go about it?

Notes

Introduction

1. *Oxford English Dictionary*, s.v. "anonymous (n. & adj.)," September 2023, https://doi.org/10.1093/OED/7754668016.

2. For an overview of this encounter of science and racism, see Tracy Teslow (2014).

Chapter 1

1. 4chan and 8chan are two imageboards that ask users to be anonymous. This is a norm that has allowed for the imageboards to welcome users to form communities with views that are controversial, radical, and often embracing nihilism. See Angela Nagle (2017).

2. In Heidegger, ontology is about Being, and ontic is about properties and characteristics of a particular class of beings (Slaby 2021). I am interested in the ontic, or in onticity, as it pertains to indexes and anonymity, and develop these issues further in the next chapter and Chapter 5.

3. Dana Snitzky (2016) writes a highly readable account of that period in the Brontë sisters' lives.

4. David Lyon (1994) uses the term "surveillance society" to attend to some of these concerns. The term is meant to encompass the way our "personal lives are collected, stored, retrieved and processed every day within huge computer databases belonging to big corporations and government departments. This is

the 'surveillance society'" (3). Our works attend to similar issues, questions, and empirical realities, but Lyon's emphasis is on social order. Indexicalization is broader than that. Indexicalization is also concerned with social order, but indexicalization also focuses on the way indexes and indexical play are crucial to daily life, identity, and self.

5. Scholarship on data and personal identifiers often uses the terms "direct identifier" and "indirect identifier" to differentiate between identifiers like personal names, Social Security numbers, and such, which point toward a singular individual, and identifiers like race or gender, which point toward categories of individuals. I believe this terminology uses metaphors of visibility (as in direct gaze, indirect gaze, or direct light and indirect light) to illustrate how these identifiers operate differently. Because my work starts with the insight that the first hermeneutic task of a human index is numerical, I prefer terminology that attends to numeracy and use instead the terms "concrete index" and "categorical index." A concrete index, like a direct identifier, refers to indexes that point toward a singular individual. Categorical indexes, like indirect identifiers, help us identify a group or a set of individuals. One identifies a unit (concrete index). The other identifies a set (categorical index).

Chapter 2

1. Let me note that this is not a chapter that engages centrally the ontological possibilities and questions of trans and/or intersex people. Other works like Katharine Jenkins's (2023) *Ontology and Oppression* more centrally deal with the issue. That said, I use cases pertaining to sexuality to work through questions of ontology. But my goal is to more generally query the connection between anonymity and ontology.

2. Nominalism is the notion that the only way that we can experience the real is with our minds and with our language. Opposite to nominalism are realism and Platonism.

3. In *The Eighteenth Brumaire of Louis Bonaparte*, Karl Marx (1926) writes: "Men make their own history, but they do not make it just as they please; they do not make it under circumstances chosen by themselves, but under circumstances directly encountered, given and transmitted from the past. The tradition of all the dead generations weighs like a nightmare on the brain of the living" (23). Echoing these concerns, E. P. Thompson writes in *The Making of the English Working Class* (1966): "I am seeking to rescue the poor stockinger, the Luddite cropper, the 'obsolete' hand-loom weaver, the 'utopian' artisan, and even the deluded follower of Joanna Southcott, from the enormous condescension of posterity. Their crafts

and traditions may have been dying. Their hostility to the new industrialism may have been backward-looking. Their communitarian ideals may have been fantasies. Their insurrectionary conspiracies may have been foolhardy. But they lived through these times of acute social disturbance, and we did not. Their aspirations were valid in terms of their own experience; and, if they were casualties of history, they remain, condemned in their own lives, as casualties" (12–13). These two thinkers and their texts speak to the ontological constraints of existence and the ontological possibilities within those moments—and how we ought to be sensitive to what seemed (im)possible in those moments.

4. I am not arguing that current technology is infallible when it comes to identifying individuals. Facial recognition failures like those documented by Timnit Gebru (see Engler 2020) or Lauren Bridges (2021) show the limits and dangers of these technologies and the discourses surrounding them.

Chapter 3

1. I want to thank Duke University Press, the publisher of my previous book *Trafficking* (2020), for authorizing me to use sections of that book in this chapter.

2. See also Torin Monahan (2022), who elaborates on companion terms like "visibility" and "transparency" (42–55).

3. The anonymous blogs include *El Blog del Narco* (elblogdelnarco.com, elblogdelnarco.net, elblogdelnarco.info), *Mundo Narco* (mundonarco.com), *Narco Violencia* (narcoviolencia.com), and several blogs and social media pages connected to *Valor Por Tamaulipas* (valorportamaulipas.com), including *Responsabilidad Por Tamaulipas*, *Esperanza Por Tamaulipas*, *Valor Por Michoacán*, and *Valor Por Veracruz*.

4. Hector Amaya, "Bloody Blogs: Publicity and Opacity," in *Trafficking: Narcoculture in Mexico and the United States*, 158–91. Copyright 2020, Duke University Press. All rights reserved. Republished by permission of the publisher. www.dukeupress.edu.

5. Rory Carroll, writing for *The Guardian* in April 3, 2013, was able to corroborate that the person he interviewed was indeed in control of *EBDN*, but some of the rest of the information in this and other interviews has not been corroborated due to Lucy's anonymity.

6. Hector Amaya, "Trust: The Burden of Civics," in *Trafficking: Narcoculture in Mexico and the United States*, 192–212. Copyright 2020, Duke University Press. All rights reserved. Republished by permission of the publisher. www.dukeupress.edu.

7. She published this in *El Blog de Lucy*, the blog started while she was on

the run. The blog was published in Spanish, and her words were the following: "Inicié Blog del Narco y mi suerte cambió. ¿Si no hubiera hecho nada? ¿Si hubiera sido una mexicana indiferente con la realidad? ¿Si me hubiera quedado callada? ¿Si hubiera decidido dejarme la venda en los ojos?" Translation by the author.

8. In Spanish, we still prefer the word *cortés*, "courteous," a word that reminds all that this aspect of trust developed first in modernity in the courts of the aristocracy.

Chapter 4

1. Changes to communication technologies, culture, religion, and economic conditions began eroding tradition, first in Europe and, seismically, through the power and violence of colonialism, in the rest of the world. The printing press began transforming knowledge distribution in the fifteenth century. Martin Luther published the *Ninety-Five Theses* in 1517, starting what would become the Protestant Reformation. In 1559, Queen Elizabeth I reestablished the authority of the Church of England and Ireland, independent from papal authority, and she was excommunicated in 1570. The British Isles and Europe were in religious turmoil while colonialism was expanding European imaginations and coffers, constituting new sources of wealth and power, and introducing the need to theorize humans anew.

2. For a more detailed look at the economic outcome of enclosures, see Joseph Inikori (2002, 49–52).

3. Evidence from LexisNexis Risk Solutions' website, accessed November 8, 2022, https://risk.lexisnexis.com/law-enforcement-and-public-safety/crime-and-criminal-investigations.

Chapter 5

1. There are many reasons why names are changed in migration processes. Some of them are forms of agency that signal the individual's willingness to reinvent themselves in the new country, and some of them are responses to bureaucratic or inscription regimes. But given that migration from Latin America to the United States is often the result of economic need or social violence, name changes that come as a result of these migrations can be understood as imposed or forced on individuals.

2. US typewriters have real material limitations. They can write only the Latin alphabet and cannot write other alphabets and forms of writing, including logographic writing, like Chinese or Vietnamese, or Cyrillic (used in Russia, Serbia, and other Slavic nations).

Chapter 6

1. Studies of Greek naming practices yield fascinating details about the importance of naming as meaning. See, for instance, Matthews and Hornblower (2000).

2. For more general analyses on naming, see the edited volume by Marjorie Elizabeth Plummer and Joel Harrington (2019), which brings different strands of onomastic research. Of particular interest to this book is the chapter by Heiko Droste on self-naming.

3. This account of Tsimshian naming practices is indebted to Christopher Roth's *Becoming Tsimshian: The Social Life of Names* (2008).

4. Different aspects of coverture, for instance, property law and inheritance, have different histories and origins. See, for instance, Amy Louise Erickson (1995) and Margaret Ferguson et al. (2004).

Bibliography

Abarry, Abu Shardow. "The Significance of Names in Ghanaian Drama." *Journal of Black Studies* 22, no. 2 (1991): 157–67. https://doi.org/10.1177/002193479102200201.

Agamben, Georgio. *Homo Sacer: Sovereign Power and Bare Life*. Stanford, CA: Stanford University Press, 1998.

Agar, Jon. *The Government Machine: A Revolutionary History of the Computer*. Cambridge, MA: MIT Press, 2016. Doi:10.7551/mitpress/3336.001.0001.

Agyekum, Kofi. "The Sociolinguistic of Akan Personal Names." *Nordic Journal of African Studies* 15, no. 2 (2006): 206–35.

Alcoff, Linda Martín. "Mignolo's Epistemology of Coloniality." *CR* 7, no. 3 (2007): 79–101. https://doi.org/10.1353/ncr.0.0008.

Alia, Valerie. *Names and Nunavut: Culture and Identity in Arctic Canada*. New York: Berghahn Books, 2007.

Alonso, William, and Paul Starr. *The Politics of Numbers*. New York: Russell Sage Foundation, 1987.

Amaya, Hector. *Citizenship Excess: Latino/as, Media, and the Nation*. New York: NYU Press, 2013. Doi:10.18574/9780814723838.

——. *Trafficking: Narcoculture in Mexico and the United States*. Durham, NC: Duke University Press, 2020.

——. "White Supremacy, Settler Angst, and Latine Immigration to the US." *Latin American and Caribbean Ethnic Studies* (2024): 1–18.

Amoore, Louise. "Biometric Borders: Governing Mobilities in the War on Terror." *Political Geography* 25, no. 3 (2006): 336–51. https://doi.org/10.1016/j.polgeo.2006.02.001.

Anon Collective. 2021. *Book of Anonymity*. Brooklyn, NY: Punctum Books.

Anzaldúa, Gloria. *Interviews/Entrevistas.* Edited by AnaLouise Keating London: Routledge, 2000.

Arendt, Hannah. *The Human Condition.* Chicago: University of Chicago Press, 1958.

——. *The Origins of Totalitarianism.* New ed. New York: Harcourt, Brace and World, 1966.

Aristotle. *Categories and De Interpretatione.* Translated by J. L. Ackrill. 1963. Reprint, Oxford: Oxford University Press, 2002.

——. *Nicomachean Ethics.* Edited by Roger Crisp. Cambridge Texts in the History of Philosophy. Cambridge: Cambridge University Press, 2014.

Asad, Asad L. *Engage and Evade: How Latino Immigrant Families Manage Surveillance in Everyday Life.* Princeton, NJ: Princeton University Press, 2023. Doi: 10.1515/9780691249049.

Asenbaum, Hans. "Anonymity and Democracy: Absence as Presence in the Public Sphere." *American Political Science Review* 112, no. 3 (2018): 459–72. https://doi.org/10.1017/S0003055418000163.

Atkin, Albert. "Peirce on the Index and Indexical Reference." *Transactions of the Charles S. Peirce Society: A Quarterly Journal in American Philosophy* 41, no. 1 (2005): 161–88. https://muse.jhu.edu/article/377477.

Atwood, Margaret. *The Handmaid's Tale.* Boston: Houghton Mifflin, 1986.

Badawy, Adam, Emilio Ferrara, and Kristina Lerman. "Analyzing the Digital Traces of Political Manipulation: The 2016 Russian Interference Twitter Campaign." In *2018 IEEE/ACM International Conference on Advances in Social Networks Analysis and Mining (ASONAM)*, 258–65. Barcelona: IEEE, 2018. doi: 10.1109/ASONAM.2018.8508646.

Baker, Lynne Rudder. "Just What Is Social Ontology?" *Journal of Social Ontology* 5, no. 1 (2019): 1–12. https://doi.org/10.1515/jso-2019-2001.

——. *Persons and Bodies: A Constitution View.* Cambridge Studies in Philosophy. Cambridge: Cambridge University Press, 2000.

Balibar, Étienne. *Politics and the Other Scene.* London: Verso, 2002.

Ball, Christopher Gordon. "Avoidance as Alterity Stance: An Upper Xinguan Affinity Chronotope." *Anthropological Quarterly* 88, no. 2 (2015): 337–72. https://doi.org/10.1353/anq.2015.0027.

Barlett, Christopher P., Douglas A. Gentile, and Chelsea Chew. "Predicting Cyberbullying from Anonymity." *Psychology of Popular Media Culture* 5, no. 2 (2016): 171–80. https://doi.org/10.1037/ppm0000055.

Barrett, Laurence. "What's in a Name?" *TIME*, 1993. https://time.com/archive/6724372/whats-in-a-name-7/.

Barthes, Roland. *Mythologies*. Translated by Annette Lavers. New York: Hill and Wang, 1972.

Behm-Morawitz, Elizabeth, and David Ta. "Cultivating Virtual Stereotypes? The Impact of Video Game Play on Racial/Ethnic Stereotypes." *Howard Journal of Communications* 25, no. 1 (2014): 1–15. https://doi.org/10.1080/10646175.2013.835600.

Benhabib, Seyla. 1993. "Feminist Theory and Hannah Arendt's Concept of Public Space." *History of the Human Sciences* 6 (2): 97–114.

Beniger, James R. *The Control Revolution: Technological and Economic Origins of the Information Society.* Cambridge, MA: Harvard University Press, 1986.

Bergson, Henri. *An Introduction to Metaphysics: The Creative Mind.* Translated by Mabelle L. Andison. Totowa, NY: Littlefield, Adams, 1975.

Bering, Dietz. *The Stigma of Names: Antisemitism in German Daily Life, 1812–1933.* Social History, Popular Culture, and Politics in Germany. Ann Arbor: University of Michigan Press, 1992.

Bertrand, Marianne, and Sendhil Mullainathan. "Are Emily and Greg More Employable Than Lakisha and Jamal? A Field Experiment on Labor Market Discrimination." *American Economic Review* 94, no. 4 (2004): 991–1013. https://doi.org/10.1257/0002828042002561.

Biavaschi, Costanza, Corrado Giulietti, and Zahra Siddique. "The Economic Payoff of Name Americanization." *Journal of Labor Economics* 35, no. 4 (2017): 1089–1116. https://doi.org/10.1086/692531.

Blackstone, William. *Commentaries on the Laws of England*. Indianapolis: Online Library of Liberty, 1753. http://files.libertyfund.org/files/2140/Blackstone_1387-01_EBk_v6.0.pdf.

Bosmajian, Haig A. *The Language of Oppression.* Washington, DC: Public Affairs Press, 1974.

Bourdieu, Pierre. *The Logic of Practice.* Stanford, CA: Stanford University Press, 1990.

Bowker, Geoffrey C., and Susan Leigh Star. *Sorting Things Out: Classification and Its Consequences.* Inside Technology. Cambridge, MA: MIT Press, 1999.

Brayne, Sarah. *Predict and Surveil: Data, Discretion, and the Future of Policing.* New York: Oxford University Press, 2021.

Brehm, Audrey L. "Navigating the Feminine in Massively Multiplayer Online

Games: Gender in *World of Warcraft*." *Frontiers in Psychology* 4 (December 2013). https://doi.org/10.3389/fpsyg.2013.00903.

Bridges, Lauren E. "Digital Failure: Unbecoming the 'Good' Data Subject Through Entropic, Fugitive, and Queer Data." *Big Data & Society* 8, no. 1 (2021). https://doi.org/10.1177/2053951720977882.

Browne, Simone. *Dark Matters: On the Surveillance of Blackness.* Durham, NC: Duke University Press, 2015.

Buckels, Erin E., Paul D. Trapnell, Tamara Andjelovic, and Delroy L. Paulhus. "Internet Trolling and Everyday Sadism: Parallel Effects on Pain Perception and Moral Judgment." *Journal of Personality* 87, no. 2 (2019): 328–40. https://doi.org/10.1111/jopy.12393.

Burnard, Trevor. "Slave Naming Patterns: Onomastics and the Taxonomy of Race in Eighteenth-Century Jamaica." *Journal of Interdisciplinary History* 31, no. 3 (2001): 325–46. https://doi.org/10.1162/002219500551550.

Burns, Thomas S. *Rome and the Barbarians: 100 B.C.–A.D. 400.* Ancient Society and History. Baltimore: Johns Hopkins University Press, 2003.

Burrough, Bryan, Sarah Ellison, and Suzanna Andrews. "The Snowden Saga: A Shadowland of Secrets and Light." *Vanity Fair* 56, no. 5 (2014): 152.

Burton, Richard D. E. "Names and Naming in Afro-Caribbean Cultures." *New West Indian Guide* 73, no. 1–2 (1999): 35–58. https://doi.org/10.1163/13822373-90002584.

Butler, Judith. *Gender Trouble: Feminism and the Subversion of Identity.* New York: Routledge, 1999.

Cardon, Dominique. *À quoi rêvent les algorithmes: Nos vies à l'heure des big data.* Paris: Editions du Seuil, 2015.

Carneiro, Pedro, Sokbae Lee, and Hugo Reis. "Please Call Me John: Name Choice and the Assimilation of Immigrants in the United States, 1900–1930." *Labour Economics* 62 (2020): 1–18. https://doi.org/10.1016/j.labeco.2019.101778.

Carroll, Rory. "Blog del Narco: Author Who Chronicled Mexico's Drugs War Forced to Flee." *The Guardian*, May 16, 2013. https://www.theguardian.com/world/2013/may/16/blog-del-narco-mexico-drug-war.

———. "'They Stole Our Dreams': Blogger Reveals Cost of Reporting Mexico's Drug Wars." *The Guardian*, April 3, 2013. https://www.theguardian.com/world/2013/apr/03/mexico-blog-del-narco-drug-wars.

Chaar López, Iván. *The Cybernetic Border: Drones, Technology, and Intrusion.* Durham, NC: Duke University Press, 2024. Doi:10.1215/9781478059035.

Cheney-Lippold, John. *We Are Data: Algorithms and the Making of Our Digital Selves.* New York: NYU Press, 2017. Doi:10.18574/9781479888702.

Chun, Wendy Hui Kyong. 2021. *Discriminating Data: Correlation, Neighborhoods, and the New Politics of Recognition*. Cambridge, MA: MIT Press.

Clark, Gregory, Neil Cummins, Yu Hao, and Daniel Diaz Vidal. *The Son Also Rises: Surnames and the History of Social Mobility*. The Princeton Economic History of the Western World. Princeton, NJ: Princeton University Press, 2014.

Coeckelbergh, Mark. *Human Being @ Risk: Enhancement, Technology, and the Evaluation of Vulnerability Transformations*. Dordrecht, Netherlands: Springer, 2013.

Coleman, Gabriella. *Hacker, Hoaxer, Whistleblower, Spy: The Many Faces of Anonymous*. Many Faces of Anonymous. London: Verso, 2014.

Corsa, Lissette. "Notes from the Underground." *Hispanic (Washington, DC)* 21, no. 9 (2008): 32.

Cosgrove, Ben. "The Invention of Teenagers: LIFE and the Triumph of Youth Culture." *Time*, September 28, 2013. https://time.com/3639041/the-invention-of-teenagers-life-and-the-triumph-of-youth-culture/.

Couldry, Nick, and Ulises A. Mejias. "Data Colonialism: Rethinking Big Data's Relation to the Contemporary Subject." *Television & New Media* 20, no. 4 (2019): 336–49. https://doi.org/10.1177/1527476418796632.

Dahlgren, Peter. *Television and the Public Sphere: Citizenship, Democracy, and the Media*. The Media, Culture & Society Series. London: Sage, 1995.

Davies, Anna Morpurgo. "Greek Personal Names and Linguistic Continuity." *Proceedings of the British Academy* 104 (2000): 15–39.

De La Fe, Rocio. "New State Bill Could Change the Way We Spell and Say Non-English Names." CBS8, 2023. https://www.cbs8.com/article/news/local/california-bill-to-allow-diacritical-marks-such-as-accents-on-document-issued-documents/509-5ff103f8-e1b6-4c7c-92f5-a8ec6e40d3f9.

De la Grange, Bertrand, and Maite Rico. *Marcos: La genial impostura (Nuevo Siglo)*. Mexico City: Aguilar, 1999.

Dean, Jodi. *Publicity's Secret: How Technoculture Capitalizes on Democracy*. Ithaca, NY: Cornell University Press, 2018.

Dean, Mitchell. *Governmentality: Power and Rule in Modern Society*. 2nd ed. Los Angeles: Sage, 2010.

DeChants, Jonah P., Myeshia N. Price, Amy E. Green, Carrie K. Davis, and Casey J. Pick. "Association of Updating Identification Documents with Suicidal Ideation and Attempts Among Transgender and Nonbinary Youth." *International Journal of Environmental Research and Public Health* 19, no. 9 (2022): 5016. https://doi.org/10.3390/ijerph19095016.

DeGloma, Thomas. *Anonymous: The Performance of Hidden Identities*. Chicago: University of Chicago Press, 2023.

Deleuze, Gilles. "Postscript on the Societies of Control." *October* 59 (1992): 3–7. http://www.jstor.org/stable/778828.

Deleuze, Gilles, and Félix Guattari. *A Thousand Plateaus: Capitalism and Schizophrenia*. Translated by Brian Massumi. 1987. Reprint, Minneapolis: University of Minnesota Press, 2005.

Derrida, Jacques. *Margins of Philosophy*. Translated by Alan Bass. Chicago: University of Chicago Press, 1982.

Díaz del Castillo, Bernal. *Historia verdadera de la conquista de la Nueva España*. Cambridge Library Collection. Travel and Exploration. Vol. 1. Cambridge: Cambridge University Press, 2010.

Dilhara, Michelle. *Social Invisibility Is Not a Fiction It Exists*. Independently Published, 2019.

Dünne, Jörg, Kathrin Fehringer, Kristina Kuhn, and Wolfgang Struck. *Cultural Techniques: Assembling Spaces, Texts & Collectives*. Berlin: Walter de Gruyter, 2020.

Edmonds, Colbi, and Adeel Hassan. "What We Know About the Death of a Nonbinary Student in Oklahoma." *New York Times*, March 15, 2024. https://www.nytimes.com/article/nex-benedict-oklahoma.html.

Eisenstein, Elizabeth L. *The Printing Revolution in Early Modern Europe*. Cambridge: Cambridge University Press, 2012.

Ellison, Ralph. *Invisible Man*. New York: Vintage Books, 1989.

Emmelhainz, Celia. "Naming a New Self: Identity Elasticity and Self-Definition in Voluntary Name Changes." *Names* 60, no. 3 (2012): 156–65. https://doi.org/10.1179/0027773812Z.00000000022.

Engler, Alex. "If Not AI Ethicists like Timnit Gebru, Who Will Hold Big Tech Accountable?" *Brookings*. Washington, DC: Brookings Institution, 2020.

Erickson, Amy Louise. *Women and Property: In Early Modern England*. London: Routledge, 1995.

Evans, Martha Noel. *Fits and Starts: A Genealogy of Hysteria in Modern France*. Ithaca, NY: Cornell University Press, 2019.

Evergates, Theodore. *The Aristocracy in the County of Champagne, 1100–1300*. The Middle Ages Series. Philadelphia: University of Pennsylvania Press, 2007.

Fanon, Frantz. *Black Skin, White Masks*. New York: Grove Press, 1952.

Fear-Segal, Jacqueline, and Susan D. Rose, eds. *Carlisle Indian Industrial School: Indigenous Histories, Memories, and Reclamations*. Indigenous Education. Lincoln: University of Nebraska Press, 2016.

Ferguson, Margaret W., Nancy Wright, and A. R. Buck, eds. *Women, Property, and the Letters of the Law in Early Modern England.* Toronto: University of Toronto Press, 2004.

Feuerherd, Peter. "The Strange History of Masons in America." *JSTOR Daily*, August 3, 2017. https://daily.jstor.org/the-strange-history-of-masons-in-america/.

Fitzpatrick, Liseli A. "African Names and Naming Practices: The Impact Slavery and European Domination Had on the African Psyche, Identity and Protest." Master's thesis, Ohio State University, 2012. http://rave.ohiolink.edu/etdc/view?acc_num=osu1338404929.

Foucault, Michel. *Discipline and Punish: The Birth of the Prison.* 1st American ed. New York: Pantheon Books, 1977.

———. *Herculine Barbin: Being the Recently Discovered Memoirs of a Nineteenth-Century French Hermaphrodite.* New York: Pantheon Books, 1980.

———. *History of Sexuality.* Vol. 1, *An Introduction.* 1978. Reprint, New York: Vintage, 1990.

———. *The Order of Things: An Archaeology of the Human Sciences.* New York: Routledge, 1989.

———. *Power/Knowledge: Selected Interviews and Other Writings, 1972–1977.* New York: Pantheon Books, 1980.

Franklin, Benjamin. *The Autobiography of Benjamin Franklin: With Related Documents.* The Bedford Series in History and Culture. 3rd ed. Boston: Bedford/St. Martin's, 2016.

Fraser, Nancy. "Rethinking the Public Sphere: A Contribution to the Critique of Actually Existing Democracy." *Social Text*, no. 25/26 (1990): 56–80. https://doi.org/10.2307/466240.

Garmonsway, George Norman. *An Early Norse Reader.* Cambridge: Cambridge University Press, 1928.

Gaskell, Elizabeth. *The Life of Charlotte Brontë.* London: Penguin, 1985.

Gavrielatos, Andreas. *Self-Presentation and Identity in the Roman World.* Newcastle upon Tyne, UK: Cambridge Scholars Publishing, 2017.

Giddens, Anthony. *Modernity and Self-Identity: Self and Society in the Late Modern Age.* Stanford, CA: Stanford University Press, 1991.

Gobineau, Arthur de. *An Essay on the Inequality of Human Races.* 1853. Reprint, London: William Heinemann, 1915.

Gramsci, Antonio. *Prison Notebooks.* Edited and translated by Joseph A Buttigieg. New York: Columbia University Press, 1992.

Greer, Allan. "Commons and Enclosure in the Colonization of North America." *American Historical Review* 117, no. 2 (2012): 365–86. https://doi.org/10.1086/ahr.117.2.365.

Griffin, Ben. "Class, Gender, and Liberalism in Parliament, 1868–1882: The Case of the Married Women's Property Acts." *Historical Journal* 46, no. 1 (2003): 59–87. https://doi.org/10.1017/S0018246X02002844.

Grosz, Elizabeth A. *Volatile Bodies: Toward a Corporeal Feminism.* Theories of Representation and Difference. Bloomington: Indiana University Press, 1994.

Guilmette, Lauren. "The Violence of Curiosity: Butler's Foucault, Foucault's Herculine, and the Will-to-Know." *PhiloSOPHIA* 7, no. 1 (2017): 1–22. https://doi.org/10.1353/phi.2017.0000.

Gutierrez-Perez, Robert M. "Warren-ting a 'Dinner Party': *Nepantla* as a Space In/Between." *Liminalities: A Journal of Performance Studies* 8, no. 5 (2012): 195–206. http://liminalities.net/8-5/nepantla.pdf.

Habermas, Jürgen. *The Structural Transformation of the Public Sphere: An Inquiry into a Category of Bourgeois Society.* Studies in Contemporary German Social Thought. Cambridge, MA: MIT Press, 1989.

Hacking, Ian. "Making Up People." In *Reconstructing Individualism: Autonomy, Individuality, and the Self in Western Thought*, edited by Thomas C. Heller, Morton Sosna, and David E. Wellbery, 222–36. Stanford, CA: Stanford University Press, 1986.

———. *The Social Construction of What?* Cambridge, MA: Harvard University Press, 1999.

Haraway, Donna Jeanne. *Manifestly Haraway.* Posthumanities 37. Minneapolis: University of Minnesota Press, 2016.

Harcourt, Bernard E. *Exposed: Desire and Disobedience in the Digital Age.* Cambridge, MA: Harvard University Press, 2015.

Harris, Cheryl I. "Whiteness as Property." *Harvard Law Review* 106, no. 8 (1993): 1017–91. https://doi.org/10.2307/1341787.

Hayles, N. Katherine. *How We Became Posthuman: Virtual Bodies in Cybernetics, Literature, and Informatics.* Chicago: University of Chicago Press, 1999.

Henderson, Timothy J. *The Mexican Wars for Independence.* New York: Hill and Wang, 2009.

Hey, David. *Family Names and Family History.* London: Hambledon and London, 2000.

Hill, Brandon J., Richard Crosby, Alida Bouris, Rayna Brown, Trevor Bak, Kris Rosentel, Alicia VandeVusse, Michael Silverman, and Laura Salazar. "Exploring Transgender Legal Name Change as a Potential Structural Intervention for Mitigating Social Determinants of Health Among Transgender Women of Color." *Sexuality Research & Social Policy* 15, no. 1 (2018): 25–33. https://doi.org/10.1007/s13178-017-0289-6.

Hill, Kashmir. "This Is Life in Metaverse." *New York Times*, October 7, 2022. https://www.nytimes.com/2022/10/07/technology/metaverse-facebook-horizon-worlds.html.

Hobbes, Thomas. *Thomas Hobbes: Leviathan. A Critical Edition*. Edited by G. A. J. Rogers and Karl Schulmann. London: Continuum, 2005.

Holbrook, Alice. "When LexisNexis Makes a Mistake, You Pay for It." *Newsweek*, September 26, 2019.

Honneth, Axel. *The Struggle for Recognition: The Moral Grammar of Social Conflicts*. Cambridge, UK: Polity Press, 1995.

Horn, Rebecca. "Gender and Social Identity: Nahua Naming Patterns in Postconquest Central Mexico." In *Indian Women of Early Mexico*, edited by Susan Schroeder, Stephanie Gail Wood, and Robert Stephen Haskett, 105–22. Norman: University of Oklahoma Press, 1999.

Howard-Wagner, Deirdre. *Indigenous Invisibility in the City*. Abingdon, UK: Routledge, 2021.

Igo, Sarah E. *The Known Citizen: A History of Privacy in Modern America*. Cambridge, MA: Harvard University Press, 2018. doi:10.2307/j.ctv24w653v.

———. "Prejudice, Social Stress, and Mental Health in Lesbian, Gay, and Bisexual Populations: Conceptual Issues and Research Evidence." *Psychological Bulletin* 129, no. 5 (2003): 674–97. https://doi.org/10.1037/0033-2909.129.5.674.

Jain, P., M. Gyanchandani, and N. Khare, N. "Big Data Privacy: A Technological Perspective and Review." *J Big Data* 3, no. 25 (2016): 1–25.

Jamieson, Kathleen Hall. *Cyberwar: How Russian Hackers and Trolls Helped Elect a President: What We Don't, Can't, and Do Know*. Oxford: Oxford University Press, 2020.

Jenkins, Katharine. *Ontology and Oppression: Race, Gender, and Social Reality*. Studies in Feminist Philosophy. Oxford: Oxford University Press, 2023.

Johnson, Austin H., Megan Nanney, and Chase Harless. "Transgender, Nonbinary, and Gender Diverse Health in the US Southeast: A Quantitative Look at the Influence of Gender Identity and Sexuality in a Sample of LGBT Southerners." In *Demography of Transgender, Nonbinary and Gender Minority Populations*, edited by Amanda K. Baumle and Sonny Nordmarken, 117–59. Cham, Switzerland: Springer International Publishing, 2022. https://doi.org/10.1007/978-3-031-06329-9_6.

Johnson, Hans, Marisol Cuellar Mejia, and Eric McGhee. *California's Popula-*

tion. Public Policy Institute of California (Report), 2025. https://www.ppic.org/wp-content/uploads/JTF_PopulationJTF.pdf.

Kai-Cheng, Yang, Onur Varol, Clayton A. Davis, Emilio Ferrara, Alessandro Flammini, and Filippo Menczer. "Arming the Public with Artificial Intelligence to Counter Social Bots." *arXiv.org*, 2019. https://doi.org/10.48550/arXiv.1901.00912.

Kant, Immanuel. *Perpetual Peace*. In *Kant: Political Writings*, edited by H. S. Reiss, translated by H. B. Nisbet, 2nd ed., 93–130. Cambridge Texts in the History of Political Thought. Cambridge: Cambridge University Press, 1991. https://doi.org/10.1017/CBO9780511809620.

Keating, AnaLouise. "From Borderlands and New Mestizas to Nepantlas and Nepantleras: Anzaldúan Theories for Social Change." *Human Architecture: Journal of the Sociology of Self-Knowledge* 4, no. 3 (2006): 5–16.

Kim, Nadia Y. *Imperial Citizens: Koreans and Race from Seoul to LA*. Stanford, CA: Stanford University Press, 2008.

Kimaid, Michael. *Modernity, Metatheory, and the Temporal-Spatial Divide: From Mythos to Techne*. Routledge Approaches to History 10. New York: Routledge, 2015.

Kittler, Friedrich A. *Discourse Networks 1800/1900*. Stanford, CA: Stanford University Press, 1990.

———. *Gramophone, Film, Typewriter*. Writing Science. Stanford, CA: Stanford University Press, 1999.

Koopman, Colin. *How We Became Our Data: A Genealogy of the Informational Person*. Chicago Scholarship Online. Chicago: University of Chicago Press, 2019.

Koselleck, Reinhart. *Critique and Crisis: Enlightenment and the Pathogenesis of Modern Society*. Studies in Contemporary German Social Thought. Cambridge, MA: MIT Press, 1988.

Kreps, David, and Jessica Muirhead. "Introduction." In *Understanding Digital Events: Bergson, Whitehead, and the Experience of the Digital*, edited by David Kreps, 1–11. New York: Routledge, 2019.

Krickeberg, Walter. *Las antiguas culturas mexicanas*. Sección De Obras De Antropología. Mexico City: Fondo de Cultura Económica, 1961.

Kripke, Saul A. *Names and Necessity*. Cambridge, MA: Harvard University Press, 1980.

Lakoff, George, and Mark Johnson. *Metaphors We Live By*. Chicago: University of Chicago Press, 2003.

Landis, Barbara. "The Names." In *Carlisle Indian Industrial School*, edited by

Jacqueline Fear-Segal and Susan D. Rose, Indigenous Histories, Memories, and Reclamations, 88–105. Lincoln: University of Nebraska Press, 2016.

Langberg, Laura. "Espaanol & Inglaes: Reinforcing English Hegemony in Library Information Systems." *The Serials Librarian* 79, no. 1–2 (2020): 19–26. https://doi.org/10.1080/0361526X.2020.1772170.

Leissner, Omi. "Naming the Unheard Of." *National Black Law Journal* 15, no. 1 (1997): 109–54.

Lenoir, Timothy. *Inscribing Science: Scientific Texts and the Materiality of Communication.* Writing Science. Stanford, CA: Stanford University Press, 1998.

Levinas, Emmanuel. *Totality and Infinity: An Essay on Exteriority.* Translated by Alphonso Lingis. Pittsburgh, PA: Duquesne University Press, 1969.

Li, Yang-Jun, Christy M. K. Cheung, Xiao-Liang Shen, and Matthew K. O. Lee. "When Socialization Goes Wrong: Understanding the We-Intention to Participate in Collective Trolling in Virtual Communities." *Journal of the Association for Information Systems* 23, no. 3 (2022): 678–706. https://doi.org/10.17705/1jais.00737.

Liu, Marian Chia-Ming. "Like Many Asian Americans, I Have Long Spurned My Full Name. A Wave of Racism Made Me Say: No More." *Washington Post*, 2022. https://www.washingtonpost.com/magazine/interactive/2022/assimilation-chinese-names-asian-racism/.

Ludemann, Dillon. "Digital Semaphore: Political Discourse and Identity Negotiation Through 4chan's /Pol/." *New Media & Society* 25, no. 10 (2023): 2724–43. https://doi.org/10.1177/14614448211034848.

Lynch, Jennifer. *What Facial Recognition Technology Means for Privacy and Civil Liberties.* Washington, DC: Senate Judiciary, 2012.

Lyon, David. *The Electronic Eye: The Rise of Surveillance Society.* Minneapolis: University of Minnesota Press, 1994.

———. "Globalizing Surveillance: Comparative and Sociological Perspectives." *International Sociology* 19, no. 2 (2004): 135–49. https://doi.org/10.1177/0268580904042897.

Lyons, Martyn. *The Typewriter Century: A Cultural History of Writing Practices.* Studies in Book and Print Culture. Toronto: University of Toronto Press, 2021.

Macaulay, Peter J. R., Lucy R. Betts, James Stiller, and Blerina Kellezi. "Bystander Responses to Cyberbullying: The Role of Perceived Severity, Publicity, Anonymity, Type of Cyberbullying, and Victim Response." *Computers in Human Behavior* 131 (2022): 107238. https://doi.org/10.1016/j.chb.2022.107238.

Madison, James. *Papers of James Madison*. Edited by William Thomas Hutchinson, William M. E. Rachal, and Robert Allen Rutland. Chicago: University of Chicago Press, 1962.

Makulilo, Alex Boniface. "Analysis of the Regime of Systematic Government Access to Private Sector Data in Tanzania." *Information & Communications Technology Law* 29, no. 2 (2020): 250–78. https://doi.org/10.1080/13600834.2020.1741156.

Martínez, Diana Isabel. *Rhetorics of Nepantla, Memory, and the Gloria Evangelina Anzaldúa Papers*. New York: Rowman and Littlefield, 2022.

Martinez, Jacqueline M. "Culture, Communication, and Latina Feminist Philosophy: Toward a Critical Phenomenology of Culture." *Hypatia* 29, no. 1 (2014): 221–36. https://doi.org/10.1111/hypa.12061.

Martínez-San Miguel, Yolanda. *Coloniality of Diasporas: Rethinking Intracolonial Migrations in a Pan-Caribbean Context*. New Caribbean Studies. New York: Palgrave Macmillan, 2014.

Marx, Gary T. "Identity and Anonymity: Some Conceptual Distinctions and Issues for Research." In *Documenting Individual Identity: The Development of State Practices in the Modern World*, edited by Jane Caplan and John Torpey, 311–27. Princeton, NJ: Princeton University Press, 2001.

———. *Windows into the Soul: Surveillance and Society in an Age of High Technology*. Chicago: University of Chicago Press, 2016. doi:10.7208/9780226286075.

Marx, Karl. *The Eighteenth Brumaire of Louis Bonaparte*. New York: International Publishers, 1926.

Matthews, Elaine, and Simon Hornblower, eds. *Greek Personal Names: Their Value as Evidence*. New York: Oxford University Press, 2000.

McKinley, Richard. *A History of British Surnames*. Approaches to Local History. London: Taylor and Francis Group, 1990. https://doi.org/10.4324/9781315846637.

Melendez Obando, Mauricio O. "En torno a un diccionario de apellidos costarricenses." *Káñina* 25, no. 2 (2001): 61–79.

Mendieta, Eduardo. "Remapping Latin American Studies: Postcolonialism, Subaltern Studies, Post-Occidentalism, and Globalization Theory." In *Coloniality at Large: Latin America and the Postcolonial Debate*, edited by Mabel Moraña, Enriqué Enrique, and Carlos A. Jáuregui, 286–306. Durham, NC: Duke University Press, 2008.

Menn, Joseph, and Elizabeth Dwoskin. "Musk's Question About Bots Is Nothing New for Twitter." *Washington Post*, May 13, 2022. https://www.washingtonpost.com/technology/2022/05/13/twitter-sale-musk-bots/.

Meszaros, Rosemary, and Katherine Pennavaria. "Govdocs to the Rescue! Debunking an Immigration Myth." *DttP* 46, no. 1 (2018): 7–12. https://doi.org/10.5860/dttp.v46i1.6655.

Meyer, Ilan H. "Minority Stress and Mental Health in Gay Men." *Journal of Health and Social Behavior* 36, no. 1 (1995): 38–56. https://doi.org/10.2307/2137286.

Mills, Charles W. *The Racial Contract.* Ithaca, NY: Cornell University Press, 1997.

Monahan, Torin. *Crisis Vision: Race and the Cultural Production of Surveillance.* Durham, NC: Duke University Press, 2022.

———. "The Right to Hide? Anti-surveillance Camouflage and the Aestheticization of Resistance." *Communication and Critical/Cultural Studies* 12, no. 2 (2015): 159–78. https://doi.org/10.1080/14791420.2015.1006646.

Monroy-Hernández, Andrés, and Luis Daniel Palacios. "Blog del Narco and the Future of Citizen Journalism." *Georgetown Journal of International Affairs* 15, no. 2 (2014): 81–92.

Morton, Samuel. *Crania Americana; or, A Comparative View of the Skulls of Various Aboriginal Nations of North and South America: To Which Is Prefixed an Essay on the Varieties of the Human Species.* Philadelphia: J. Dobson, 1839.

Moss-Racusin, Corinne A., Christina Sanzari, Nava Caluori, and Helena Rabasco. "Gender Bias Produces Gender Gaps in Stem Engagement." *Sex Roles* 79, no. 11–12 (2018): 651–70. https://doi.org/10.1007/s11199-018-0902-z.

Mullan, John. *Anonymity: A Secret History of English Literature.* Princeton, NJ: Princeton University Press, 2007.

Muñoz, José Esteban. *Disidentifications: Queers of Color and the Performance of Politics.* Minneapolis: University of Minnesota Press, 1999.

Nagle, Angela. *Kill All Normies: Online Culture Wars from 4chan and Tumblr to Trump and the Alt-Right.* Lanham, MD: John Hunt Publishing, 2017.

Naone, Erica. "Anonymous Won't Expose Mexican Cartel's 'Servants.'" Reuters, November 4, 2011. https://www.reuters.com/article/us-mexico-drugs-hackers/anonymous-wont-expose-mexican-cartels-servants-idUSTRE7A408C20111105.

Narco, Blog del. *Dying for the Truth: Undercover Inside Mexico's Violent Drug War.* Port Townsend, WA: Feral House, 2013. https://books.google.com/books?id=e4lWeQxlIjoC.

Nissenbaum, Helen. "The Meaning of Anonymity in an Information Age." *Information Society* 15, no. 2 (1999): 141–44. https://doi.org/10.1080/019722499128592.

Nitschinsk, Lewis, Stephanie J. Tobin, and Eric J. Vanman. "The Disinhibiting Effects of Anonymity Increase Online Trolling." *Cyberpsychology, Behavior and Social Networking* 25, no. 6 (2022): 377–83. https://doi.org/10.1089/cyber.2022.0005.

———. "A Functionalist Approach to Online Trolling." *Frontiers in Psychology* 14 (2023). https://doi.org/10.3389/fpsyg.2023.1211023.

Ocampo, Ambeth. "A Sense of Order." *Inquirer.net*, February 15, 2013. https://opinion.inquirer.net/46885/a-sense-of-order.

Ongweso, Edward, Jr. "Palantir's CEO Finally Admits to Helping ICE Deport Undocumented Immigrants." *VICE* (blog), January 24, 2020. https://www.vice.com/en/article/palantirs-ceo-finally-admits-to-helping-ice-deport-undocumented-immigrants/.

Ortega, Mariana. *In-Between: Latina Feminist Phenomenology, Multiplicity, and the Self.* Suny Series, Philosophy and Race. Albany: State University of New York Press, 2016. doi:10.1515/9781438459783.

Pagden, A. *The Languages of Political Theory in Early-Modern Europe.* Cambridge: Cambridge University Press, 1990. https://books.google.com/books?id=q7-7pqloLqAC.

Painter, Nell Irvin. *Sojourner Truth: A Life, a Symbol.* New York: W. W. Norton, 1996.

Papacharissi, Zizi. *A Private Sphere: Democracy in a Digital Age.* Digital Media and Society. Cambridge, UK: Polity, 2010.

Pateman, Carole. *The Problem of Political Obligation: A Critical Analysis of Liberal Theory.* Chichester, UK: Wiley, 1979.

———. *The Sexual Contract.* Stanford, CA: Stanford University Press, 1988.

Peirce, Charles. *The Essential Peirce: Selected Philosophical Writings.* 1895. Reprint, Bloomington: Indiana University Press, 1998.

Peters, John Durham. *Speaking into the Air: A History of the Idea of Communication.* Chicago: University of Chicago Press, 1999.

Piepmeier, Alison. *Out in Public: Configurations of Women's Bodies in Nineteenth-Century America.* Chapel Hill: University of North Carolina Press, 2004.

Plummer, Marjorie Elizabeth, and Joel F. Harrington. *Names and Naming in Early Modern Germany.* Spektrum: Publications of the German Studies Association. Vol. 20. New York: Berghahn Books, 2019. https://doi.org/10.2307/j.ctv287sk2d.

Pohl, Walter, and Rutger Kramer. *Empires and Communities in the Post-Roman and Islamic World, C. 400–1000 CE.* Oxford Studies in Early Empires. New York: Oxford University Press, 2021.

Poovey, Mary. *A History of the Modern Fact: Problems of Knowledge in the Sciences of Wealth and Society.* Chicago: University of Chicago Press, 1998.

Putnam, Robert D. "Bowling Alone: America's Declining Social Capital." *Journal of Democracy* 6, no. 1 (1995): 65–78. https://doi.org/10.1353/jod.1995.0002.

Quijano, Aníbal. *Aníbal Quijano: Foundational Essays on the Coloniality of Power.* Edited by Walter D. Mignolo, Rita Segato, and Catherine E. Walsh. Durham, NC: Duke University Press, 2024. doi:10.1515/9781478059356.

Radin, Margaret Jane. *Boilerplate: The Fine Print, Vanishing Rights, and the Rule of Law.* Princeton, NJ: Princeton University Press, 2013. doi:10.1515/9781400844838.

Rainie, Lee, and Janna Anderson. "The Future of Free Speech, Trolls, Anonymity and Fake News Online." *Pew Research Center* (blog), 2017. https://www.pewresearch.org/internet/2017/03/29/the-future-of-free-speech-trolls-anonymity-and-fake-news-online/.

Récanati, François. *Direct Reference: From Language to Thought.* Oxford, UK: Blackwell, 1993.

Rondilla, Joanne L., and Paul Spickard. *Is Lighter Better? Skin-Tone Discrimination Among Asian Americans.* Blue Ridge Summit, PA: Rowman and Littlefield, 2007.

Rose, Carol M. *Property and Persuasion: Essays on the History, Theory, and Rhetoric of Ownership.* New York: Routledge, 1994. doi:10.4324/9780429303227.

Roth, Christopher F. *Becoming Tsimshian: The Social Life of Names.* Donald R. Ellegood International Publications. Seattle: University of Washington Press, 2008.

Rubinstein, Ira S. "Privacy Localism." *SSRN Electronic Journal* 93, no. 4 (2018): 1961–2049. https://doi.org/10.2139/ssrn.3124697.

Rubinstein, Ira S., Gregory T. Nojeim, and Ronald D. Lee. "Systematic Government Access to Personal Data: A Comparative Analysis." *International Data Privacy Law* 4, no. 2 (2014): 96–119. https://doi.org/10.1093/idpl/ipu004.

Sagi-Vela González, Ana, and Ursula Thiemer-Sachse. "Nombres entre los Ayuuk (Ayuuk Ja'ay) o mixes, Oaxaca, México." *Anthropos* 100, no. 1 (2005): 151–71.

Sasaki, David. "Citizen Journalism and Drug Trafficking in Mexico." *Weblog World* (blog), September 27, 2010. https://weblogtheworld.com/formats/videos/citizen-journalism-and-drug-trafficking-in-mexico.

Saussure, Ferdinand de. *Course in General Linguistics.* New York: Philosophical Library, 1959.

Scott, James C. *Domination and the Arts of Resistance: Hidden Transcripts.* New Haven, CT: Yale University Press, 1990.

———. *Seeing like a State: How Certain Schemes to Improve the Human Condition Have Failed.* Yale Agrarian Studies. New Haven, CT: Yale University Press, 1998. doi:10.12987/9780300128789.

Seligman, Adam B. *Problem of Trust.* Princeton, NJ: Princeton University Press, 1997.

Sest, Natalie, and Evita March. "Constructing the Cyber-Troll: Psychopathy, Sadism, and Empathy." *Personality and Individual Differences* 119 (2017): 69–72. https://doi.org/10.1016/j.paid.2017.06.038.

Shelley, Mary Wollstonecraft. *Frankenstein; or, The Modern Prometheus.* Hertfordshire, UK: Wordsworth Editions, 1993.

Siegert, Bernhard. *Cultural Techniques: Grids, Filters, Doors, and Other Articulations of the Real.* Translated by Geoffrey Winthrop-Young. Meaning Systems. New York: Fordham University Press, 2015. doi:10.1515/9780823263783.

Simmel, Georg. 1971. *On Individuality and Social Forms: Selected Writings.* Edited by Donald N. Levine. The Heritage of Sociology. Chicago: University of Chicago Press.

Slaby, Jan. "Ontic (*Ontisch*)." In *The Cambridge Heidegger Lexicon*, edited by Mark Wrathall, 542–46. Cambridge: Cambridge University Press, 2021.

Smith, Michael, and Jim Waldo. "Anonymity, De-identification, and the Accuracy of Data." *Harvard Online*, August 28, 2023. https://www.harvardonline.harvard.edu/blog/anonymity-de-identification-accuracy-data.

Smith, Rogers M. *Stories of Peoplehood: The Politics and Morals of Political Membership.* Contemporary Political Theory. Cambridge: Cambridge University Press, 2002.

Snitzky, Dana. "How the Brontes Came Out as Women." *Longreads*, September 1, 2016. https://longreads.com/2016/09/01/how-the-brontes-came-out-as-women-2/.

Spade, Dean. *Normal Life: Administrative Violence, Critical Trans Politics, and the Limits of Law.* Rev. and exp. ed. Durham, NC: Duke University Press, 2015.

Spillers, Hortense J. *Black, White, and in Color: Essays on American Literature and Culture.* Chicago: University of Chicago Press, 2003.

Spivak, Gayatri Chakravorty. "Can the Subaltern Speak?" In *Marxism and the Interpretation of Culture*, edited by C. Nelson and L. Grossberg, 271–313. Basingstoke, UK: Macmillan Education, 1988.

Standing Bear, Luther. *My People, the Sioux.* Boston: Houghton Mifflin, 1928.

Story, Joanna. *Charlemagne: Empire and Society.* Manchester: Manchester University Press, 2005.

Stowe, Harriet Beecher. "Sojourner Truth, the Libyan Sibyl." *The Atlantic*, 1863.

https://www.theatlantic.com/magazine/archive/1863/04/sojourner-truth-the-libyan-sibyl/308775/.

Tatalovich, Raymond. *Nativism Reborn? The Official English Language Movement and the American States.* Lexington: University Press of Kentucky, 1995.

Taylor, Paul C. *Black Is Beautiful: A Philosophy of Black Aesthetics.* Foundations of the Philosophy of the Arts. Vol. 6. Hoboken, NJ: John Wiley and Sons, 2016.

Teslow, Tracy. *Constructing Race: The Science of Bodies and Cultures in American Anthropology.* New York: Cambridge University Press, 2014.

Thomas, Hugh. *The Slave Trade: The Story of the Atlantic Slave Trade, 1440–1870.* New York: Simon and Schuster, 1997.

Thompson, E. P. *The Making of the English Working Class.* New York: Vintage Books, 1966.

Tirzo, Jorge. "5 lecciones del Blog del Narco para el periodismo tradicional." *Revista Mexicana de Comunicación*, 2013. http://mexicanadecomunicacion.com.mx/rmc/2013/04/22/5-lecciones-del-blog-del-narco-para-el-periodismo-tradicional/.

Turkle, Sherry. *Alone Together: Why We Expect More from Technology and Less from Each Other.* New York: Basic Books, 2011.

Turner, Cheryl. *Living by the Pen: Women Writers in the Eighteenth Century.* London: Routledge, 1992. https://books.google.com/books?id=VIXSVDSi1-UC.

Upton, Sarah de los Santos. "An Anzaldúan Theory of Identity." In *This Bridge We Call Communication: Anzaldúan Approaches to Theory, Method, and Praxis*, edited by Leandra Hinojosa Hernández and Robert Gutierrez-Perez, 123–42. New York: Rowman and Littlefield, 2019.

Vareschi, Mark, "Frankenstein and Anonymous Authorship in Eighteenth-Century Britain." *University of Minnesota Press* (blog), January 13, 2019. https://uminnpressblog.com/2019/01/18/frankenstein-and-anonymous-authorship-in-eighteenth-century-britain/.

Vogels, Emily A. "The State of Online Harassment." Pew Research Center, January 13, 2021. https://www.pewresearch.org/internet/2021/01/13/the-state-of-online-harassment/.

Wilson, Stephen. *The Means of Naming: A Social and Cultural History of Personal Naming in Western Europe.* London: UCL Press, 1998. doi:10.4324/9780203214497.

Wiszewski, Przemyslaw. *Domus Bolezlai: Values and Social Identity in Dynastic Traditions of Medieval Poland (C. 966–1138).* Boston: Brill, 2010.

Wrathall, Mark A. 2022. "The Question of Ontological Dependency." *British*

Journal for the History of Philosophy 30, no. 3 (2022): 547–59. doi:10.1080/09608788.2021.1991270.

Wu, Ellen Dionne. "'They Call Me Bruce, but They Won't Call Me Bruce Jones': Asian American Naming Preferences and Patterns." *Names* 47, no. 1 (1999): 21–50. https://doi.org/10.1179/nam.1999.47.1.21.

Zawawi, S. *African Muslim Names: Images and Identities.* Trenton, NJ: Africa World Press, 1998. https://books.google.com/books?id=eUVmAAAAMAAJ.

Zuboff, Shoshana. *The Age of Surveillance Capitalism: The Fight for a Human Future at the New Frontier of Power.* New York: PublicAffairs, 2019.

Index

absolutism, 2–3, 89, 236
Accenture, 182
accountability, 4, 17, 27, 61–62; anonymity, 51; identification, 251; legal, 29, 34–35, 39–40, 43; power of, 209; register of enumeration, 52; register of obligations, 52; social order, 51–52
acoustic gunshot detection systems (AGDs), 146
Afghanistan, 172, 226
Africa, 214–15
African American studies, 24
Agamben, Georgio, 218
Agar, Jon, 167, 189, 194
agency, 7, 100, 196, 244; name changes, 258n1
agentic anonymity, viii, 6–8, 11–12, 36–37, 50, 65, 71, 74, 211, 243–44, 250, 252; ethics, in tension with, 251; misrecognition, 251; mythological meanings, 35; political progress and change, 237; public actions, 252; rebellion, association with, 236
agentic dissociation, 200–201
agentic indexical dissociation, 210; of anonymous publishing, 212; women in literature, 211
agora, 102–3, 108
Alcoff, Linda Martín, 165, 167, 195
Alcohols Anonymous (AA), 239
Alexander, Gregory, 139, 161
Alia, Valerie, 213
Alonso, William, 157–58
alphanumeric indexes, 22, 25, 27; advantages of, 26; as institutional, 26; statistical thinking, rise of, 26
Althusser, Louis, 247; interpellation, notion of, 246
American Library Association (ALA), 187; diacritics, 186

American Revolution, 105
American Standard Code for Information Exchange (ASCII), 187–88
Amoore, Louise, 173, 180, 182, 191, 195–96
Andor (television series), 235–38, 240, 242
Anduril Industries, 182
Anglo-centrism, 168, 172; diacritics, 187; library catalogues, 187; name loss, 187; nativism, 186; transliteration, 187–88; Unicode, 188; writing technologies, 183
Anon Collective, 8
anonymity, 2–3, 38, 40, 48, 62, 65–66, 75, 86, 89, 98, 113–14, 120–21, 125, 127, 133, 163, 167–68, 195–96, 233, 236; accountability, 51–52; affect, 58; analytics of, 243; anonymity condition, 250–51; autobiographical pathways, 56; "Big Brother," 164; built on mistrust, 108; censorship, 96; by changing names, 23–24, 174; citizenship and civic agency, 35–36; as contextual, 21; contracts, 138; control, 238–39; of crowds, 1, 7–8, 10, 21–22, 129; as cultural technique, 37, 60, 100, 243; in datafication, 36; digital, 241; digital opacity, 122; directed downward, 240–41; directed upward, 240–41; disindentification, 246; dissidence, importance to, 42; dynamic nominalism, 73–74; economy of anonymity, 238; economy of identification, 199; elements of, 60–61; entropic power of, viii; ethics, 250–51; eye of power, 4–6, 12; erasure of, 6; in everyday life, 126; freedom, intertwined with, 6–8, 35, 37, 90, 211; heroicity, 100; horizontal, 250, 253; human ontology, 248–49; identification, 20, 34–35, 42–43, 198, 246; identities, hiding of, 7–8, 10; in-between, 10, 41; of indexes, 53, 60–61, 87; as indexical, 20, 44–46; as indexical dissociation, viii, 8–11, 15–16, 18–19, 22, 33, 37, 43, 71, 108, 179, 194, 244; as indexicalization, 35, 42, 53–54, 60, 92, 154, 189, 237; individual and collective, 7; invisibility, 102; materiality, 102, 170; mediality of, 43; migrants, 194; multiplicity, 252–53; myth of, 6–8, 36, 90, 105–6; names, 197–98; of names, hiding and substitution of, 37; naming practices, 53, 166; nepantla, 57; ontic effects, 35; ontology, 64, 67; as opposite of identification, 17; political and agentic capacities, 124; power, effects on, 238; by powerful, 241–42; privacy, as different from, 18; and pseudonymity, 118; public actions, 18; publicity, 101; public sphere, 252; relational technologies, 60–61; secrecy, 102; self-recognition and identity, crucial to, 242; signification, 19; signs, 43–44, 53; in slavery, 77; as social good, 12; social life, 35; as socially useful, 51; statistical turn, 27–28; stigmatization, 51–52; subalterns, 241, 253; subaltern theory of, 14; subjectivity, shaping of, 243, 253; technical di-

mensions of, 43, 253–54; technical side, as process of anonymizing, 41; technologies of inscription, 37, 60–61; trickster element, vii–viii; vectorial property of, 239; as vertical, 240; as word, 7, 9
anonymizing, 9, 10, 11, 33, 41, 55, 56, 60, 64, 86, 166, 180, 186, 188, 195, 197, 212–13, 232, 241, 244, 246; complexities of, 42; horizontal forms of, 239–40; identification, dependent on, 42; immigrants, effects over, 36; of natural language indexes, 24; social subjective manifestations, 42; standardization, 206; tactics, 12; techniques, 11; types of, 210, 249
Anonymous (organization), 5, 40–41, 60–61, 113, 235, 240; collective persona of, 38–39; Guy Fawkes mask, use of, 38, 43; as performance, use of, 38; vulnerability of, 114
anonymous absences, 154; datafication, 163
anonymous contract: "good fences make good neighbors," 138
anonymous contractarianism, 132
anonymous copresence: contractarianism, based on, 163
anonymous kin, 126
anonymous publicity, 91, 104, 106–7, 112; civic notion of, 101; as contradiction, 102, 109; cultural techniques, 92; as heroic, 109; as logical contradiction, 102, 109; materiality, 92; as "mere talk," 113; myth, 92; as sociotechnical practice, 93; as term, 108; and trust, 115
anonymous publishing, 37, 41, 50, 233; as agentic indexical dissociation, 212; copyright, 212; pseudonyms, as form of artistic expression, 211–12
anonymous strangers, 125–26, 129, 144, 159, 161; archetypes, 128; civility and politeness, 127; in digital environments, 253; ontological security, challenging of, 128; politeness, 140; prediction, 158; trust, 128, 153, 155; as types, 128, 132
Anzaldúa, Gloria, 14, 43, 67, 74, 167, 189–91, 193, 195, 244–45, 248; birthing metaphor, use of, 58, 198, 233; borderlands, as in-between space, 188, 249; identity, as river metaphor, 79–81, 85, 88; in-between worlds, 56, 198; as inner exiles, 62–63; *los atravesados*, 86, 247–48; nepantla, notion of, 35, 42, 53, 56–57, 59, 154, 198, 233, 249
Arendt, Hannah, 5–6, 102–3, 108, 114, 121; action and speech, 112; agnostic publicity, notion of, 112–13
Aristotle, 67–68, 70, 74, 82, 88, 135, 148, 207
artificial intelligence (AI), 242–43
Asad, Asad L., 181
Asia, 168, 175
assimilated identity, 173
Athens (Greece), 108
Atkin, Albert, 44–45
Atwood, Margaret, 3, 244, 247
Austen, Jane, 5, 64, 212, 233, 240
Austin (Texas), 177
Australia, 155

authorial identity, 120; self-disclosure, 119
authoritarianism, 2–3, 89–90, 236, 253
authorship, 38, 98, 117, 119
automated license plate readers (ALDRs), 146
Azerbaijan, 156
Aztec Empire, 220–21

Bacon, Francis, 184
Bahrain, 156
Baker, Lynn Rudder, 66–67, 69–70, 73–75, 81, 88; first-person perspectives, 72, 79–80, 83, 86; identity continuity, 72, 79, 82
Balibar, Étienne, 191
Barbin, Herculine, 76–78, 83–88, 246
Barrett, Laurence, 174
Barthes, Roland, 6–8
belonging, 7, 52, 87, 156, 157, 226–27; categorical, 49
Benedict, Nex, 63–65, 77–78, 83–86, 246
Benhabib, Seyla, 112
Beniger, James, 184–85
Bennet, Chloe, 23
Bentham, Jeremy, 2, 235–36
Bertrand, Marianne, 208
Biden, Joe, 51
big data, 5; privatization of, 157–58
"Big Other": anonymity of, 164
biological indexes, 22, 23, 27, 28, 30, 32–33, 87–88, 143–44; fingerprints, 29; legal accountability, 29; phenotypes, 209; shaping humanity, 31
biometrics, 167, 180, 195; biometric and cybernetic borders, 196
biopolitics: and slavery, 217–18; as term, 206–7; third space, 218
biopower, 196
BitTorrent, 75
Blacks, 105
Blackstone, William, 230
blogosphere: and recognition, 118
Blumenbach, Johann Friedrich, 31–32
bodies: as indexical archives, 177
borderlands, 35, 42, 244–45, 249; biometric borders, 182; bordering process, 189–91, 195; writing systems, 188–89
Bosmajian, Haig, 213
Bowker, Geoffrey, 50
Brayne, Sarah, 144, 146
Brazil, 33, 111
Bridges, Lauren, 257n4
British Columbia, 227
Brontë, Anne: pseudonym, use of, 39, 41
Brontë, Charlotte, 5, 16–17, 23, 42, 107, 212, 235; pseudonym, use of, 20, 39, 41, 45, 106
Brontë, Emily, 5, 16–17, 23, 42, 107, 212, 235; pseudonym, use of, 39–41, 48–49, 58, 60, 106
Browne, Simone, 6
Burton, Richard, 215–16
Bush, George H. W., 179
Butler, Judith, 76–77, 88
Butler, Octavia, viii
Byatt, A. S. (Antonia Susan Drabble), 106

Cady Stanton, Elizabeth, 230–31
Caird, Mona Alison, 106

Calderón, Felipe, 93, 110
CalGang, 145
California, 77, 171–72, 191, 194; AB77 state bill, 186, 192; diacritics, banning of, 186; Proposition 63, Anglocentrism of, 186
Calgary (Alberta), 176
Canada, 171–72, 176, 179, 200–201
capitalism, 6, 136, 147–50
Cardon, Dominique, 159
Carley, Kathleen, 156
Carlisle Indian Industrial School, 218, 220
Carroll, Rory, 110, 118–20, 257n5
Catálogo alfabético de apellidos, 206
categorical indexes, 24, 28, 35, 49, 69, 71, 73, 76, 78, 125, 141, 143–44, 177, 182, 245, 256n5; of names, 208; as ontological, 66–68, 79; power of prejudice, 209
Categories (Aristotle), 67
Catholic Church, 149, 184, 221–22, 224
Chaar López, Iván, 180; cybernetic border, 167
Charcot, Jean Martin, 32
Charles III, 210
Cheney-Lippold, John, 160
Chicano studies, 24
China, 89, 156, 168, 172, 174–75, 205
Chun, Wendy, 126–27, 159–60, 162
Cicero, 203
citizen journalism, 100–101
citizenship, 35, 93, 136, 144, 165, 210
civic duties, 100–101; as public morality, 93
civil indifference, 132, 140, 163; recognition, rooted in, 141
civility, 118; democracy, 116; in modernity, 131; politeness, 116, 127
Clark, Gregory, 208–9
classifications, 68, 70, 74; classificatory systems, social order, as central to, 51
Clavería y Zaldúa, Narciso, 206
Clinton, Bill, 179
Coeckelbergh, Mark, 123–24; being-at-risk, 122
coffee houses, 103; as open self-disclosure, 107–8
Coleman, Gabriella, 39
colonialism, 5–6, 32, 126, 132, 135–36, 200, 210, 222, 224–25, 239, 244, 258n1
coloniality, 149, 152, 165–66, 172
colonization, 22, 229
Common Sense (Paine), 5, 105
computation, 17, 26
concrete indexes, 3, 17, 23, 27, 28, 35, 50, 66, 75–76, 87, 118, 125, 141, 182, 198, 245, 256n5; accountability, power of, 209; duality of, 49–50; life processes, marking of, 73; of names, 207–8; oneness of, 74; as ontological, 66–67, 74, 79; personal name, 198
Conrad, Joseph (Jozef Korzeniowski), 211–12
contradiction, 91, 101, 109; logical, 102, 107
contextual anonymity, 8, 10, 12, 37, 65, 124
contractarianism, 36, 127–28; anonymous, 132–33, 138–39, 143–44; anonymous copresence, 163; colonialism, framed by, 149; digital,

contractarianism (*cont.*) 150–52, 156; fables of, 144; of heterogeneity, 135–36; homophily, 162; informal, 156–57; massification of contracts, 150–51; modern, 132–33; ontological security, 135–36; pastoralism, 158; property, 135; statistical turn, 158; subaltern critique of, 141–42, 144, 161–63
contract theory, 150–51
contradiction, 91, 101, 109; logical, 102, 107
copresence, 103, 112, 116–19, 156, 177; indexicalization of, 176; prediction, 158
Cortés, Hernán, 222–23
Cosgrove, Ben, 70–71
Cosmopolitans, 104
Couldry, Nick, 6, 14, 126–27, 148–52, 156, 158, 242
counterhegemony, 124
coverture, viii, 10–11, 22, 24, 32, 137, 143–44, 201, 231, 239–40, 244; as system of subjugation, 229–30
COVID-19 pandemic, 51, 156
Cremona, 204
Crime Analysis Mapping System, 145
critical algorithm studies, 2
critical platform studies, 2
critical race theory, 56
critical theory, 65
Critique and Crisis (Koselleck), 103
Cronkite, Walter, 121–22
Cuba, 111, 115
cultural techniques, 53, 55, 91–92; anonymity of, 60, 100; indexicalization, 54, 59, 61, 102, 152; media concept, at root of, 108; as method, 54; as term, 54
Cultural Techniques: Grids, Filters, Doors, and Other Articulations of the Real (Siegert), 91–92
cyberbullying, 253
cybersecurity, 26

Dante Alighieri, 30
Darwin, Charles: survival of the fittest, 177–78
dasein, 14
data anonymization, 28
data colonialism, 149–50, 157, 253
data extraction, 6
datafication, 2–3, 17, 19, 75, 89, 127, 146, 149, 154–55, 157, 162, 164, 241–42; anonymous absences, 163; digital contractarianism, 156; economy of anonymity, transforming of, 163; indexicalization, 148, 153; prediction, models of, 156; social order, 163; surveillance, 147
data relations, 158
David (Michelangelo), 178
Dean, Mitchell: assemblages, 195; routines of bureaucracy, 196
De Beauvoir, Simone, 165–66
DeChants, Jonah P., 78
DeGloma, Thomas, 8
Derrida, Jacques: *différance,* concept of, 88, 170; signs, 175–76
diacritics: erasure of, 186–87; name loss, 185–87
Díaz del Castillo, Bernal, 222
digital anonymity, 96; incivility, 253; trolls and fakers, 155
digital indexes, 22, 33, 157, 164; ma-

teriality of, 178–79; as ubiquitous, 27; uniqueness of, 27
digital revolution, 2
digital walls, 109
digitation, 36
disciplinary indexical dissociation, 201, 210–11, 220–25, 227, 232; effects of, as massive, 226
disindentification, 57, 246–47
dispositif, 60–61, 198, 242
drug criminal organizations (DCOs), 93–96, 122–23
Dünne, Kathrin, 55
Dupin, Amantine-Lucile-Aurore (George Sand), 106
Durkheim, Emile, 75
Dussel, Enrique, 165
Dying for the Truth: Undercover Inside the Mexican Drug War (Blog del Narco), 97, 110
dynamic nominalism, 69–70, 75; anonymity, 73–74; indexical dissociation, 73–74; mythical status of anonymity, dependence on, 90

Earl of Arundel, 228
economy of anonymity, 15, 34, 36, 43, 62, 64, 90, 124, 126–27, 136, 155, 168, 194–96, 201, 210, 235; datafication, transforming of, 163; distribution systems, 238; economies of identification, 198–200; ethics of, 250–54; inequality, based on, 162; intersubjectivity, 249; personal name, 198; as phrase, 11; properties of, 37; social properties of, 238–43; subjective properties of, 243–50; as term, 237; as transforming, 12
economy of identification, 198–200
Ecuador, 156, 186
8chan, 255n1
Eighteenth Brumaire of Louis Bonaparte, The (Marx), 256–57nn3
Eisenstein, Elizabeth L., 184
El Blog del Narco (EBDN) (blog), 90–91, 96–99, 107, 114, 118, 120, 122, 257n5
El Historiador (anonymous blogger), 98–99
Eliot, George (Mary Ann Evans), 106, 212
Ellison, Ralph, 10, 64, 140–41, 244
Emancipation Proclamation, 216, 232
Engage and Evade (Asad), 181
Engels, Friedrich, 13
England, 105, 136, 205; naming practices, 204, 230; second names, 230. *See also* United Kingdom
Enlightenment, 5, 31–32, 94–95, 99–101, 107
entropy, vii–viii
erasure, 8, 28, 124, 166, 168, 173–74, 206; of anonymity, 6; of diacritics, 186; by imposition of names, 9–10; invisibility, 9, 246; social, 9, 167
Erasure (Everett), 244
Espinoza, Nancy Chaires, 186
Espinoza, Pablo, 186
ethics, 52; anonymity, 250–51; identity, 251; prudential rationality, 252; publicity and openness, reliance on, 250; “rational actor,” 250
Ethiopia, 205
ethnicity, 23
ethnocentrism, 165–66
eugenics, 162, 177–78

Europe, 129, 136, 168, 170, 184–86, 200–201, 204–5, 226, 228, 230, 258n1
European Union (EU), 28
Everett, Percival, 244
existential continuity, 88

Facebook, 27, 156–57
facial indexicality, 48
facial recognition, 2, 242, 257n4
Fanon, Frantz, 165–66, 246
fascism, 236
Fear-Segal, Jacqueline, 218
feminist theory, 56
feudalism, 135
fingerprinting, 242
First Amendment, 241
First Nation, 201
first-person perspective, 72–73, 79–80, 83, 86–88
Fiszalan-Howard, Edward, 228
Florence (Italy), 204
forced dissociation, 201; in slavery, 214
forced indexical dissociation, 210, 214–20; master-slave hierarchies, 213
Foucault, Michel, 40, 47–48, 76–77, 88, 151, 173, 185; biopolitics, 217–18; eye of power, 1–2; panopticon, as metaphor, 2
4chan, 19, 38–39, 60, 156–57, 255n1
France, 186, 230
Frankenstein; or, The Modern Prometheus (Shelley), 7, 30–31, 238
Franklin, Benjamin, 39, 49, 104, 107, 236–37; pseudonyms, 105

gait recognition, 2
Galbraith, Robert, 106
gaming, 156–57
Gaul, 204
Gebru, Timnit, 257n4
gender studies, 24
Gender Trouble (Butler), 76
Generation Y (blog), 111
German media theory, 92
Germany, 111, 186
Giddens, Anthony, 126–27, 140, 142, 144, 153, 161, 163; being safe in modern world, 129; civil indifference, and trust, 131–32; knowledge environments, 130, 146; natural attitude, 129–30; ontological security, 128, 135, 146, 155; self-identity, 138–39
Gilroy, Tony, 235
Global North, 94–95
Global South, 152, 172, 194
Gobineau, Joseph-Arthur de, 31
GoDaddy, 123
Godfather Part II, The (film), 169; aurality, depiction of, 170
Goffman, Ervin, 131–32, 135, 137–38, 140, 142, 161; civil indifference, 141
Google, 158
Gramsci, Antonio, 13
Grosz, Elizabeth, 30, 32
Guatemala, 223
Guha, Ranajit, 13
Guilmette, Lauren, 76, 87
Gutierrez-Perez, Robert M., 59

Habermas, Jürgen, 5–6, 62, 92, 102–3, 108, 117
habitus, 116

hackers, 26
Hacking, Ian, 40, 69–70, 72; dynamic nominalism, 75
Haley, Alex, 58, 244
Handmaid's Tale, The (Atwood), 3, 244–45, 247–48
Harcourt, Bernard, 160
Harris, Cheryl, 137
Hegel, G. W. F., 101
Heidegger, Martin, 65–66, 73, 81–82, 87–88, 255n2; being-in-the-world, 86
Henderson, Timothy, 105
Herculine Barbin (Foucault), 76
Heraclitus, 79, 88
heroicity, 100, 114, 124; myth of, 92
Hobbes, Thomas, vii, 126, 129, 132–33, 136–38, 142, 151, 161–63
Homer, 112
homophily, 126–27, 160, 163, 253; contractarianism, 162; feudal township, 132; personalization, 159; through property, 128, 152; recognition, as core of, 135
Honneth, Axel, 251
Horn, Rebecca, 222–23
Human Condition, The (Arendt), 102, 112
human indexes, 20, 44–46, 48, 68–69; accountability of, 51; as archival mechanisms, 56; as iconic, 48; as numerical, 49; as propositional, 47; shaping social order, 51
human onticity, 66, 71, 82
human ontology, 61, 68, 75; anonymity of, 35, 64, 124, 248–49; dynamism of, 69, 71
hybridity, 245–48
hypersurveillance, 89, 166
hypervisibility, 21, 36–37

Iceland, 205
identification, 25, 53–54, 241; accountability, 51, 251; anonymity, 34–35, 43, 198, 246; liminality in, 42
identity, vii, 34, 42, 53, 62, 81, 85, 88, 117, 131–32, 249; accountability, 51; and ethics, 251; as fragmented, 248; indexical dissociation, 248; and indexicalization, 130; institutionalized, 122; interpellation, notion of, 246; liminality in, 42; as multiple, 59–60; power in, 200; relational, 245
identity continuity, 82; first-person perspective of, 72–73, 79; in world, 81
identity dissociation, 38–39, 48–50
identity politics, 24
identity scholarship, 245
identity theory, 237; in ethnic studies, 245
Igo, Sarah, 17
Illuminati, 104
immigrants, viii, 84, 125, 166, 169–70, 175, 183, 186, 240, 246, 249; acculturation, 226; assimilation, 239; bordering, bureaucratic processes of, 189; dehumanization of, 180; name changes, 36, 168, 174, 177, 191, 194, 226–27, 239; radical surveillance of, 167; self-creation, 226; undocumented, 179, 181–82; unnaming and renaming, 238

in-between, 10–11, 20, 37, 41, 84; as indexicalization, 55; as liminal space, 40, 42; ontological effects, 42
indexes, 27, 33–35, 37, 39, 47, 50, 56, 76, 169; absences, 88; accountability, 52–53; anonymity of, 51, 53, 87; asserting nothing, 45–46; association, creating of, 20; biographical losses, reminders of, 59; characteristics, retaining of, 45; copresence, 177; defining capacity of, 19–20; *différance,* as endemic to, 88; digitalization of, 178; embodied beings, 58; erasure of, 173–74; features of, 44–46; hermeneutics of, 48–49; human onticity, 40; in-between of, 42; individuals, referring to, 45; life transitions, marking of, 71; materiality of, 173; as ontological, 68, 79; physical contiguity, 44–45; privacy, 51; semiotic work of, 43, 46, 53; signification, 130; signifying, 74; as signs, 44, 53; social life of, 173, 177; specification, 49; technologies of inscription, 170
indexical association, 67, 71, 120
indexical dissociation, 4, 14, 34–35, 64, 77, 81, 84, 100, 120, 125, 197, 220, 245, 246–47; agentic, 210, 249–50; anonymity of, viii, 8–11, 15–16, 18–19, 22, 33, 37, 43, 50, 71, 108, 179, 194; in crowds, 22; disciplinary, 210–11, 249; dynamic nominalism, 73–74; experience, 57; forced, 210–11, 249; identity, 248; inscription, 194; multiplicity of, 54; as ontological, 67, 79; rebirth, promise of, 59; as self-creation, 201, 210–11, 232–33, 249; slavery, 58, 213–14; subalterns, 242, 248; traditional, 249; types of, 210–11; in writing systems, 188
indexical inscription, 166–67
indexicality, 44, 66, 83, 87, 108, 152; of names, 207
indexicalization, 42, 131–32, 139, 157, 195–96; anonymity, 42, 53–54, 60, 92, 154, 189, 237; computational turn, 69; in copresence, 176; as cultural technique, 55–56, 59, 61, 102, 152; datafication, 148, 153; door, metaphor of, 55, 61; individuation, crucial to, 74; and identity, 130; materiality, 171; of migrants, 180–81; ontic capacities, 35, 61; ontology, centrality of to, 70; privacy, 54; publicity, *posteriori* to, 92; as space in-between, 55; as term, 56, 61; walls, 108
indexical reassociation, 213–14
indexing, 42–43, 50, 53, 60–62, 171, 242
India, 13, 33, 156, 174
Indigenous communities, 201
industrialism, 129, 132, 148, 256–57nn3
industrialization, 126; typewriters, 184–85, 258n2
information society, 184–85
inscription, 174–75, 177, 182–83, 190; indexical dissociation, 194; mate-

riality of, 170, 178; name changes, 189; technologies of, 180
Institute for Advanced Study, viii
Institute for the Future, 156
institutional anonymity, 8, 11–12, 36–37, 65, 124
interpellation, 246
intersubjectivity, 252
invisibility, 10–11, 21, 36–37, 64, 86, 92, 102, 246
Invisible Man (Ellison), 10, 64, 140–41, 244
Iran, 156
Isaac, Oscar (Oscar Hernández), 226

Jamaica, 216
James, P. D., 211
Japan, 32, 177
Jefferson, Thomas, 33–34

Kaling, Mindy, 23
Kapipal (crowdfunding site), 111, 114
Kant, Immanuel: ethics, notion of, 251; publicity condition, 53, 250–51
Katz, Elihu, 160
Keating, AnaLouise, 57
Kimaid, Michael, 105
Kim, Nadia, 32
King, Larry, 23
King, Martin Luther Jr.: "I Have a Dream" speech, 144
kinship, 129; chronotypes, 225, 227, 229; as property, 138
Kingsley, Mary Harrison, 106
Kittler, Friedrich, 55, 100, 184–85
Koopman, Colin, 17
Korea, 177, 226. *See also* South Korea
Korean War, 32
Koselleck, Reinhart, 5–6, 104, 108; conceptual history, 103
Kripke, Saul, 48; semiotic rigidity, 47

Landis, Barbara, 219
Langberg, Laura, 187
Latin America, 13, 59, 165, 172, 174, 179, 185–86, 223, 226, 258n1
Latin American studies, 13
Latine studies, 56, 245–47
Latinidad, 245
Lazarsfeld, Paul, 160
L-Diverse, 28
Leissner, Omi, 213
Lenoir, Timothy, 175–76
Leonard, Erika, 106
Leviathan (Hobbes), 126, 133, 135, 163
Levinas, Emmanuel, 251
Lewes, George Henry, 212
LexisNexis, 145–47, 154, 157, 163
LexisNexis Risk Solution, 157
liberalism, 94–95, 150, 249; as illiberal, 161
liminality, 42
Liu, Marian Chia-Ming, 168, 172–73
Locke, John, 132–33, 135–37, 148, 151
logical contradiction, 102
Lopez, Jennifer, 245
Los Angeles (California), 2, 49, 77, 125; Compton, 145
Los Angeles County, 144
Los Angeles Police Department (LAPD), 145; LexisNexis, 157; Palantir Gotham computational system, 145–47, 154
Los Zetas, 99, 114

Lucy (anonymous blogger), 36, 90–91, 94, 96–99, 103, 108–15, 122–23, 235–37, 241, 244–45, 257n5, 257–56nn7; anonymous publicity, embrace of, 106–7; authorial standing, 118; civic duty, 100–101; digital anonymity, 96; myth of heroicity, 92–93, 114; trust, conveying of, 119–21
Lugones, Maria, 82–83, 165
Luna, Diego, 235
Luther, Martin, 184, 258n1
Luther Standing Bear, 219, 220
Lyon, David, 17; surveillance society, 255–56nn4
Lyons, Martin, 184

Macho, Thomas, 55
Macías, María Elizabeth, 99
Madison, James, 137, 151
Making of the English Working Class, The (Thompson), 256–57nn3
marginalization, 29–30, 83
marginality, 173
Married Women's Property Act, 212
Mars, Bruno (Peter Hernandez), 226
Martínez, Diana, 58, 167–68, 189–90, 192–93
Martinez, Jacqueline, 74, 81, 82
Marx, Gary, 22
Marx, Karl, 13, 148–49, 165–66, 256–57nn3
Marxism, 13, 148–49
Masons, 104–5, 107, 109
materiality, 18, 55, 92, 101–2, 105, 108, 118, 168–69; anonymity, 170; of aurality, 170; of digital indexes, 178–79; of forms, 172; of indexes, 173; of inscription, 170, 178; indexicalization, 171; material multiplicity, 253–54; of names, 171; of sound and memory, 175; of writing, 183
matrilinearity, 203
Mauss, Marcel, 228
McLaren, Margaret, 87
media concept: cultural technique, at root of, 108
mediality, 42–43
media studies, 92
mediation, 55, 114
Meillassoux, Claude, 216
Mejia, Ulises, 6, 14, 126–27, 148–52, 156, 158, 242
Melendez Obando, Mauricio, 223
memory, 72, 112, 114, 152, 168–69, 174–78, 221, 228; cultural, 217
Mendieta, Eduardo, 13–14, 19
mercantilism, 126, 132, 135
Meszaros, Rosemary, 169
Meta, 156–57
metadata, 27
Mexico, 33, 59–60, 73, 90, 97, 99, 106, 110–11, 113, 115, 118, 121–22, 172–73, 176, 186, 200–201, 234, 241; acculturation, 224; anonymity in, 105; Ayuuk community, 223–25; Christian and Spanish names, adopting of, 223; "drug war," 93–94, 109; *encomienda*, 221–22; *hacienda* system, 222; Indigenous names, 221–25; Mixtecs, 221; naming practices, 220–24; naming tradition, 171; Nahuas, 221–23; Oaxaca, 223–24; public sphere, erosion of, 95–96; securitization of border between US, 179–80; War of Independence, 105; *xemabie*, 224

Meyer, Ilan, 84
Middle Ages: naming practices, 203–4
Middle East, 185–86
Middle Passage, 220; removal of names, 214
Mignolo, Walter, 165
migrants, 166, 168, 171, 174; anonymity of, 194; assimilated identity, 173; as datafied bodies, 180; dehumanization, 179–80; indexicalization of, 180–81; migration process, in movies, 169; naming transformations among, 172–73; radical identification, 167; securitization of border, 179; systemic identification of, 182–83
Millard, Dr. Ralph, 32
Mills, Charles, 142, 161–62; racial contract, 143
Minority Report (film), 6
mobility, 123, 129, 170, 225; of bodies, 196; social, 126, 208–9
modernity, 5–6, 11–12, 34, 36, 85, 103, 124, 126–27, 130, 156, 161, 184; civility, 131; first, 150; inscription, 189; personhood and property, 139; as post-traditional order, 129; second, 150; social contract, 131–32; third, 150; traditional societies, erosion of, 132; trust versus familiarity, 131
Modernity and Self-Identity (Giddens), 128
Monahan, Torin, 6, 10, 21, 36–37
Mongolia, 172
Monroy-Hernández, Andrés, 100
Morton, Samuel, 31–32
Moss-Racussin, Corinne, 208
Mullainathan, Sendhil, 208
multiplicity, 26, 30, 43, 82–83, 85–86, 182, 220, 247, 249–50; anonymity, 252–53; ethical, 254; indexicalization, 54; material, 254; ontological, 254; phenomenological, 254; social, 237
Muñoz, José Esteban, 244, 246–47
Musk, Elon, 156, 241
Myanmar, 205
My People, the Sioux (Luther Standing Bear), 219

name changes, 168, 170, 175, 177, 193, 195; agency, 258n1; bordering, 189; erasure, 173–74; as erasure and anonymizing, 166; forgetting, 173; forms, 191–92, 194; of immigrants, 36, 191; transliteration, 174; WASP-dom, 174
names, 44, 197–98, 234; ambiguity, 207, 209; anonymity, 198; biopolitics, 206–7; gendered names, power of, 208; hiding and substitution of, 37; identity, 198; as indexes of personality, 206; indexical capacity of, 207; losing of, 58, 185–86, 189; naming traditions, 171–72; personal names, 47; power work of, 200, 208–9; as propositional, 48; race, context of, 208; as referential, 207; significations, 200, 209; signifying capacity of, 209; social mobility, 208–9; systems of power, connection to, 208; women's married names, 50

naming, 47, 54, 202, 233, 239, 249; act of, 53; anonymity, 53, 166; dissociational, 226; obligation, 53; renaming, 144, 199–201; unnaming, 144, 199–201; Yoruba names, 214
naming practices: in Africa, 214; agnatic and cognatic practices, 203, 230; animal names, 205; family names, 205; in Ghana, 214; invisibility of women, 203; master-slave hierarchies, 213; nicknames, 205; Native Americans, 218–20; in Nigeria, 214; second names, 204–5; surname standardization, 205–6; three names, 202–3; two names, 204; women's names, 230–31
National Security Agency (NSA), 111, 160
nation-states, 136, 157, 205
Native Americans, 218–20
nativism, 128, 140, 186
natural language indexes, 22–24, 26, 29, 33, 65, 198, 233; signifying of, 74
neocolonialism, 94–95
neoliberalism, 150
nepantla, 53, 58, 154, 198, 211, 248–50; autobiography and affect, as intertwined, 59; birthing, 233; borderlands and in-between, 42; as in-between space, 56–57, 84, 217–18; reflexive agency, 59; subalterns, importance to, 35; as term, 56–57
New Spain, 105, 167, 222–23
New York City: COMPSTAT, 146; Ellis Island, 226
Nicomachean Ethics (Aristotle), 135
Nigeria, Yoruba of, 214
1984 (Orwell), 6, 89
9/11, 179
Ninety-Five Theses (Luther), 184, 258n1
Nissenbaum, Helen, 4–5, 17, 51, 236–37
nominalism, 256n2
nonbinary individuals, 63–65, 78, 84

Oklahoma, 63–64
onticity, 34–35, 40; signification, 74
ontological security, 128, 130, 135–36, 138, 146, 155; social order, 163
ontological theory, 86
ontology, 65–69, 74, 86, 256n1
OpCartel, 114
Order of Things, The (Foucault), naming in, 47
Ortega, Mariana, 14, 65–67, 74, 81, 83, 86, 244, 246–48, 254; existential continuity, 82; identity in borderlands, 35; in-between, 10; multiplicitous self, 82, 249
Orwell, George (Eric Arthur Blair), 6, 89, 211–12
Otis, James, 104–5

Pacheco, Blanca, 186, 192
Pagden, Anthony, 136–37
Paget, Violet, 106
Paine, Thomas, 5, 10, 17, 37, 105, 107, 235, 240
Pakistan, 156
Palacios, Luis Daniel, 100
panopticon, 2, 8
Papacharissi, Zizi, 19
Parable of the Sower (Butler), viii
Parable of the Talents (Butler), viii
Pateman, Carole, 142–43, 161–62

patriarchy, 6, 54, 106, 140, 142, 210, 229; invisibility of women, 203; racial, 32, 162; White, 162
Peirce, Charles, 20, 34–35, 43, 45; physical contiguity, principle of, 47–48; signs, 44, 46–47
Pennavaria, Katherine, 169
Penn, Kal, 23
Pennsylvania, 218
Perpetual Peace (Kant), 250
personalization, 124; computer algorithms, 159; eugenics, 126; homophily, 159; as misnomer, 159; as ubiquitous, 158
Persons and Bodies (Baker), 72
Peru, 223
Perugia, 204
Philip III, 215
Philippines, 156, 205–6
Phillips, Captain Thomas, 215
Platonism, 256n2
pluralism, 104, 133, 135
polarization, 160
policing, 144–46
politeness, 21–22; anonymous strangers, 140; reciprocity, 140
Politics of Numbers, The (Alonzo and Starr), 157–58
Poovey, Mary: facticity of an individual, 25
Portugal, 205
postcolonialism, 13
postcolonial theory: subaltern studies, difference between, 13–14
posthumanism, 68–69
prediction, 161, 164; anonymous copresence, 163; anonymous stranger, 158; datafication, 156; digitation, 153; social contractarianism and copresence, 158
Predict and Surveil (Brayne), 144
printing press, 183–84, 258n1
privacy, 2, 17, 19–20, 28, 51, 89, 104, 163; anonymity, as different from, 18; and classification, 42; indexicalization, 54; as spatial category, 18
Problem of Political Obligation, The (Pateman), 142
property, 137, 151; kinship, 138; personhood, 139; subaltern critique of, 136
Protestant Reformation, 258n1
prudence, 252–53
prudential rationality, 251–52
pseudonyms, 1, 39, 41, 54, 58, 60, 90, 105, 235; artistic expression, as form of, 211–12; pen names, 105; on social media, 75, 238, 249; by women, 106
publicity, 121, 252; anonymity, 101; cultural technique of indexicalization, 102; ethics, 250; materiality, rooted in, 102, 108; as media concept, 102; openness, tied to, 92, 101–2, 107–8; secrecy, 108; self-disclosure, 112; trust, built on, 108
publicity condition, 53, 250–51
publicity theory, 6, 91; material genealogy of, 101; reciprocity of trust, 115
publicness, 102, 121; openness, 103; secrecy, 103; as spatially reflexive action, 103; trust, 117
public sphere, 5–6, 89–90, 92, 95–96, 101–3, 137; anonymity, hiding behind, 252; re-feudalization of, 117; sociability, erosion of, 117
Puerto Rico, 218

queerness, 246
queer studies, 24
queer theory, 56
Quijano, Anibal, 165

racism, 111, 140, 165–66, 223, 226
Radin, Margaret, 150–51
Ramé, Maria Louise, 106
Rawls, John, 132–33, 151
Reagan, Ronald, 179
realism, 175, 256n2
Récanati, François, 207
reciprocity of trust, 116; anonymous publicity, 115; openness, 121
reflexivity, 84, 86, 164, 193, 249
renaming, 50, 210, 213, 215, 225, 231–32, 234, 239, 245; as form of rebirthing, 233
representation, 30, 39, 88, 170, 175, 180
republicanism, 139–40
Republican Party, 77–78
Requerimiento, El, 149–50
Revere, Paul, 104–5
Rodríguez, Ileana, 13
Rogue One (film), 235
Roman Empire: *cognomen*, 203; *gens*, 202–3; *gentilicium*, 202; naming practices, 202–4; praenomen, 203; *tria nomina*, 202–3
Rome (Italy), 201–3, 213, 216
Roots (Haley), 58, 244
Rose, Carol, 136, 139, 161
Rose, Susan, 218
Rousseau, Jean-Jacques, 132–33, 142, 151
Rowling, J. K., 106, 211
Russia, 155–56, 226, 258n2
safety, 51, 103, 115, 116, 127–29, 133, 136, 144
Sagi-Vela González, Ana, 223–24
Sánchez, Yoani, 110–15, 121
Sasaki, David, 100
Saudi Arabia, 156
Saussure, Ferdinand de, 29, 47
Schreiner, Olive, 106
Schurz, Carl, 219
science and technology studies (STS), ix
Scott, James C., 6, 201, 205–6, 240
Scott, Walter, 211
Second Treatise of Civil Government (Locke), 136
secrecy, 49, 50, 92, 103, 106–8; anonymity, 101–2; disguises, 105; secret societies, 104
secularism, 5
segregation, 160, 162
self: as multiplicitous and fragmented, 88; selfhood, 82; self-identity, 129, 138–39, 239
Seligman, Peter, 117, 122
semiosis, 22–23
semiotics, 53; semiotic rigidity, 47; semiotic systems, 56
Serbia, 258n2
settler colonialism, 137, 218, 220, 229, 232
Sexual Contract, The (Pateman), 142
Sheen, Martin, 23
Shelley, Mary, 5, 7–8, 10, 18, 23, 30–32, 37, 238, 240
Siegert, Bernhard, 35, 42–43, 56, 85, 91–92, 166–68, 171, 173; cultural technique, 54–55; door, metaphor of, 55, 152

signification, 19, 54, 56, 130, 170; onticity, 74
signs, 175–76; icons, 44, 46; indexes, 44, 46; symbols, 44, 46–47
Silo (television series), 6
Simmel, Georg, 126–27, 129–30, 132, 135, 140–41, 144, 155; nativism, alignment with, 128; stranger, as foreigner, 125
Slaby, Jan, 66
slavery, viii, 5–6, 11, 22, 24, 137, 143–44, 200–201, 210, 219–20, 225, 233, 239–40, 244; adopting surnames, 216; anonymity of, 77; biopolitics, 217–18; branding of, 214–15; changing of names, 33–34; erasure of, 9–10; forced dissociation, 214; indexical dissociation, 58, 213–14; indexical reassociation, 213–14; loss of names, 58; married women, simile between, 230–31; names, 198; naming of, as mark of possession, 216; naming practices, 217–18, 232; renaming of, 214–16; resistance, 218; secret real names, 216; unnaming of, 215; vestibular space of in-betweenness, 216–17
Snowden, Edward, 110, 112–15, 121, 241; as whistleblower, 111
social constructivism, 68–70, 74
social contract, 131–32, 155, 161–62; anonymous, 133; impossibility of equality within, 142–43
social invisibility, 9, 21
sociality, 112, 116, 147
social media, 1, 75, 96, 99, 155–56, 163, 238, 249; online harassment, 251; unethical behavior, 251
social ontology, 68–70, 74
social order, vii, 51, 133, 135, 161; accountability, 52; datafication, 163; ontological security, 163
social sciences, vii, 27–28
Somalia, 205, 226
Sons of Liberty, 105
South Africa, 214
South Asian studies, 13
South Korea: plastic surgery industry, 32–33. *See also* Korea
Spade, Dean, 64, 84–85
Spain, 110, 167, 185
Spillers, Hortense, 218; vestibular space, 84, 216–17, 233
Spivak, Gayatri Chakravorty, 10
Starbucks, 130–31
Starr, Paul, 157–58
Star, Susan, 50
Star Wars (film series), 235
Structural Transformation of the Public Sphere, The (Habermas), 102, 117
subalterns, viii, 6–7, 9, 14, 19, 22, 28, 30–31, 89–90, 143, 152, 240, 249–50; anonymity, 241; burden of, 18; contractarianism, critique of, 141–42, 144, 161–63; hiding of, 23; indexical dissociation, 248; material multiplicity, 253–54; nepantla, importance to, 35; policing, 146; property, critique of, 136; as term, 13; writing systems, 188
subaltern studies, 14–15, 247
subaltern theory, 250
subjectivity, 14, 30–31, 53, 73, 138, 140, 160, 214, 229, 243, 247, 252–53
Sumer, 201

surveillance, 2–3, 6, 17, 19–20, 38, 75, 89, 180, 236, 241–42, 253; CCTV technologies, 15–16; datafication, 147; of immigrants, 167; institutional, 181; mutuality of, 181–82; radical, 167, 195; social, 16
surveillance capitalism, 147, 149–50, 157, 253, 255–56nn4
surveillance studies, 2

T-closeness, 28
technologies of inscription, 36, 56, 60–61, 166–68, 170, 175, 180, 189, 196, 198, 200, 240, 243; anonymity, shaping of, 37; Form I-485, 171, 191, 194
teenagers, 70–71
temporality, 102, 152; temporal immediacy, 119
Texas, 190–91
Theuderic I, 204
Thiemer-Sachse, Ursula, 223–24
Thirteenth Amendment, 33–34
Thompson, E. P., 256–57nn3
TikTok, 19, 27, 101
Tirzo, Jorge, 98
totalitarianism, 6
traditional indexical dissociation, 201, 210, 227–31
traditionalism: erosion of, 129
transgender, 78, 84
trolling, 212, 252; anonymous, 253; bots, 156; state-sponsored, 155–56; veil of anonymity and sadism, 155
Trump, Donald, 168, 179, 241
trust, 119, 120, 124, 127, 129–30, 144, 163; anonymous publicity, 115; anonymous strangers, 128, 153, 155; civil indifference, 131; definition of, 117; digitation, 153; "divide and conquer," 253; versus familiarity, 131; publicness, 117; recognition, 135; safety, 116; social contract, 131–32; as word, 116
Truth, Sojourner (Isabella Bomfree), 197–99, 201, 233, 244–46; renaming, 231–32
Tsimshian people, 230, 233–34, 246; kinship chronotype, 229; naming practices, 227–29
Turkey, 156, 186
Turkle, Sherry, 154
Turner, Cheryl, 212
Tuscany, 204
Twitter, 156

uniqueness: as social fact, 75, 87
United Kingdom, 155, 210. *See also* England
United States, 2–3, 5, 36, 60, 93, 105–6, 124–25, 143, 156, 166–67, 169, 171, 173–74, 177, 184–85, 200–201, 208, 213, 216, 218, 224, 226, 230–32, 241, 243, 247, 258n1; Anglo-centrism of administrative practices, 168, 172, 181, 188; gender classifications, tracking of, 84–85; gender and sexual norms, 77; Mexico, securitization of border with, 179–80; SSN numbers, 25–26
unnaming, 50, 210, 215, 225, 232, 234, 245; as form of rebirthing, 233
Upton, Sarah de los Santos, 59
urbanism, 126
urbanization, 1, 129, 135

Venezuela, 156
Venice, 204
Vicente, Rafael Sebastián Guillén, 113
Vietnam, 177, 186
visible invisibility, 21
Vismann, Cornelia, 55–56
voluntarism, 142

war on terror, 196; biometrics, 180
Washington, George, 33–34, 104–5
whiteness, 23, 137
WikiLeaks, 5
Wu, Ellen D., 174–75
Wuthering Heights (Brontë), 40

YouTube, 101

Zapatista Army of National Liberation (EZLN), 113
Zedillo, Ernesto, 113
Zuboff, Shoshana, 17, 126–27, 149–51, 156, 242; "Big Other," 164; surveillance capitalism, 147

The authorized representative in the EU for product safety and compliance is:
Mare Nostrum Group
B.V Doelen 72
4831 GR Breda
The Netherlands

www.ingramcontent.com/pod-product-compliance
Lightning Source LLC
Chambersburg PA
CBHW031406270326
41929CB00010BA/1344